FINDING

FORGIVENESS

FINDING

FORGIVENESS

·····················

A 7-Step Program for Letting Go of Anger and Bitterness

·····················

Eileen R. Borris-Dunchunstang, Ed.D.

New York Chicago San Francisco Lisbon London Madrid Mexico City
Milan New Delhi San Juan Seoul Singapore Sydney Toronto

Library of Congress Cataloging-in-Publication Data

Borris-Dunchunstang, Eileen R.
    Finding forgiveness : a 7-step program for letting go of anger and bitterness /
Eileen R. Borris-Dunchunstang.
        p.   cm.
    Includes bibliographical references.
    ISBN 0-07-147469-2 (hardcover)
    ISBN 0-07-171375-1 (paperback)
    1. Forgiveness.   I. Title.

    BF637.F67B67   2006
    158.2—dc22   2006009945

1 2 3 4 5 6 7 8 9 10 11 12 13 14 15 16 17 18 19 20   DOC/DOC   0 9

ISBN 978-0-07-171375-7
MHID   0-07-171375-1

Interior design by Monica Baziuk

McGraw-Hill books are available at special quantity discounts to use as premiums and
sales promotions or for use in corporate training programs. To contact a representative,
please e-mail us at bulksales@mcgraw-hill.com.

Some of the names in this book have been changed to protect the privacy of the
individuals involved.

In loving memory of my parents,
Sarah Mayrsohn and Henry Borris

Contents

Foreword

by His Holiness the Dalai Lama

IN THE COURSE of our lives we often make misguided decisions that harm ourselves or others. We do this out of ignorance. We think that a certain mode of behavior will bring us happiness when in fact it brings us suffering. Feelings of self-righteous anger and the urge for revenge may sometimes lead us to harm others in the mistaken conviction that it will benefit us and bring us some form of happiness. Actually, it creates suffering not only for the victims of our deeds but also for us. However justified we may feel, doing others harm, even in the name of revenge, severely disturbs our own peace of mind and creates conditions for our own suffering.

Human beings need to live together and are dependent on each other in many essential ways. In human society we, therefore, need moral codes of behavior in order to live in peace and harmony with one another. Although victims may have a psychological need to feel that justice is being done, the infliction of pain on someone else only serves to add to the suffering already done and does not increase the potential for happiness of anyone involved. Instead of revenge, it is the notion of forgiveness that should be encouraged and developed.

If we truly act out of concern for others' well-being we will recognize the potential impact of our actions on others and order our conduct accordingly. When we become angry, we stop being compassionate, loving, generous, forgiving, tolerant, and patient altogether. We deprive ourselves of the very things that happiness consists of. And not only does anger immediately destroy our critical faculties, it tends toward rage, spite, hatred, and malice—each of which is always negative because it is a direct cause of harm to others.

If, on the other hand, we can let go of anger and hatred, if we can apply reasoning to analyze the situation, adopt a wider perspective and look at other angles of the situation, the end result—the product of patience and tolerance—is forgiveness. When we are truly patient and tolerant, then forgiveness comes naturally.

Although we may have experienced deep hurt in the past, with the development of patience and tolerance it is possible to let go of our sense of anger and resentment. If we analyze the situation, it is possible to realize that the past is past, that continuing to feel anger and hatred serves no purpose. They do not change the situation, but just give rise to further disturbance within our minds and cause our continued unhappiness. Of course, we may still remember what happened, but forgetting and forgiving are two different things. There's nothing wrong with simply remembering what happened, but with the development of forgiveness, it's possible to let go of the negative feelings associated with what took place. This is why the author of this book, Eileen R. Borris-Dunchunstang, has referred to forgiveness as the ultimate freedom. Forgiveness is not about letting off the perpetrator of some wrong; it is about freeing the victim. If you can forgive, you no longer have to concern yourself with who did what to you and how you are going to make them pay for it. You will be free of that entire burden.

It is my sincere hope and prayer that the fundamental theme of this book, the importance of forgiveness, may be seen as effective not only in individuals' private lives, but equally in the arena of public and even international relations. The idea that concern for others is a matter for our private lives only is simply short-sighted. Compassion and the forgiveness and tolerance it gives rise to belong to every sphere of activity. As the source both of inner and external peace, they are fundamental to the continued survival of our species. On the one hand, they constitute nonviolence in action; on the other, they give meaning to our lives and allow us to be truly constructive.

Acknowledgments

—◆ ◆—

MANY YEARS WENT INTO writing this book. It began when Ken Wapnick first introduced me to the concepts of *A Course in Miracles*, a book that reflects Ken's kindness. He patiently taught me the profound meaning of forgiveness. Without the many weekends spent in Roscoe, New York, this book could not have been written.

I am also very deeply grateful to Ambassador John McDonald, who was the first to encourage me to speak about forgiveness in international affairs and who has supported my work in forgiveness and reconciliation throughout the years.

I am enormously grateful to all those in this book who shared their stories of struggles and eventual triumph on their paths toward forgiveness. You have taught me so much and inspired me to continue this work.

I would like to give a very special thank-you to Tenzin Geyche Tethong, who helped arrange my interview with His Holiness the Dalai Lama and who graciously helped with the arrangements of the writing of the Foreword for this book.

My heartfelt thanks goes to my agent, Barbara Zitwer, whose unwavering faith in this project kept me going during the most critical times.

With profound gratitude I want to thank my family, dear friends, and meditation group, who kept encouraging me to keep moving forward. Your thoughts, prayers, and phone calls always uplifted my spirits.

And, finally, I am so deeply grateful for my beloved husband, Yak, whose love and laughter in his very uniquely Tibetan way has filled my heart with joy.

Introduction

Why Should We Forgive?

"Anger makes you smaller, while forgiveness forces you to grow beyond what you were."
—CHERIE CARTER-SCOTT

OUR LIVES ARE faced with many challenges concerning forgiveness. Incidents happen on a daily basis where we get angry about something that someone else said or did and then carry that anger way past its due. Before we realize it, we have become angry people.

Perhaps one day you come home to find your spouse has left you and that you have been betrayed. How can you forgive someone who has caused you so much pain? Consider the Jenny Sanfords and Elizabeth Edwards of this world, grappling with how to forgive their husbands for deception and infidelity. And as if forgiving your spouse isn't difficult enough, how are you supposed to forgive yourself for the messes you're in that you feel responsible for and that bring you great hardship?

We are told to forgive to prevent becoming embittered people. Yet forgiveness can be difficult to understand and to achieve. It's essential to remember, though, that the key is forgiveness is *not* a gift to the wrongdoer—it is a gift to ourselves, a gift that allows us to be freed of our emotional burden. Forgiveness is *our ultimate freedom.*

When it comes to deception, financier Bernie Madoff tops the list of those who have shattered the lives of many others. On December 11, 2008, Madoff was arrested for perpetrating one of the greatest investment frauds in history by allegedly losing at least $50 billion of investors' money. The former chairman of the NASDAQ stock index was surprised that his Ponzi scheme was not uncovered sooner. The victims of Madoff's Ponzi scheme felt deeply betrayed and angry. Some lost all their life savings and had to begin living on social security checks. Others felt as though they were discarded like road kill. Many people spoke of unpaid bills and lost homes, dreams destroyed, and sleepless nights.

Burt Ross, the former mayor of Fort Lee, New Jersey, and one of Madoff's victims, condemned the fraud as "the worst of sins, the ultimate evil." Madoff sank so low as to steal from Elie Wiesel, the Nazi concentration camp survivor and Nobel Prize winner, as if Wiesel hadn't suffered enough in his lifetime. Wiesel conjured a vision of torment for Madoff: he wanted Madoff to be in solitary confinement for five years, forced to watch a movie played continuously in which photos of his victims appeared, one after the other after the other. The narrative would repeat, "Look what you have done to this old lady, look what you have done to that child, look what you have done" (Strom, 2009). Did Elie Wiesel forgive him? No. Could you if you were one of his victims? Could you forgive Madoff, who looked people squarely in the eye as they turned over their life savings, all the while knowing that he was going to ruin them?

Because of the magnitude of the crime, people questioned whether Bernie Madoff could or should be forgiven. Elie Wiesel felt that Madoff needed to get on his knees and ask for forgiveness for there to be forgiveness given. Some believe that forgiveness can only be accomplished with the participation of the one being forgiven. Yet the true meaning of forgiveness may take us someplace else. Forgiveness doesn't come because someone has asked for it or has earned it. Forgiveness is a gift of grace given to those who choose to forgive because they don't want the cancer of hatred to spread within them and eat them up. Therefore, Madoff cannot earn forgiveness; forgiveness is not about someone else. It is about our own personal inner healing.

As unbelievable as it may seem, there are some of Madoff's victims who have been able to forgive him. One example is Ian Thiermann, who lost his entire life savings of $750,000 to Madoff. Ninety-year-old Thiermann subsequently needed to go back to work. The grocery store where he was a customer for years created a greeter position just for him. According to Ron Clements, the store manager, Thiermann was an inspiration to many of his customers because of his ability to forgive. Although Thiermann still had house payments and his wife's medical bills to pay, he chose not to be a victim twice over. He made the decision to let go of his hatred and need for revenge and to forgive so the poison of bitterness wouldn't ruin his life.

What Ian Thiermann was able to accomplish you, too, will be able to do *if you choose to*. Don't worry; don't be afraid of what this book will tell you. It will *not* tell you that what people have done wrong to you is OK. It will *not* tell you that you must excuse someone who has treated you vilely. It will *not* tell you that you have no right to vengeance or to the anger that fuels it. It will tell you something quite different.

What this book does is expose the complexities of forgiveness—a misunderstood process that frequently hides in robes of morality, self-righteousness, and woundedness. It will tell you that you have a right to that anger, and that your desire for justice and retribution are perfectly normal and recognizable human emotions. It will also tell you that you have a right *not* to excuse someone who has wronged you.

But it will also tell you that the path to freedom requires you to shed the baggage caused by persons, circumstances, fortunes, fate, and bad experience so that you are light and limber enough to travel that road. There is a process to shedding that baggage, and this book will tell you how to develop that technique. Shedding that burden is what I call the process of forgiveness, not in the sense of excusing or ignoring a wrong done to you, or of being passive in its wake, as you may have been taught by religion. It is forgiveness in the sense of forgiving debt, of recognizing that full repayment may not always be possible, even at the cost of someone's life, and that justice may be better done more practically through the process of forgiveness.

Do not misunderstand. If people commit a crime, they should suffer the legal consequences. This book does *not* tell you to forgive crime in the legal sense. That would be foolish and injurious to you and to society. This book does *not* tell you that you must love your enemies. This might add to the pain of the wrong done you and is completely unnecessary. And this book does not tell you that you must simply forget debt owed to you. For civilized society to run properly and sensibly, people must all pay the debts they incur, whether they are financial or behavioral. Pickpockets, cheaters, and murderers must all suffer the consequences of their actions.

Why We Need to Forgive

The purpose of forgiveness is not to make you holy or to elevate you in the divine sense. The purpose of forgiveness is not to humiliate you further in the human sense. The purpose of forgiveness is to empower you above and beyond those who have made you their victim. Forgiveness makes one strong, not weak. But forgiveness must be defined in terms that can be applied appropriately. For example, the terrible fires that take place in California, the earthquakes that take place in Asia, and the tidal waves that wreak havoc in Japan are all wrongdoers in a sense. If one is the victim of such natural disaster, is there a process of forgiveness for that person?

And what about institutionalized horror, such as the Holocaust, for which justice can truly never be done? In some cases, it is not even possible to identify the criminal whose behavior is responsible for the crime. Consider the damage done when entire lifesavings are wiped out when loyal employees are cheated by wealthy, powerful corporate executives who hide behind corporate charters and obscure legal defenses that entangle justice rather than serve it? Can we forgive in these situations as well?

Forgiveness is understood differently by different people. The Old Testament teaches us one kind of justice, as in "an eye for an eye and a tooth for a tooth." The New Testament teaches us to "turn the other cheek" and "vengeance is mine, sayeth the Lord." To most human beings, the latter seems more immediately satisfying, but it is also horrifying to contemplate. When Americans learned that in Iran first-time pickpockets had their right hands amputated, they were horrified. Americans want justice, but they want civilized justice.

Turning the other cheek, on the other hand, seems terribly unfair to one who, for example, has been the victim of a horrible crime. The pope might have been able to forgive his would-be assassin, but we are not all so well disposed to excusing a murderer who has taken the life of a loved one, or to a thief who has stolen a valued possession. It is more likely that we will feel too angry about the terrible injustice done to us, and we will wish that the injustice be avenged. If we are lucky, we will allow this anger to fade with time and will move on to more productive pursuits in our lives—pursuits that will better us by making us happier and freer. If we are not so lucky, we will allow the anger to fester. We may even feed it by fantasizing vengeful plots against the wrongdoers. And this cultivation may lead us to spend more and more of our energy over time, consuming that energy and that time—consuming our lives or a significant portion of it. To free ourselves from that anger would be liberating and that freedom is what we call *forgiveness*.

There are many interpretations of the concepts of forgiveness and reconciliation. People view these in many ways, depending on the culture from which they come and their personal experiences or what they have been taught, directly by instruction (as in many religions) or subtly by the examples presented to them (intentionally or unintentionally through parental behavior or authority). However people learn these concepts, there is a finite and definitive meaning to them.

The values of these concepts, however, are not taught in direct terms regarding personal human experience. We may be told that to forgive is divine or that reconciliation is practical. But we are rarely taught that there is power in both forgiveness and reconciliation—the power of personal freedom. To survive, human beings must have freedom. We are not speaking merely of freedom from want or freedom to pursue one's ambitions or goals, or even the freedom to love. We are speaking here of the freedom of a human being to *be human and to pursue life by embracing the totality of who we are.* In order to do this, we must recognize and accept all that is human, including those strengths and weaknesses that *make* us human, and we must be free to act on those qualities, to enhance them or control them as required in order to live a full and joyous life.

This brings up a uniquely human emotion, the capacity to hate. Hatred, whether discriminate or indiscriminate, is uniquely human. Animals do not hate. They may fear and they may kill, but they do not hate, because hate in its own way requires the faculty of conceptual thought.

Human beings, on the other hand, are capable of hate and vengeance for long periods of time, even their entire lives. They can act on this hatred many years after perceiving that they have been wronged. Although it is frequently *felt* by such people that their dedication to revenge is fulfilling, in reality it is the opposite. When we nurse hatred with the intention of revenge, we have dedicated energy to that one purpose and have taken that energy away from other pursuits that might prove to be infinitely more fulfilling. It is possible for hatred and the desire for revenge to be perceived as energizing, rather than enervating. Yet if we examine this carefully using that unique faculty of the human mind, the ability to think rationally and logically, then we reach the irresistible conclusion that the ability to move on from the ill done to us will free us and energize us far more than nursing the old, debilitating hatred.

This does not mean that it is wrong to want justice. But justice must be weighed in terms of spiritual gains. If justice is done when we take revenge on the person who has harmed us, it may well be that greater justice will be done and felt if we let go of that hatred. This can only happen if we are able to release ourselves from the lurking sense of revenge. Justice gives us a kind of spiritual freedom, but only if it is an ethical justice, born of our potential for spiritual freedom. And to experience this form of justice, we must be able to forgive in the *true* sense of the term.

What This Book Is About

This book is dedicated to teaching you skills that can serve as a guidepost on your journey to forgiveness. Yes, *skills* because forgiveness is not always easy. These tools will help you learn how to heal the raw emotions that make people feel stuck and vulnerable. They will also help you grow in compassion and see situations differently. Anyone can learn these skills. Forgiveness will often require great strength, and it will always require reason, because the human mind is the embodiment of the human spirit. We refer to this as the "heart" of our nature.

All of us will be faced with situations in which we will grapple with issues of forgiveness. We may have dealt with a betrayal, some form of violation, or of being deceived. For many of us, coming to terms with what has happened has been very difficult. On a larger scale, our world is filled with violence and conflict. We need to do something to help humanity become more human.

To hold anger and hatred in our hearts takes a toll on our bodies. Negative thinking can affect our immune and cardiovascular systems. Negative thoughts elevate blood pressure. The energy we use to fight and hate people creates hormonal changes that are linked to cardiovascular disease and, possibly, impaired neurological function and memory. Relationships are destroyed when we only focus on the deed that has made us angry. What about those really difficult events in our lives that we say we can never forgive?

Ironically, these are precisely the events that we need to practice forgiveness the most or we become a victim twice over. It is hard enough to lose a loved one to a senseless murder or to be sexually assaulted, but then to imprison ourselves in a vortex of hatred and fear will only create a life filled with pain.

If we are willing to welcome forgiveness, as difficult as it may be, we are releasing ourselves from the powerful hold of being victims. Not only is there healing of our emotional pain, but our lives can take on new meaning. A life filled with compassion is a life well lived.

Included in this book are stories of incredible individuals from the person who could be your next door neighbor to one of the holiest men in the world, the Dalai Lama. Each of the storytellers shares his or her struggles and eventual triumphs in being able to forgive. You will learn how different people became skilled in being able to forgive. You will also learn the specific steps in the forgiveness program, an active program that will help you change the way you relate to other people. Interspersed between the stories are chapters that give a further explanation of what forgiveness is about, how it applies to the inspirational stories read, and how you can apply the lessons learned to yourself.

Finding Forgiveness: A Seven-Step Program for Letting Go of Anger and Bitterness is about the healing power of forgiveness and the ultimate freedom it can bring to our lives. This is a book about our journey into wholeness, written to inspire those who have a desire to forgive others and themselves and to make a difference for future generations. Its purpose is to provide the help you need to open your heart to forgive and to chart the territory that needs to be covered for forgiveness to occur at a transformational level. By being able to forgive, we learn how to extend ourselves to others and to realize that this action is part of *our* healing. Through stories of personal struggle and tragedy, you will gain a deeper understanding of the psychological and spiritual landscape of forgiveness, from its difficulties to its greatest rewards.

Forgiveness is a radical way of living that openly contradicts the most common beliefs of this troubled world. It is radical because it involves a transformation of our thinking from thoughts of "an eye for an eye" to compassion and understanding. Forgiveness is the science of the heart, a discipline of discovering all the ways of being that will extend your love to the world and discarding all the ways that do not. Forgiveness is the accomplishment of mastery over a wound. It is a process through which an injured person first fights off, then embraces, then conquers a situation that has nearly destroyed him or her.

Paul Tillich wrote that forgiveness is the divine answer to our existence. It restores our hearts to the innocence that we once knew—an innocence that allows us the freedom to love. It is the means for taking what is broken and making it whole. This book teaches us about forgiveness, one of the most awesome powers of the human spirit. It is about the struggles and courageous acts of people who chose to demonstrate forgiveness and, ultimately, love in their lives.

We are on the threshold of a new stage of development, and if we are willing to do the hard work of forgiveness and recognize what a powerful healing agent that forgiveness is, it is possible to create a more loving and peaceful world. The results of this will be dramatic. With all the violence that has taken center stage on the world arena, we can either take the path of self-destruction or take a path leading to a radical transformation. Forgiveness is pivotal in creating the kind of transformation that will not only bring peace in our lives, but peace in our world.

FINDING

FORGIVENESS

1

How Do We Forgive?

"The knowledge that illuminates not only sets you free, but also shows clearly that you are free."

—*A COURSE IN MIRACLES*

THROUGHOUT OUR LIVES most of us have been taught about forgiveness. Each one of us thinks differently about what forgiveness means, ranging from emotional weakness to high moral standards. To be able to forgive, we need to understand what forgiveness means. Otherwise, our misconceptions can become obstacles in our ability to forgive.

Forgiveness is a process that shows us how to heal emotional pain by choosing to see the person who caused the pain differently. It is about changing the way we think about ourselves and the way we see the world. Forgiveness is an essential part of *our* healing, enabling us to release *our* anger, pain, and suffering. As we learn to forgive and heal our emotional pain, we begin to experience the gift of inner peace.

Forgiveness is not about letting someone get away with murderous acts. It is about asking us to look at the totality of who we are, to accept the shortcomings within ourselves, and to embrace that truth with compassion, understanding, and unconditional love. As we face ourselves with courage and acceptance, we get in touch with our humanity and vulnerabilities. This gift of self-acceptance helps us grow in understanding and compassion, which we can then, ideally, extend to others.

There are many misconceptions concerning forgiveness. For example, many of us believe that we forgive in order to repair the relationship with the offender. Although this can be an outcome, the relationship that we are repairing is that within ourselves. Another misconception is that if we forgive someone, we cannot seek forms of justice. As we shall learn, forgiveness is about creating attitudinal changes within ourselves. Our outer actions may be the same whether we forgive or not. What is important is the motivation behind the actions we choose to take.

From its inception, forgiveness involved a process that required a change in perceptions and judgments. Changing perceptions directly effects the healing of anger and hatred. In our willingness to see the situation differently, these emotions begin to diffuse to the point that we no longer want to act out revenge. As we face truths about ourselves that make it possible for us to see others differently, we are taking the first steps in becoming more compassionate human beings. This brings us to a point where, because of our own development of compassion, we are willing to help others regardless of whether there has been acknowledgement from the offender.

Forgiveness is a voluntary act in which a person makes a *decision*—a *choice*—about how he or she will deal with an event concerning the past. One of these choices may be based on the belief that people can judge events, measure the magnitude of an offense, and decide that receiving an equal amount of retribution somehow balances the account (Hope, 1987). Another choice is to practice an attitude of forgiveness. This attitude allows us to let go of anger and resentment by deciding to absolve what we perceive as wrongs committed by the other (Hope, 1987). This involves recognizing how our attitudes and beliefs color the actual situation. We form our attitudes and beliefs based on our judgments and perceptions. Judgments and perceptions are based on our fears and needs at the time of the event. They are not facts, although we want to interpret them as such. The attitude of forgiveness is founded on the understanding that we screen and create the past through the process of judgment in the same way that we screen and create the present through the process of perception, and that our judgments and perceptions are subjective and unreliable (Hope, 1987). Therefore, it is through our filters of judgment and perception that we dictate our reality and not our deeper understanding of the actual event.

There are a few important points to make about this definition. First, those who forgive must have suffered a deep hurt, such as betrayal, that elicits anger and/or resentment. Although it is clear that those offended have a right to this resentment, they *choose* to overcome it. There are many reasons people make this choice. It could be they want to move on with their lives, they recognize that by holding on they are giving the perpetrator power, or they realize that by wanting revenge they become just like the perpetrator. Whatever the reason for this choice, a new response emerges that results in a change in perception based on understanding, compassion, and/or love. These responses occur because of the offended person's *choice*, not his obligations. The paradox is that as people let go of their feelings of anger, hatred, or the need for revenge, it is *they* who are healed. By accepting and coming to terms with what took place, those who can see the situation from a perspective of understanding and compassion can lay the past to rest and experience inner peace.

There are many complexities and misunderstandings concerning forgiveness that are important to clarify. The first point to understand is that forgiveness can only occur between two people. We cannot forgive a natural disaster or a war because forgiveness is about resolving the misperceptions we have projected on someone else. It is about healing a deep psychological injury we believe someone did to us. If we did not personally experience harm from someone else then we are not in a position to forgive.

One of the more difficult concepts to understand about forgiveness deals with perceptions. Perceptions are our views in how we choose to see the world. We all see the world differently according to our chosen lens. The events in our lives that are otherwise neutral derive meaning according to how we perceive what has happened. That is why two people can experience similar hurts but one gets stuck in the victim role while the other becomes empowered and takes action. Our reactions are based on our unconscious motivation. This unconscious motivation, be it guilt or fear, is colored by thoughts about ourselves that are too painful to acknowledge. What we cleverly do is sweep the negative thoughts we hold about ourselves under the carpet by only seeing these things in other people. This is what the psychological term *projection* means. We place on others what we don't want to see about ourselves. These lenses, which also serve as filters for our unconscious needs and desires, give meaning to our life events. This dynamic is important to understand because it explains how we create enemies of people we instantly do not like. It also explains why we can be standing in a hotel lobby and see someone we don't know, yet automatically decide we don't like that person. Part of the forgiveness process is to recognize our projections and reclaim them. In accepting the rejected aspects of ourselves, we begin to see the world more clearly. We cannot change the event itself, but we can change the way we see it. This is part of the forgiveness process.

An issue intertwined with forgiveness is justice. Most often we call for justice based on retribution. When we can finally understand forgiveness at its deepest level, we also get a deeper understanding of what is taking place within the perpetrator. We understand that just like us, other people's behavior is based in *their* woundedness, fear, and guilt. We recognize that twisted behavior is a call for help, and so it is help we need to give. That doesn't mean that we don't take the necessary actions to protect ourselves, but justice takes on a new meaning—a restorative one—when we begin to see the world differently, through the eyes of forgiveness.

Another difficult aspect of forgiveness deals with the issue of apology. Many people believe that it is necessary to receive an apology before they can forgive. Because forgiveness is about *our* inner healing, it is not dependent on an apology from someone else. Therefore, we do not need to have someone apologize to us. If we were dependent on an apology from someone else, we would become trapped in a state of unforgiveness, experiencing prolonged anger and pain (Enright, et al., 1992). This is where the power of forgiveness lies. Forgiveness is the gift from someone who has been hurt to give when there is a healing. Making the choice to forgive is part of the healing process that only comes from within.

Ultimately, forgiveness is about changing the way we think. Its transformational power moves us from being helpless victims of our circumstances to powerful cocreators of our reality. We learn to see people anew every day in terms of their future potential, not their past deeds. In becoming more loving, compassionate, and understanding human beings, we gain the ability to have a deeper relationship with ourselves and with the significant people in our lives.

Rethinking Forgiveness

In order to attain a better understanding of forgiveness, we have to clear up some common misperceptions that many people hold about its meaning. Some of these misperceptions focus on the terms *pardoning*, *condoning*, and *reconciliation* (Mawson and Whiting, 1923).

Forgiveness is not pardoning. Forgiveness is an inner emotional release. Pardoning is a public behavioral release. To pardon someone usually involves an authority who oversees laws by which the degree of punishment is established for each violation. If a person breaks the law and his punishment is reduced or suspended, there is a pardon. When officials pardon someone for their wrongdoing, they always reassert that wrong was done. The Hebrew-Christian tradition long ago understood forgiveness in this light (Frost, 1991). It is a way of affirming norms in the very process of seeking to lift from wrongdoers the full penalty due for breaking the norms. Here lies the misunderstanding of forgiveness. *To forgive the wrongdoer does not mean that we abolish the punishment for what was done.*

 Forgiveness is not condoning. Certain behaviors such as unprovoked violence, abuse, and aggression are totally unacceptable. Sometimes the most compassionate acts require taking action to stop the behaviors and to prevent them from happening again. Forgiveness does not mean that you support behaviors that cause pain to yourself or others. It does not mean that you don't take action to change a situation or protect yourself or others. Remember, forgiveness is a process that happens internally on a personal level. *We do not have to accept someone else's behavior in order to forgive.*

 Forgiveness is not reconciliation. Forgiveness is a personal, internal release that only involves oneself. Forgiveness may be a necessary step in bringing people together to reconcile and includes a willingness to reconcile, but it only involves ourselves. Reconciliation is a coming together of two or more people. We can forgive someone and demonstrate that in our behavior, but we may not reconcile until changes in the offender's behavior take place. *We can forgive someone, but it does not mean we have to reconcile.*

Some people believe that those who forgive are emotionally weak and fearful, without the courage to do what is "right" and necessary. They believe that forgiveness and strength cannot coexist within an individual. Yet, it is those people who *cannot* forgive who truly live with fear. Forgiveness is not about weakness and giving into the "strengths" of others. Forgiveness is about finding the strength in ourselves to see beyond the immediate harm inflicted upon us by others (and even ourselves), discovering the weaknesses that cause harm, and forgiving those shortcomings. Forgiveness is about seeing the *humanness* in others, seeing beyond their surface actions and realizing their pain that causes such actions.

It takes a generous spirit to understand that people do not always hurt us because they choose to. Oftentimes, they have no more control over their actions than we, their victims, do. Only from our wisdom and compassion can we recognize that when people harm us, it is *their* weaknesses that compel them to act. People who attack us act out of fear to protect themselves. Fear drives us into a hard shell. It shuts the door on our capacity to understand, empathize, and love, while allowing distrust and enmity to guard against being touched from the outside world. The truth is that behind the plague of violence and war lies confusion about ourselves, including the painful guilt we sense about our own failings. To compensate for this perception, we often harden ourselves so that others cannot gain access to our inner selves or discover our shortcomings.

The fact that we are struggling against our own unconscious feelings about our personal inadequacies and evils only makes us more desperate, destructive, and, ultimately, more self-destructive and leaves us with the unhealed wounds of our perceptions. The prospect of having to confront unbearably frightening aspects of our experience sometimes even leads to excessive outward violence. From this unhealed place, we find the acts of criminals committing random crimes, including individuals who hurt children or who commit war crimes. Such destructive behavior is evident not only from individuals, but it also can be found in the more global interactions of communities acting against other communities.

Forgiveness is a process that engages us in a search for significance not readily apparent to us by outward appearances. As we begin to look beneath the surface, we develop an understanding of hidden forces that we did not recognize before. We realize that within all of us is hidden bad and good, both of which have to be brought to the surface and dealt with. We are so accustomed to the doctrine of inherent sinfulness that we overlook our inherent goodness—our innate divinity. In fact, the tendencies of the majority of people are predominantly good. Forgiveness is about finding the unique good in ourselves and others and letting go of judgments that consequently predispose us toward harshness in our view of others. In suspending judgment, we experience the unity of life instead of defining the world in terms of opposites. We remember the connection to a greater source of being in which we know that no man is the "other." Forgiveness provides us the opportunity to recognize and strive toward the practical realization of what we innately are—good, caring people.

The Forgiveness Process

Forgiveness is a process that happens over time. Following the initial injury, we experience pain or anger. We can feel a loss of personal control. At times, we psychologically replay the hurt over and over so that the pain deepens. Then we compare the hurt to the perceived lack of pain of the offender's experience. We invariably come to the conclusion that life is not fair and that the world is not just. As the injured persons, we slowly deal with the anger and begin to gain insight into the behavior of the perpetrator, and we give meaning to the event. When we can finally let go of our pain we begin to heal.

Before we can truly forgive, we need to realize that forgiveness is about *our inner healing* and not necessarily about behavioral change. Until then we may needlessly deal with resistance about forgiving someone.

We heal by remembering, by bringing back into our awareness everything we have kept hidden from ourselves. It takes time to bring all these pieces together. This process begins by telling our story and validating our feelings and experiences. Too often, because of the pain and cutting of a deep wound, we gloss over a traumatic event at the time it happens. There is a tendency to set up psychological defense mechanisms that separate us from the pain we feel. Telling our story can help us reconnect with this pain so that we can eventually be freed from it.

Sometimes the pain we desperately deny resurfaces in various ways, such as anger or hatred toward the person who has hurt us. In order to forgive the person we have to listen to our anger and other strong emotions and learn to understand what they are telling us. Only after time and being in a safe environment can we allow ourselves to feel and express our strong emotions and to explore the issues concerning our pain and circumstances. As we become more aware and accepting of all our emotions as valid messengers about our interaction in the world, we begin our healing. And if someone is willing to listen to us and share our pain and sorrow, the burden becomes lighter and even bearable.

After we focus attention on our emotions, especially anger, and understand its meaning, it is very important to look at our reactions to pain and how we may be subtly nurturing our pain. If we are holding onto something, we need to recognize that, despite any other person's role in creating the situation, we are responsible for what we do with the hurt. Forgiveness is about accepting responsibility for our emotional reactions to our hurt. We need to let go of the feelings from the past, especially those that nurture our pain, and experience the power that comes from their release This growth requires that we remove the obstacles created by our anger and guilt and deal with them appropriately by facing them, however painful and difficult this may be. It may also require the recognition that what we have condemned in another is indeed what we have condemned in ourselves. Because this is sometimes too painful for us to acknowledge about ourselves, we see shortcomings only in someone else and not in ourselves, thus diverting our attention from the true source of the problem.

As we bring our shortcomings to our awareness, it is normal and expected for us to have feelings of guilt. However, unhealthy guilt causes us to reject our own worth as human beings. It causes us to retreat from life with the need to avoid fear rather than engage in life in a loving way. When guilt takes over our life, our faults and fears seem to stand out at the expense of our joys and pleasures. Unhealthy guilt keeps us stuck in our feelings of presumed unworthiness, and we hurt others because of this.

Guilt and responsibility are mutually exclusive. Guilt holds onto the wound and prevents it from healing. Taking responsibility for what we have done and making other choices heals guilt.

Holding on to guilt represents a decision that can always be changed. Certainly, the shift is not something that mysteriously happens; it must be something we want and are willing to work toward. Releasing guilt and our self-judgments allows us to have a change of heart for others. If we are successful in releasing our guilt, we are psychologically ready to consider forgiveness as an option. The commitment to forgive will not happen unless *we want it to happen*. We must go beyond the feeling level and make forgiveness a cognitive decision.

By learning what anger and guilt need to teach us, we begin to develop new perspectives. We recognize that pain and suffering in others can lead them to horrific actions. Forgiving someone becomes easier once we understand how *our* pain and suffering has colored *our* world. This insight helps us contemplate the suffering of others, or it may help us acknowledge something deeper within ourselves that leads us to a greater personal healing. As we begin to consider the situation in a different conceptual context, we gain greater empathy for the situation and the perpetrators. Consequently, we are then able to ask the questions, "Are you willing to see the person as a member of the human community? Are you willing to see this person as possessing value? Are you able to see his or her weaknesses, fears, and sufferings that led to the event?" As we learn to walk in others' shoes, we are able to feel their situations and perhaps come to recognize that given similar circumstances we may not have acted much differently. This realization is the moment of *our* release.

When we have reached this point in our journey of forgiveness, some of our experiences are so profound that they transform. An inner shift takes place and the love and compassion that have begun to grow in our hearts enable us to think about the other person, who needs forgiveness. We are able to shift the focus away from our pain and ourselves to the person who caused the pain. This is the place in the forgiveness process that provides us with the opportunity to grow in compassion, by entering into the life of another and experiencing that person's pain as though it were ours. To have compassion toward another is to have the ability to include *everything* about this person in our hearts, which allows us to view this person anew. When we feel compassion toward another, we open ourselves up to that individual and become sensitive to that person's feelings and receptive to the possibility of accepting that person unconditionally with love and sensitivity. Compassion comes from the heart. If we could know the past history of the person who has hurt us so deeply, we would likely find intense pain and suffering, enough to disarm our anger. Compassion does *not* condone the wrong that has been committed. It assists us in understanding the hurt from an entirely different perspective, seeing the pain or fear behind the actions of another.

Perception is our reality. It is what we have chosen to see. We possess the capacity to change our view of an event and the participants of that event to create for ourselves any reality we select. The healthiest and most productive manner in which to view an event is through the eyes of compassion and forgiveness. We develop the willingness to "accept" pain, a perspective that is always better than coping with revenge and resentment. Emotional or psychological pain leaves more than a mental scar. It leaves a memory. Although time heals most hurts, it does not completely remove feelings. In accepting and absorbing pain, we diffuse the need for revenge and can move on. Absorbing pain is extremely difficult to do. Such thorough acceptance is at the heart of forgiveness, which stops the cycle of pain from being passed on.

Discovering the meaning in our pain is central to the process of forgiveness. In knowing our suffering, we come to know the suffering of others. Strangely enough this helps us release our own pain. The process of giving meaning to our pain may take the form of spiritual currency, such as doing something with our lives so our tragedy doesn't befall others. It may also happen when we can view the situation through the eyes of compassion and come to a spiritual understanding gained because of our pain. When we are able to transform our lives in some way because we have allowed forgiveness to open our hearts, we have discovered that our pain was not in vain.

Once we have unlocked our hearts, we are ready to forgive. When we make the commitment to forgive others, we are enriching ourselves. We open ourselves to the entirety of what life has to offer, giving ourselves permission to be at one with the situation, or with life as a whole. The opening of ourselves to something beyond ourselves is sometimes called the *third factor* in the process of forgiveness (Muller-Fahrenholz, 1989). It calls upon us to trust the unknown and unexplainable (i.e., a leap of faith). The third factor is that specific element of strength, faith, or trust that makes us sufficiently free from the feelings of guilt, shame, anger, or distrust in order to act independently and to make the forgiving, reconciling move. The transcending spark of courage that the third factor brings opens us up to the moment of daring and trust that causes hearts to jump over the fence. This surprising energy dissolves the dividing walls between us and paves the way for unions between individuals. During the moment of grace, illusions of judgment and hatred are lifted from our experience. Now we can accept love within a world filled with fear.

The last step in the forgiveness process is about reflecting on what we have learned in our psychological and spiritual growth and then integrating the wisdom gained into our lives. This is when the inner transformation becomes solidified in the outer world in the most gracious acts of kindness and goodwill. Many stories in this book are illustrations of how tragedy and forgiveness led people to help lessen the suffering of others.

A spiritual transformation of an individual or of humanity as a whole is not an easy undertaking, nor is it quickly accomplished. This is the spiritual challenge we face. It requires a certain amount of spiritual stamina to appreciate and accept that our efforts lead to very slow growth at best. It is gratifying to know that this stamina can be summoned by all of us when we are ready to access and receive the spiritual reserves that we all have.

2

Learning to Forgive
The Seven-Step Forgiveness Program

"To err is human, to forgive divine."
—ALEXANDER POPE

WE KNOW THAT as difficult as forgiveness may be, the psychological case for practicing forgiveness is compelling. If we are unable to forgive, we are imprisoned by the past, and we remain under the control of the one who has hurt us. Holding on to our hurt and pain negatively affects our physical and emotional well-being. Anger, in particular, affects our cardiovascular system. Psychologically, when we are stuck in anger, it becomes nearly impossible to change the circumstances of our lives. The end result is that we lose all the way around.

Although forgiveness can happen in an instant, for many of us it can take weeks, months, years, or possibly a lifetime. The work of forgiveness is different for each of us, yet there are certain predictable steps all of us will go through. This program will describe what these steps are and how we go about achieving them. Some steps will be more difficult than others depending upon our personal circumstances. Other steps may be more relevant for some than for others. We may also find that we move back and forth between steps. That's OK. Focus on what is important. We use these steps as a guide to get through the process. For example, we may find that we thought we had worked through a lot of emotions in Step Two only to find in Step Three that more emotions come to the surface. It will be important to work with those emotions when they arise. When dealing with painful situations, sometimes the emotional content can be so overwhelming that we may not be able to deal with it all at once. We may need to go back to Step Two a number of times before we feel we have released what we needed to in order to move on. These steps are very fluid so we may find that we are working on more than one step at the same time. Keep in mind, none of us forgive in the same way, and the forgiveness process is not a rigid process.

Getting Started

As with any difficult emotional work, it is important to have a strong and healthy emotional support network. You need to be around people who love you and who can support you in healthy ways. You need a companion throughout your forgiveness journey, someone to comfort you and help you through your pain and who can be used as a sounding board, especially when you begin to delve into anger, guilt, and grief. If there is no one in your life you feel comfortable to do this work with, find a therapist who can guide you. Make sure you are under the care of a therapist if you are dealing with difficult issues such as trauma, depression, anxiety, or suicidal thoughts.

The first thing you will need is a journal or a notebook. This will become an invaluable tool and is for you only. Writing what comes to mind is one way to give all the stuff trapped inside of you voice. You can write during moments of reflection or for a pouring out of whatever needs to be expressed. Just keep writing. Don't sensor anything. Let your stream of consciousness take you where you need to go, even if you think "This is silly!" or "I don't want to do this." If you feel stuck, ask yourself what you are feeling at that moment and write down whatever comes up. Keep writing no matter what comes up. Eventually, something will come to mind that will surprise you. By writing things down, you are giving your emotions voice, dissipating their energy. You will know when you are done and will probably experience a sense of release.

A journal is a wonderful way to tap into deeper parts of yourself and access thoughts and feelings that would not normally come up in talking with someone. It allows you to expose what is hidden in a deeper way that aids tremendously in the release of suppressed emotions. It is a nonthreatening way of telling your story, which no one else needs to see.

Write in your journal for a few minutes every day while working on this program. Some people like to write first thing in the morning when their mind hasn't become preoccupied with the day's events. Others prefer the evenings when things quiet down. Commit to a time that works best for you, and get into a routine of writing at that same time every day. Below are some guidelines you may find helpful.

- Find a quiet and comfortable place to do your writing where you will not be disturbed.
- Use this same place every time you write.
- Make sure you will not be disturbed by anyone or anything, including the telephone.
- Before you begin, take a few very deep, relaxing breaths to help quiet your mind and body.
- Begin journaling by allowing whatever needs to come up to be written even if it seems totally off the wall. Follow the stream of consciousness. It will take you where you need to go.

Allow your writing to guide you. If you are working on a particular situation in your life or a particular step in the forgiveness process, you can ask yourself certain questions to help clarify what you are feeling and what you need to do. You will find some of these questions, which you can use as guides, at the end of each step.

Practice some relaxation techniques at least once a day either using techniques you have liked in the past or with relaxation tapes. Learning how to relax is an important skill to develop and to use, especially if you sense that you are becoming overwhelmed with emotion. If this does happen where your emotions are too much to handle and you need to stop, end your journaling session with one of these relaxation activities.

One more skill that you will find invaluable is visualization. Visualization or imagery techniques can help you learn how to relax as well as give you insight into your thoughts and behavior. You will find visualization exercises on each step in the forgiveness process in Chapter 15, "What *You* Can Do for Yourself." Visualization is a skill anyone can learn. With practice you will develop better concentration skills and your visualizations will deepen. It is important to remember that images are symbols from our unconscious mind, part of ourselves that we are unaware of. Because of their symbolic nature, imagery techniques are nonthreatening, meaning that if you are not ready to understand what the images have to say, you will not. The wonderful thing about using imagery is that once you start experiencing your symbols, a healing process is started, even if you do not understand what the images mean.

You can also use imagery to reinforce certain behaviors. For example, if you want to be doing more of something, visualize yourself doing it. This action will reinforce your desire and get you moving! If you are new to this kind of work, there are a few tips to give you.

- Before you begin any visualization exercise, make sure that you have gone to a very quiet place where you will not be distracted.
- Sit or lie in a comfortable position, making sure that your clothing is loose and you do not feel any restriction.

- Take a number of deep, relaxing breaths until you feel that your body and thoughts are slowing down. This is an extremely important step. The more relaxed you are, the easier it is to experience images.
- If at first you feel as though you are making things up, go with it. Those made up images are coming from some place and are very important. Just go with it. Create your own scenes. That is part of the process.
- Try to make your images as vivid as possible. Notice colors, sound, who or what is in the scene, and so on.
- After your session is over, write your experience in your journal. Ask yourself, "Why did I have this image or scene now? What is going on in my life now that may relate to this experience?"
- Most important, have fun!

Rating Scales

Rating scales are used to help you chart your progress. You will be asked to complete these rating scales before you start this program, when you feel you are ready to move from one step to the next, and at the end of the program. The purpose is to help you see the progress you have made in the forgiveness process and where you have improved and, possibly, where more work needs to be done.

Many of you will see progress. Others may not. Don't be discouraged if you aren't progressing the way you might have liked. Change takes time, especially when it involves adopting a totally different world view. Congratulate yourself for your willingness and your efforts. That is monumental in and of itself. As you work with the rating scales, circle the number that best describes where you are in the process. There is a rating scale for each of the steps of the forgiveness program. Take a moment now and rate all of the following questions. Record that number in your journal so you will be able to go back to it at a later time.

Step One: Becoming Clear

How clear is your understanding concerning forgiveness?

VERY CLEAR   **NOT CLEAR AT ALL**

| 1 | 2 | 3 | 4 | 5 | 6 | 7 |

How often do you think about getting even with the perpetrator?

I DON'T THINK ABOUT IT   **I AM OBSESSED WITH IT**

| 1 | 2 | 3 | 4 | 5 | 6 | 7 |

How willing are you in wanting to forgive?

TOTALLY WILLING   **NOT WILLING AT ALL**

| 1 | 2 | 3 | 4 | 5 | 6 | 7 |

Step Two: Telling Your Story

How much emotional pain are you experiencing as you start this program?

NONE   **FEELINGS ARE OVERWHELMING**

| 1 | 2 | 3 | 4 | 5 | 6 | 7 |

How difficult is it to share your emotional experiences as you start the program?

NOT DIFFICULT AT ALL   **VERY DIFFICULT**

| 1 | 2 | 3 | 4 | 5 | 6 | 7 |

Step Three: Working with Anger

How angry are you at the person who hurt you as you start this program?

NOT ANGRY   **INFURIATED**

| 1 | 2 | 3 | 4 | 5 | 6 | 7 |

How well do you understand the deeper meaning of your anger?

TOTAL UNDERSTANDING   **NO UNDERSTANDING**

| 1 | 2 | 3 | 4 | 5 | 6 | 7 |

Do you see ways in which you are subtly nurturing your pain?

VERY AWARE TOTALLY UNAWARE

| 1 | 2 | 3 | 4 | 5 | 6 | 7 |

Are you open to making changes to your own behavior according to what your anger may be teaching you?

VERY WILLING NOT WILLING AT ALL

| 1 | 2 | 3 | 4 | 5 | 6 | 7 |

Step Four: Working with Guilt

How aware were you of your own feelings of guilt?

VERY AWARE NO AWARENESS

| 1 | 2 | 3 | 4 | 5 | 6 | 7 |

Are you willing to step back and accept that you were not seeing the total situation that needed to be forgiven?

TOTALLY WILLING NOT WILLING

| 1 | 2 | 3 | 4 | 5 | 6 | 7 |

Are you acknowledging your guilt and taking responsibility for your actions?

TAKING TOTAL RESPONSIBILITY TOTALLY DENYING GUILT

| 1 | 2 | 3 | 4 | 5 | 6 | 7 |

Step Five: Reframing the Situation

Are you willing to shift your focus from yourself to the other person who needs forgiveness?

VERY WILLING NOT WILLING AT ALL

| 1 | 2 | 3 | 4 | 5 | 6 | 7 |

How difficult is it for you to walk in the offender's shoes?

EASY VERY DIFFICULT

| 1 | 2 | 3 | 4 | 5 | 6 | 7 |

How willing are you to see your situation differently?

VERY WILLING   NOT WILLING AT ALL

| 1 | 2 | 3 | 4 | 5 | 6 | 7 |

Step Six: Absorbing Pain

How difficult was it for you to accept your pain before you
started this program?

EASY   IMPOSSIBLE

| 1 | 2 | 3 | 4 | 5 | 6 | 7 |

How complete is your process for mourning your losses?

COMPLETE   NOT BEGUN

| 1 | 2 | 3 | 4 | 5 | 6 | 7 |

Have you been able to make your pain meaningful?

VERY MEANINGFUL   NO MEANING AT ALL

| 1 | 2 | 3 | 4 | 5 | 6 | 7 |

Did you have a deep commitment to forgive before you started
this program?

VERY DEEP COMMITMENT   NO COMMITMENT

| 1 | 2 | 3 | 4 | 5 | 6 | 7 |

Step Seven: Gaining Inner Peace

How well have you forgiven the offender before you started this
program?

COMPLETELY   NOT AT ALL

| 1 | 2 | 3 | 4 | 5 | 6 | 7 |

Were you able to view the situation by seeing that this person was
worthy of love?

TOTAL SPIRITUAL INSIGHT   NO INSIGHT

| 1 | 2 | 3 | 4 | 5 | 6 | 7 |

Has practicing forgiveness changed your life in anyway before you started the program?

VERY MUCH						NOT AT ALL
1	2	3	4	5	6	7

Seven-Step Forgiveness Program

The seven-step forgiveness program was developed as a result of working with many clients wanting to learn how to forgive. Over time, a pattern began to emerge as people moved forward in their healing journey. There were certain predictable steps people went through and certain issues or tasks people faced along the way depending upon their personal circumstances. Although this program is very fluid, many people find it helpful to have an idea of what can be expected along their journey. Below is a description of this process that has helped many people learn how to forgive.

With each step are journal exercises and questions to answer. It is also important that you write in your journal every day. For the journal writing, you can allow anything to come up, even if it doesn't seem to relate to what you are doing. Whatever it is needs expression. You may also focus on the step you are working on and journal with whatever issue is on your mind. You may find that as you do the journal exercises you may want to go over them a few times, or that it takes more than one sitting for everything to emerge that needs expression. That's OK. Once you feel you have finished these exercises, complete the rating scales. At the end of the book, you will have a chance again to complete a final scale.

Step One: Becoming Clear

Before we can actually begin the work of forgiveness, we need to prepare ourselves. One of the greatest obstacles in learning how to forgive is that people do not have a clear understanding of what forgiveness means. If you have gotten this far in the book, you should

have a greater understand of what forgiveness is about and realize
that forgiveness has greater benefits for yourself than for others.
Become clear in what forgiveness means to you. Remember that
forgiveness focuses on your *inner healing* and is not necessarily
about an outward behavior. It is not about letting someone else off
the hook. You are releasing *your* emotional pain so you can have a
happier and more fulfilling life. Part of becoming clear about what
forgiveness is involves the acknowledgement of our need for
revenge. This stems back to the notion of an "eye for an eye," and
it is also what our natural tendencies are. If someone attacks us, we
feel that justice is not served until there is some form of retribution. We will talk more about this later, but for now we recognize
that retribution is only one way to handle a situation and it never
gets us what we really want.

The last important issue to think about in this step is your
motivation. A lot of emotional healing may need to take place
before you are truly ready to forgive. Acknowledging this is healthy
and normal. If you understand the true meaning of forgiveness
and realize that revenge will not get you what you really want,
then you have set the stage for forgiveness. At the beginning of
this process, all you need is a little willingness to entertain the
idea that forgiveness can be an option in terms of what you would
like to do. A little willingness means that you are receptive to the
idea of forgiveness and are willing to let the forgiveness process
work itself out, however long it takes. This includes the willingness to put aside any thoughts of revenge and to focus on healing. That little willingness is what will help you open the door
for forgiveness to enter your life when you have done your emotional healing work.

Tasks for Step One

Understand what forgiveness truly means.

Recognize that we have a universal need for revenge.

Consider choosing a little willingness to entertain the thought of
forgiveness.

Journal Exercise for Step One

Step One focuses on getting clear regarding what forgiveness is and why you are thinking about the forgiveness process now. Write down your understanding of what forgiveness means and what is happening in your life right now that may be serving as a catalyst for thinking about forgiveness. Some of you may want to write a revenge fantasy. If you do, ask yourself after you finish your story what you will have gained by revenge. Does revenge complete anything, and what are the repercussions of revenge? Explore revenge and ask what the need for revenge inside of you is saying. Write about how revenge will hurt you and what you will need to do to bring about a little willingness to entertain the thought of forgiveness.

Questions to Think About for Step One

What healing effect will forgiveness have on my life?

Is there anything blocking me from entertaining the idea of a little willingness to forgive and, if so, what do I need to do to be able to change my mind?

Rating Scales

How clear is your understanding concerning forgiveness after Step One of the program?

VERY CLEAR　　　　　　　　　　　　　　　　**NOT CLEAR AT ALL**

1	2	3	4	5	6	7

How often did you think about getting even with the perpetrator after completing Step One?

I DON'T THINK ABOUT IT　　　　　　　　**I AM OBSESSED WITH IT**

1	2	3	4	5	6	7

How willing are you in wanting to forgive at the end of Step One?

TOTALLY WILLING　　　　　　　　　　　　**NOT WILLING AT ALL**

1	2	3	4	5	6	7

Step Two: Telling Your Story

Once you recognize the healing effect that forgiveness can have in your life and that revenge will not take your pain away, you are ready to take the next step in the forgiveness process. Step Two is about telling your story to those you trust. You begin with what is inside of you right now. Most of us feel some very strong emotions and the need for revenge may still be lurking not far behind. Tell your story as completely, and with as much depth and detail, as possible. You may want to start with a review of your life and the circumstances that led up to the event. Talk about important relationships and whatever else is pertinent to provide a context within which the particular meaning of the event or events can be understood. Then give a detailed account, your response to it, and the responses of the important people in your life. If it is difficult to talk about it, write or draw your story. Drawing pictures can be tremendously healing in working through painful material. Tell your story as though you were watching a movie with as much vivid description as possible. What are you seeing, feeling, hearing, smelling, and thinking?

When you first tell your story, it may be incomplete. It is important to bring all the pieces together, including what you felt and the meaning of the event to you and to the people around you. Talk about the question of guilt and responsibility. This may help you later in reconstructing a system of belief that makes sense of undeserved suffering.

As you tell your story, some of you may feel a great deal of anxiety. This is when you stop and use relaxation techniques to help manage strong emotions. Once you feel in control, you can continue where you left off or return to it on another day.

Tasks for Step Two

Tell your story to those who will be supportive and whom you can trust.

Talk about your emotional experiences.

Journal Exercise for Step Two

Write a script describing the event in detail. This description should include the context of the situation, facts, emotions, and meaning. If there were several events, develop a separate script for each one. Don't be surprised if new memories are recovered as you explore old ones. Write down everything you feel about the situation and the person causing you pain. Allow a stream of consciousness to flow across the pages of your journal and spare nothing. Remember that this is your private journal for no one else to see. After you have written everything down, ask yourself, "If I were face to face with this person, what would I say?" Let out the anger and the hurt in what you write and keep on writing until there is nothing left to say.

Questions to Think About for Step Two

Why did this situation happen to me?

Why did this situation happen to the others included?

Rating Scales

How much emotional pain are you experiencing as you finish Step Two?

NONE   FEELINGS ARE OVERWHELMING

| 1 | 2 | 3 | 4 | 5 | 6 | 7 |

How difficult is it to share your emotional experiences after finishing Step 2?

NOT DIFFICULT AT ALL   VERY DIFFICULT

| 1 | 2 | 3 | 4 | 5 | 6 | 7 |

Step Three: Working With Anger

Anger tells us that our circumstances need to change. If we can't let go of our anger it is also telling us that *we* need to change.

This is the time when we get into the trenches of our emotions and have the difficult dialogue with ourselves about what happened and how we will choose to deal with it in a *healing* capacity. It is the time when we roll up our sleeves and become very honest with ourselves. Our tendencies are to want to feel sorry for ourselves and stay stuck in a victim role. By playing "poor me," we disempower ourselves or continue to play the blame game and not take responsibility or positive action in our lives. Instead of seeing the situation as the good guy versus the bad guy, we would be better served to learn the lessons our emotions are trying to teach us and to understand what is making the person behave that way.

This is a difficult phase because it requires introspection and honest soul searching. Although we may think we are angry at someone else if we are having difficulty letting go of anger it is an indication that we are in the need of healing. Don't be afraid to dialogue with the anger inside of you. Ask your anger what it wants to tell you. You can have this conversation by either writing down whatever comes to mind or sharing what is inside of you with someone you trust. Honor what your anger says to you. You may need to journal many times focusing on your anger. You can also draw it. There may be multiple meanings to your anger. Your anger could be protecting you. It could also be telling you what *you* need to do to heal.

Tasks for Step Three

Accept your emotions as valid messengers.

Acknowledge anger.

Look at the origins of your pain.

Feel the depth of your rage.

Take responsibility for your own behavior.

Ask yourself if you are subtly nurturing your pain.

Listen to your anger for its deeper message.

Look inward and make necessary changes.

Journal Exercise for Step Three

Rewrite your story. Focus on your anger and give your anger voice. Ask your anger what it is trying to tell you. How is your anger protecting you? If you are having difficulty letting go of your anger, ask yourself what are you accusing the offender of? Deep down inside, you are secretly accusing yourself of the same thing. The form may be different but the content will be the same. For example, if you are accusing someone of betraying you, you may have never betrayed someone in the same way but perhaps you have betrayed *yourself* or others in some other way. Ask yourself, have I ever betrayed (or whatever the issue may be) someone else or myself in a different way and journal with whatever comes up. Explore your anger until you find out what needs to change inside of you and, possibly, what outer changes you may also want to make. Ask your anger how it can be used in a *healing* capacity.

Questions to Think About for Step Three

What are the lessons my anger is trying to teach me?

What do I emotionally experience as I tell my story?

Rating Scales

How angry were you at the person who hurt you while you worked through this step?

NOT ANGRY   INFURIATED

1	2	3	4	5	6	7

How well did you understand the deeper meaning of your anger after you finished Step Three?

TOTAL UNDERSTANDING   NO UNDERSTANDING

1	2	3	4	5	6	7

Did you see ways in which you were subtly nurturing your pain after you ended Step Three?

VERY AWARE   TOTALLY UNAWARE

1	2	3	4	5	6	7

Were you open to making changes to your own behavior according to what your anger taught you at the end of Step Three?

VERY WILLING   **NOT WILLING AT ALL**

1	2	3	4	5	6	7

Step Four: Working with Guilt

Underneath your anger, you will find guilt. No one wants to be aware of their guilt and the possible shame that goes with it. Work with these emotions in the same way you worked with your anger. Guilt is particularly hard to get in touch with and deal with. Guilt includes all those negative feelings we believe to be true about ourselves. It is something we don't want to know about ourselves. We would much rather pretend that it doesn't exist. The problem is if we don't look squarely at our guiltly feelings we have to put them somewhere else, namely on other people. Whenever we attack someone even in times when we think it is in self-defense, we need to become sensitive to the motivation behind our actions. Often our actions are based in guilt and fear, not in genuine concern for ourselves and others. As soon as something happens to us, we can only see the situation through *our* negative thinking caused by our guilt. Until we recognize what we are doing, we will continue to blame others and have a distorted view of what is actually happening. We need to learn how to see through our smoke screens and own our guilt. We heal guilt by taking responsibility for our choices. Keep in mind that holding on to guilt and being stuck in a victim role is a choice, too. As we begin to heal our guilt, the prison walls around our heart begin to fall away. The healing that takes place during this phase will ultimately enable us to accept and absorb our pain, which is a pivotal point in the healing process.

The way to work with guilt is to recognize that when you are experiencing feelings ranging from a slight irritation to a full-blown fight, you are covering up feelings of guilt. Once you ask what you are accusing others of, and recognize that you are also accusing yourself of the same kind of thing, you are beginning to uncover your guilt. When these feelings are exposed, you can begin to take responsibility for them, which begins the healing process. Once these feelings are exposed, you can begin to take responsibility for them, which, in turn, heals guilt. When you recognize that you are capable of committing a similar kind of act in a different form as your offender, you begin to recognize that we are all capable of doing things that hurt ourselves and others. In some respects, we are more alike than different. In acknowledging that all of us are capable of doing similar things, we begin to see the situation differently.

This may be the time when we need to forgive ourselves for something we may have done in the past. As we learn how to forgive ourselves, our interpretation of reality begins to shift. When we begin to peel away our guilt, we begin to see the situation differently, not through the eyes of guilt any more, but with eyes of compassion. Once we take responsibility for our actions, holding on to guilt becomes a choice. We can choose to hold on or to let go. Healing guilt is about looking at what *we* have done, taking responsibility, making other choices, and realizing that we are greater than our thoughts and behaviors. That is not to say that other people's behavior may not need to be changed. The important issue here is our motivation. Are we coming from a place of guilt or compassion that is influencing what we do? There is something far greater inside of us that we have covered by our guilt. The more guilt we can heal, the closer we come to the truth of who we are, and the more we can hear the voice of our higher nature. When we can recognize the truth in ourselves as we heal, we will also see the truth in others. This is the work of Step Four.

Tasks for Step Four

Face your guilt.

Understand that what you attack in others you condemn in yourself.

Be willing to change your interpretation of reality.

Recognize that holding on to guilt is a choice, too.

Accept responsibility for your emotional reactions.

Listen within.

Journal Exercise for Step Four

To be able to forgive others you need to be able to forgive yourself. Begin this journal exercise by asking yourself, "What do I *feel* guilty of in relation to this situation or at other times in my life?" Explore whatever comes up without judgment. Don't be afraid to reach back in time for feelings of guilt. This is part of *your* healing process. Feel your feelings as they surface and be open to what they want to say to you. "Is there something now or in the past that needs healing and, if so, what actions can I take to heal it?" Even if it is clear that you did nothing to the perpetrator, you still may have feelings of guilt. If there is something that you feel ashamed of, explore those feelings to get to the roots of *your* wound. This action will uncover something you need to forgive yourself for. Guilt will also surface after you ask yourself, "What am I secretly accusing myself of?" If you are honest with yourself, you will find guilt associated in some way with what has happened. Explore this in your journal. It could be that you recognize something about your actions or inaction that has caused these feelings or thoughts about certain things. Journal with whatever comes up. You will probably have to repeat the journal exercise in this step a number of times before you are able to release some of your guilt. Guilt runs so deeply that if we worked on it for a lifetime we would still find more! What's important is to be gentle with yourself as you do this work. After you have explored your guilt feelings ask yourself, "How have I placed my feelings of guilt on others, such as through blaming or judging? What can I do differently now?" Go deep within and listen.

Questions to Think About for Step Four

How has my unresolved guilt affected my life?

How has guilt kept me trapped in the victim role?

How has guilt kept me from forgiving myself and others?

Rating Scales

How aware were you of your own feelings of guilt after you finished Step Four?

VERY AWARE						NO AWARENESS
1	2	3	4	5	6	7

Were you willing to step back and accept that you were not seeing the total situation that needed to be forgiven after you finished Step Four?

TOTALLY WILLING						NOT WILLING
1	2	3	4	5	6	7

Could you acknowledge your guilt and take responsibility for your actions after you finished Step Four?

TOOK RESPONSIBILITY						TOTALLY DENIED GUILT
1	2	3	4	5	6	7

Step Five: Reframing the Situation

This step entails changing our thinking about the situation. We have healed a lot of our anger and guilt, which helps us to see things differently. Once we have learned the lessons our emotions want to teach us, the reins of pain loosen. At this point in the forgiveness process, we are ready to think about the other person who needs forgiveness, and *not* the incident or the pain it has caused. We begin to reframe the situation in a different conceptual context. We recognize that outward appearances don't tell the entire story of what is inside a person. This realization helps us shift our focus from ourselves to thinking about the perpetrator. We begin to ask the questions, "Why did *this* person behave in a certain way? What life events brought this person to do this particular act at this particular time?" When we ask these questions, we eventually recognize that a healthy and happy person would not do harm to others. Only those who are wounded themselves would continue to perpetuate suffering. That's why *our* healing is important; so we do not react from our pain, creating more pain for others.

We learn how to become more compassionate by being willing to walk in someone else's shoes and see the world from that person's psychological perspective. Compassion involves being open to the suffering of oneself and others in a nonjudgmental way. We are willing to look at *their* life events and how those events have affected them. We recognize how their pain has caused them to behave in the ways we have experienced them. This may help us appreciate how lucky we have been that our life circumstances have been much better than theirs. The more you grow in compassion, the more resilient you become in dealing with painful situations and the greater your ability to transform these situations into more positive conditions. Compassion becomes a source of inner strength. As we grow in compassion and begin to develop a spiritual understanding that an outward behavior does not negate the true essence of who this person is, our commitment to the forgiveness process deepens.

Tasks for Step Five

Shift focus from ourselves to the other person who needs forgiveness.

Walk in someone else's shoes.

Be willing to see the situation differently.

Journal Exercise for Step Five

Rewrite your story to create a "healing" story that reflects an understanding of the perpetrator. Put yourself in his or her shoes and include a description of the perpetrator and what motivated the action. Where were the wounds? What was this person's life like that possibly led to the action? If you found that a lot of anger or resistance came up and you could not put yourself in the perpetrator's shoes, explore that. Did a shift in your thinking take place and, if so, how did it happen? If not, journal with what is blocking you in making that shift. Describe how you are able to see the situation differently now.

Questions to Think About for Step Five

What are some things you can do to grow in compassion?

What are your spiritual beliefs about who we are as human beings?

Can these spiritual beliefs help deepen your commitment to forgive?

Are you willing to consider forgiveness and, if not, what is getting in your way?

Rating Scales

Were you willing to shift your focus from yourself to the other person who needs forgiveness after you finished Step Five?

VERY WILLING | NOT WILLING AT ALL

| 1 | 2 | 3 | 4 | 5 | 6 | 7 |

How difficult was it for you to walk in the offender's shoes after you finished Step Five?

EASY | VERY DIFFICULT

| 1 | 2 | 3 | 4 | 5 | 6 | 7 |

How willing are you to see the situation differently after finishing Step Five?

VERY WILLING | NOT WILLING AT ALL

| 1 | 2 | 3 | 4 | 5 | 6 | 7 |

Step Six: Absorbing Pain

Pain can feel devastating. We may try to deny it or cover it up, sometimes using alcohol and drugs, but eventually, if we want to forgive we will have to learn how to deal constructively with our pain. You have already begun healing your pain by uncovering and working through your anger and guilt. The next part of the process involves mourning.

To release pain, we need to grieve, especially for the loss the offense has brought, be it the loss of innocence or some ending that needs to be mourned. Mourning is essential for healing and moving on in our lives. It is also something we would rather avoid. Sometimes we refuse to grieve as a way of denying victory to the perpetrator. To the extent that we are unable to grieve indicates how much we are cut off from an important part of our own healing process. When we allow ourselves to mourn we discover that our inner strength is indestructible. Mourning means that we will have to live tomorrow differently than before, usually with a void to fill. This is the time we give ourselves permission to cry. For some of us, this could be for the first time. Often, especially if the offense happened when we were children, we had to keep in or deny feelings concerning what befell us as a way of survival. Now we can do things differently. Only when we give ourselves permission to feel the pain can we absorb it.

Absorbing our pain is the most difficult part of the forgiveness process. Paradoxically, by absorbing the pain, the pain slowly dissipates until we are freed from it. By absorbing the pain, we accept it and, instead of being a victim, we become survivors. In accepting the pain, we discover that we can begin to handle it and we become stronger. This is how the pain lessens. Accepting pain is a pivotal step in the forgiveness process. As we learn how to do this for ourselves, our hearts begin to open, and we gain a greater ability to care for ourselves and others. When we finally begin to hurt and grieve, we free ourselves of those emotional burdens. This is how we heal. In taking responsibility for our emotional life, as difficult as this may be, we become stronger and more complete.

Part of our healing is to give our pain meaning. It brings us peace when out of a tragedy something good comes from it. Many organizations have been formed in the name of a loved one, usually with the hope that their work will make a difference in the lives of others. By helping others heal, we are developing "spiritual currency" for ourselves, which has a dramatic effect on our healing process. By giving to others and helping to create a better world, we give meaning to our life. This spiritual currency helps to fill a void that many tragedies bring. Often when we make these kinds of decisions a spiritual transformation takes place within us. Even if we don't begin something new, by creating something positive, however small, it will begin to give us peace.

Tasks for Step Six

Accept your pain.

Mourn your losses.

Absorb your pain.

Give meaning to your pain.

Develop spiritual currency.

Journal Exercise for Step Six

For this journal exercise, allow yourself to feel your pain and grief and whatever it is that is festering inside of you. Explore these emotions and ask what they want to tell you. What does your grief need to be healed? What does your pain need to be healed? How can you give pain meaning? What will your life be like once you are able to absorb your pain? If you are having difficulty absorbing your pain, what is getting in the way? Explore the resistant part of yourself. Ask your resistance what it wants and needs from you. Examine all these emotions until nothing is left. Then describe what your life would look like if you could accept your pain, heal your grief, and bring new meaning to your life.

Questions to Think About for Step Six

What does it mean for you to accept your pain? Can any of your beliefs help you in this process?

Are there feelings you are holding onto that nurture your pain?

How can you give meaning to your pain?

Is there a way you can create spiritual currency that will make you feel better about the situation?

Is there something you can do that will symbolize the acceptance of your pain?

Rating Scales

How difficult was it for you to accept your pain at the end of Step Six?

EASY   IMPOSSIBLE

| 1 | 2 | 3 | 4 | 5 | 6 | 7 |

How complete was mourning your losses at the end of Step Six?

COMPLETE   NOT BEGUN

| 1 | 2 | 3 | 4 | 5 | 6 | 7 |

Have you been able to make your pain meaningful at the end of Step Six?

VERY MEANINGFUL   NO MEANING AT ALL

| 1 | 2 | 3 | 4 | 5 | 6 | 7 |

Do you have a deep commitment to forgive after completing Step Six?

VERY DEEP COMMITMENT   NO COMMITMENT

| 1 | 2 | 3 | 4 | 5 | 6 | 7 |

Step Seven: Gaining Inner Peace

Once we have reached Step Seven in the forgiveness process, we have come to a very special place. There are certain things we have come to realize about our minds and the way we think. We may have realized that in a sense we have operated from two minds—one we call the *lower self* or *ego*, and one of a spiritual self or the place of our divinity. When we function from the lower self, we believe that responsibility for whatever has taken place is outside of ourselves, not within. When we work through our higher or spiritual nature, our divinity helps us see through our illusions and misperceptions. Our spiritual essence is that part of our self that is in touch with the creative force and reminds us that this force is always within us. It is the part that tells us that there is another way we can go about living and interacting in this world. In Step Seven, the spiritual self is awakened, setting the stage for a transformation to take place that only forgiveness can bring.

This step not only asks us to understand what has taken place in another person's life but also to recognize that what we see in them is the outer covering and not their true inner being. When we are able to see their inner light, no matter what the outer actions are, we are seeing with spiritual sight. All of us wear different outer clothes but are the same at the depth of our being, and so we look for their light and do not focus on the outer covering. When you can open your heart to others, no matter what the circumstances are, and not lose sight of *their* spiritual essence, a transformation within you takes place. Your life changes to a more meaningful existence and you experience the wonderful fruits of your labor. For some people these changes happen gradually, and they may not notice how profoundly they have changed. For others, their transformation can be so deep that not only is it a profound moment in their lives, what they chose to do becomes an incredible service to mankind.

When we make the commitment to forgive others, we are sometimes given a gift. If we find that we are struggling to forgive but know in our heart the commitment is there, sometimes a mysterious energy intervenes. We can experience this force as a surge of energy or the feeling of inexplicable love. Some people call it grace, and others call it a third factor that transcends anything they have ever experienced. At this point in our healing process, we open ourselves to the entirety of what is. In that opening we allow ourselves to be at one with a situation, or with life as a whole, and a profound healing takes place. There is nothing we can do to create this experience except to say to ourselves, "I take responsibility for my anger, guilt, and pain and give it over to that which is greater than me." If our request is heartfelt, we will get the help we need. This can be one of the most profound moments of our life when our prayers are answered.

Once we complete the forgiveness process it is important to look back and see how far we have come. We note the changes that took place, especially in our thinking. We have recognized that forgiveness is a better way to deal with life's challenges, and this recognition has become firmly established at this step. By learning not to judge by outer appearances alone, we have developed an open-mindedness, which in turn, strengthens spiritual vision. Forgiveness becomes a lot larger than what we first thought it would be. It has brought about true learning by enabling us to heal the misperceptions we once held about another. Once this shift in perception happens, healing is accomplished. We understand at a much deeper level that the world we see is because of what we choose to see. This is the shift that true perception and spiritual vision brings.

With forgiveness the past, although not forgotten nor rationalized away, is no longer a haunting or burdensome issue. Instead, we experience a restoration of a sense of wholeness and of inner direction and an opening up of our heart to others. We can acknowledge that others act in a way human beings do, out of their fears, needs, and perceptions, and that we are no different. This understanding makes it possible for us to live in a new and fuller way.

Last, the spiritual dimension of forgiveness cannot be overlooked. It is the transforming nature of forgiveness, coupled with what some experience, that involves more than our own will that makes forgiveness so profound. Once forgiveness is experienced at this deeper level, we can realize the larger meaning of the injury. The sense of relief from the hurt itself seems to be only one aspect, perhaps even small, compared to the freedom we experience from forgiveness. The future opens with amazing possibilities, and we feel a fuller kinship with others and at the same time humbled by what seems to be a gift that only forgiveness can bring.

Tasks for Step Seven

View the situation differently through spiritual sight.

Be open to grace.

Reflect on what you have learned and on your psychological and spiritual growth.

Journal Exercise for Step Seven

Rewrite your forgiveness story, this time with the understanding you have gained going through the forgiveness process. Include in your story the understanding you have gained about yourself and the perpetrator. How has your thinking changed in terms of how you choose to see the world? Did you struggle with letting go of your anger and guilt and, if so, what happened or what did you need to have happen to finally let go? Did you experience a moment of grace and, if so, how has that changed you? Finish your story with what you would like to do or say that you may not have been able to do yet.

Questions to Think About for Step Seven

What has seeing the world through spiritual sight taught you?

What have you learned and gained from the forgiveness process?

Rating Scales

How well have you forgiven the offender at the end of Step Seven?

COMPLETELY   NOT AT ALL

| 1 | 2 | 3 | 4 | 5 | 6 | 7 |

Were you able to view the situation with spiritual insight at the end of Step Seven?

TOTAL SPIRITUAL INSIGHT   **NO INSIGHT**

1	2	3	4	5	6	7

Has practicing forgiveness changed your life in any way at the end of Step Seven?

VERY MUCH   **NOT AT ALL**

1	2	3	4	5	6	7

Although you may have worked through the entire forgiveness process, as you read the following stories you will want to revisit these seven steps. As you work through the forgiveness process, remember that the changes that will take place are slow and gradual. Keep in mind that it takes a while for our emotions to heal and for our thinking to change. What is being asked of you is something very hard to do, and for many of us it will require discipline and stepping out of a thought system that has kept us stuck in unhappiness.

Forgiveness is the science of the heart. It is the anchoring of a new wisdom rooted in compassion. For those who have the courage to follow its path, forgiveness reminds us how to live with love in a world filled with guilt and fear. Gregg Braden, in his book *Walking Between the Worlds: The Science of Compassion* (1997), eloquently describes the opportunity forgiveness brings to all of us.

> *Without exception, each event, every relationship, every love, and every betrayal that you have ever experienced have provided you key emotions and feelings leading to your mastery. How you perceive those emotions and feelings, how you define them in your life, is your way of training and teaching yourself, reminding yourself of the promise of compassion.*

We are the ones who determine how much anger and hatred we will experience in our lives, as well as how much compassion and forgiveness we will extend to others. We have been given opportunities to hate and the wisdom to transcend our hate. Think of the personal power we must have to move beyond old choices and to respond to life from a place of spiritual wisdom. Our pain and suffering provide us with the chance to learn how to forgive and to know our truest, most beautiful nature. Forgiveness is the gift given to us to transcend our darkness and, like alchemy, turns it to gold.

3

Beginning the Journey

The Struggle with "Sweet" Revenge

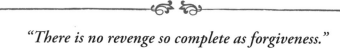

"There is no revenge so complete as forgiveness."
—Josh Billings, writer

I was reading a story in *Newsweek* about a man who grew up in India who recounted horrifying stories of suffering from his family elders. He spoke of a British ruling that took effect on August 14, 1947, in which Britain partitioned colonial India into India, a majority Hindu nation, and Pakistan, a majority Muslim nation. Unprecedented violence broke out. Almost two million people were murdered because of the partition. Murder, arson, and rape continued until November of that year. Several million people, including this person's clan, became refugees.

Unfortunately because of fate's hand, the ancestral village where this man's family lived became the place where the boundary commission had drawn an invisible border line. Suddenly the man's family, who were Hindus, found themselves living in an Islamic state. Many uncles and granduncles were murdered by Muslim mobs. Aunts were raped and abducted. Those lucky enough to survive had to flee.

Unbelievable chaos and violence sent this family in many different directions. This man's fate was to grow up in a refugee colony in India and feel the effects of the violence his elders had witnessed and been subjected to. He could sense the deep hatred his family felt toward Muslims.

After living in the United States for sixteen years, this man returned to India for a visit. To his surprise, he was told about an ugly family secret. His father took him to visit a granduncle, someone he had not seen since the partition fifty-four years before. The granduncle began to retell the story of what happened the day when his uncles and two aunts were killed while trying to flee a Muslim mob, and how he narrowly escaped by swimming across the flooded Ravi to the Indian side. When he got there, he had to walk over fields of dead refugees on his way to the nearest town.

Then the dirty secret came out about his family. His granduncle joined a group of young men who were attacking Muslim refugees in caravans going west to Pakistan. The granduncle was asked, "Do you know how many people were killed?" The granduncle did not know how many people died but justified what was happening by saying that no one could imagine what was going on. Muslims were butchering entire trains of Hindu refugees, and they were just retaliating.

The shocked younger man commented, "Our family members were killed by Muslims in Pakistan. They were desperately trying to escape, leaving behind their homes and land. Don't you think that the people you killed were also innocent refugees who were trying to escape to Pakistan?"

The granduncle was quiet for awhile before he spoke. "Yes, those were also poor, innocent people. But there must have been some sinners among them, too."

The younger man tried to argue this faulty logic but to no avail. Then the younger man realized, "suddenly the moral certainty I felt about my family's legacy as victims and survivors of a brutal massacre was gone. I had never imagined that they were killers, too. My granduncle was probably not the only member of my family to wander Punjab with vigilantes. Like thousands of other killers who roamed the countryside, killers who lived respectably after the carnage as husbands and uncles, he never had to face the law for what he had done."

The younger man went away thinking about how easily victims of crimes can lose their moral bearings and turn into criminals themselves. He also thought about how often we focus on punishing the guilty while leaving the victim to suffer with no support, especially in terms of a healing process. He recognized that this may be one reason why cycles of violence continue.

As he continued his inner dialogue, he knew the pain his family had endured. He came to the conclusion that revenge-based justice is no justice at all. He knew that nothing came out of the killing his granduncle perpetrated in 1947. The action brought no satisfaction to his family. They were never able to return to their ancestral homes, and the dead relatives could not be brought back to life because Hindus had killed Muslim refugees to even the score. After all the pain and suffering he and his family had gone through, he realized that only forgiveness and compassion can put an end to violence (Dutta, 2004).

We often hear about "sweet" revenge. When we have been hurt or continually abused by someone, the first thing we think about is how we are going to get this person to pay for what was done. What drives that very first thought of ours that wants revenge? Our thinking tells us that we should pursue punishment because those who have hurt us should get what is coming to them. After all, that is only fair, right? Revenge is the impulse to retaliate when we experience wrongs being done to us. In our thinking, we keep score, a tabulation of who did what so we know how to balance the scales. All of us have adapted to a way of thinking that likes to keep track. This is the same kind of thinking that leads us to believe "an eye for an eye," but as Gandhi has told us everyone would then be blind.

In our minds, revenge is about maintaining some sort of balance between the pain and suffering the victim has experienced and what the perpetrators must feel. We hurt and we want to get even. We feel that revenge is absolutely justified and that those who created pain in our lives need to know how it feels. We believe these scales must be balanced for us to move on with our lives. If we follow this through, victims become the perpetrators by their need for revenge. By our need for revenge, we have set the stage for more conflict and violence. Unfortunately, we have made no attempt to allow for healing or any transcendence of the suffering, only replicate it.

There are other issues involving revenge. We get stuck in a way of thinking that we don't want to change. We only choose to hear our voice of anger, and we don't know how to appropriately deal with that. We are all capable of lashing out to such degrees that we may become very malicious. Ugly divorces are examples of this. We all have been in situations where trivial arguments escalate to full-blown fights. Revenge can lead to horrific vendettas being passed down from one generation to the next. On a societal level, it can lead to death and destruction of people's lives. In either case, the results can be devastating.

What happens to victims when revenge is carried out? In her book *Trauma and Recovery* (1992), psychologist Judith Herman tells us that although traumatized people believe that revenge will bring relief, satisfaction never comes. In effect, it does the reverse. Although there may be a momentary feeling of relief, their post-traumatic symptoms worsen. Even for us who may not be suffering from post-traumatic stress disorder, revenge does not change our situation or bring back a loved one. Only momentarily do we feel relieved and that justice has been served. Those feelings are fleeting, often leaving us in a worse mental and emotional state. When we recognize this, we hopefully can also recognize that avoiding hatred and revenge becomes very pragmatic because of the emotional cost of revenge.

This holds true for societies as well. Especially in the context of collective violence and genocide where there is legitimacy for outrage and hatred, a need for social restraint becomes more compelling. Therefore, finding an alternative to vengeance becomes not only an emotionally significant moral imperative, it is also necessary for our survival. This is when forgiveness becomes essential.

Why People Seek Revenge

Olga Botcharova (2001), a conflict resolution specialist, has described a process of what she terms "stages of victim development." Within this process is what leads us to want to seek revenge. The process begins with the injury and then the shock, pain, and denial that follow. When we first experience a painful situation, we often go into shock, which is a protective mechanism giving us time to slowly absorb what may have just happened. As the shock begins to wear off we tend to go into denial, which temporarily protects us from facing the ugly gaping wound caused by severe loss.

Eventually, victims move to the second stage and begin to realize their loss. Many times victims are overwhelmed by the horrible truth of what has just happened. Because of this, we continue to deny and distance ourselves from this new reality. This action leads to the third stage—suppression of grief and fear.

Our feelings of anger, grief, and fear can be so overwhelming that we sometimes shut down as a way of attempting to deal with these emotions. Suppression of grief is also a way of hiding from shame, a factor that negatively affects one's self image and sense of identity. Regrettably during times of trauma people may not be able to grieve for their survival and may require strength to enable them to take action to prevent further tragedy. Suppressing our emotions may be helpful during the initial stages of dealing with tragedy, but this becomes a double-edged sword because we need to grieve in order to heal and move forward in a more integrated way. Unfortunately, suppressing feelings doesn't make them go away and sooner or later they begin to manifest them in more painful ways such as flashbacks or nightmares. We may begin to feel very fatigued physically or develop psychosomatic illnesses, all of which need to be treated.

Suppression leads to heightened feelings of anger, the fourth stage of victim development. In many respects, this is justifiable. No one deserves to suffer and be caught up in unjust situations that bring pain and possibly death. Yet suppressed anger needs to go somewhere, and it is usually projected on the perpetrator and anyone or anything associated with the perpetrator. Sometimes anger is expressed in the question, "Why me?" Within that question lies the blame of the abuser, feelings of pain and despair, the assertion of our own innocence, and a need for justice. This is where the sense of "victimhood" takes hold. As the anger builds, the victim begins to think that healing can come about once the perpetrator and everything associated with him or her pays a price. Revenge, healing, punishment, and justice become one and the same, leading the victim to the fifth stage.

The need to hurt and sometimes even to kill is what motivates victims to seek revenge. They feel that an eye for an eye will help them heal their pain. Even when revenge is carried out or retributive justice is achieved, it never seems like enough to the degree of the victim's suffering. The reason for this lies in the fact that these mechanisms fail to provide healing due to the pain of loss. Yet the revenge cycle is perpetuated in the attempt to fill the gaping hole created by the woundedness.

Before many seek revenge, they not only need to feel that it is right within themselves, they also need to strengthen this rightness in the eyes of others. They have to reinforce their innocence and they do this by repeating their story. The reason the hurt party does this is to deprive the perpetrator of getting any sympathy and to deny the possibility of the wrongdoer being human. This reinforces a good guy/bad guy way of thinking that eliminates any possibility of hearing other points of view. Even when engaging in acts of revenge, the victim preserves the image of suffering. The victim, although unaware of this behavior, becomes more manipulative. It is under these conditions that demands for justice are reinforced. The only time revenge is not acted out during this time is if any doubts emerge in the mind of the victim, and he or she begins to view the perpetrator differently. But if the demands for justice are carried forward, the victim sees these acts as justified aggression. This becomes the last stage in this process.

Once we come to this part of the cycle, the roles of victim/perpetrator are now reversed. The aggressor now feels victimized, seeks revenge, and demands that justice be done. The former innocent victim is now in the place of power. Roles can continually change over the course of the conflict, making it confusing as to who is on the defense and who is on the offense. Both sides feel extremely victimized by the other. Without the acknowledgement of harm, a place to express anger, the mourning of losses, and grappling with the issues of justice, there cannot be a coming together.

There is one other important point to mention that can turn this situation around, and that is the role of changing perceptions and the way we think. We can only begin to see things differently if we can accept the belief that there is a divine essence, a basic goodness within each of us. That universal goodness is what gives us the ability to love and to recognize the interconnectedness with all of humanity. Some people call it the divine light that shines in everyone's heart. This inner spiritual resource enables us to view the world differently. When we can't hear our inner voice, our world becomes more frightening and appears to have great power over us. Our fear drives us to violence. Therefore, part of our work in healing wounds is to help people get in touch with themselves at a deeper level. Forgiveness is the process that gets us there. A transformation takes place in the way we see the world and in the way we think about it. Events causing so much pain are seen with a different meaning and purpose. When victims can view their experience from the wisdom of their inner voice, they are ready to heal through the work of forgiveness.

Steps in Breaking the Cycle of Revenge

Before anyone can introduce the concept of forgiveness in breaking the cycle of revenge, we have to look at what happens to the victim after he or she acts out revenge. Momentarily, people may feel better, but shortly thereafter feelings of pain resurface, fears of how to cope with loss are still there, and the anger continues to burn. Feelings of emptiness fill that momentary feeling of relief. People have lost their sense of identity because of acting out with no past to hold onto. The challenge is to develop a sense of self different from the one that was destroyed. Restorative justice will not take place until an inner transformation of the self occurs. *We have to find our own inner peace and strength to cope with the new reality.* Instead, we haven't taken the responsibility of confronting our pain and grief, expecting that seeking justice would do the job for us. An outside factor can never provide inner healing and spiritual growth. The only way healing comes is to understand the meaning of the event from a spiritual perspective. When we are successful in doing so, it culminates in forgiveness. Forgiveness is the means by which the victim can let go of the sense of being victimized. The victim can release the past by opening up to the acceptance of the present and an unknown future. For a deep inner transformation to occur, it will require a reframing of how we view the tragedy we experienced and how we view suffering. We begin by mourning our losses and coming to terms with the experiences that took place.

For people to heal from loss, they have to begin with feeling the pain of that loss. Staying with the pain and not ignoring it will help process it. The mere awareness of our tendency to deny the pain can become the opening for us to let the pain out. As we release these emotions, they lose power over us. Giving ourselves time to mourn helps us to begin a reintegration process for a new life.

Mourning opens the process of identifying and confronting our fears. Usually we are more afraid of the emotions that accompany the fear then of the fear itself. Expressing these emotions will help the victim to release the anger that is often just underneath the surface of the fears.

Only after we have worked through our anger and fear can we take the next step—recognizing the humanness in the person or people we hate so much. This may be one of the most difficult steps to take and is usually met with a great deal of resistance. As victims, people are invested in seeing the others as "nonhuman" people with no redeeming qualities. To think of the motives of the person or people who caused us so much pain as being deeply rooted in their own fears and needs would mean that we would have to understand something about them, which makes them more like us. Given similar circumstances we could behave in very similar ways. If we look for an honest answer to "Why them?" and what led them to do these terrible things, our anger can turn more into sorrow and possibly even compassion. This begins a rehumanization process. Although the act of aggression or wrongdoing is seen for what it is, the person who committed the act is seen as someone who is acting out of their woundedness. At this point, the victim is beginning to separate the person from the act committed. Viewing someone who is struggling with their own pain lessens the need for revenge.

Once we have some understanding of who the perpetrator is, we are at the point where we can begin to entertain the thought of forgiveness. More than anything else forgiveness is a conscious choice, a decision. You cannot skip any steps to get there, but you can clear the way to make that decision. Forgiveness is not about excusing someone's behavior. It is about the victim's inner healing that will eventually allow him or her to see the past differently and help move into a brighter future. Forgiveness is the victim's ultimate freedom.

Before any inner healing, victims would seek retributive justice or revenge, wanting to create at least as much pain as they experienced. For those who have been able to forgive, they view justice in a different way. The purpose of justice is not retribution but restoration. Forgiveness provides a different imperative for seeking justice—integration not of the way things were, but in a way that reintegrates the relationship of the victim and perpetrator in a safe and productive manner built by both sides. This shines a light on one of the mysteries of forgiveness. As the victim opens up to the process of forgiveness, a deep mystical transformation takes place. People experience this in very different ways, but it is usually described as feeling the power of love. As we get connected to the essence of who we are, a shift takes place in our thinking. We are now able to see the world through the eyes of forgiveness. It is through these eyes and the wisdom that has been gained that people are able to view justice and make decisions about what restorative justice should look like based on this new experience.

Finally, when people accept responsibility for the past and begin to work together to create something new, they can begin to build a secure future. This journey can be a long, painful process. It needs to be built on the truth of what took place in the past and a clear vision that makes way for newly gained recognition and respect for the suffering that took place. Only then can a reconciliation process begin and address the practical issues of restoring relationships, if that is appropriate.

What is asked of victims is sometimes very difficult to do. The victims should not seek revenge and become perpetrators, but, instead, they are asked to break the cycle by forgiving those who have caused so much suffering. In this case we are asked to recognize our human bond and to forgive to strengthen our commonality. We are also asked to give up our preoccupation with the past, which can paralyze the victim. In our ability to forgive, we are able to release anger and our sense of victimhood and not suffer the consequences of its self-destructive effect. Forgiveness can empower victims and give them back their dignity while sending a message to the perpetrators concerning their harmful actions. In the act of forgiving, what we offer is the creation of a new relationship that can heal by absorbing pain and breaking the cycle of violence. Victims can seek the reintegration of oppressors into society for their own sake, the sake of reconciliation, and the rebuilding of a more fair and humane world.

As we think back to the beginning of the chapter to the man who grew up in India, he was on the right track when he realized that only forgiveness can put an end to violence. When we recognize that people react out of fear and the greatest healer of fear is forgiveness, we know what to do. Violence begets violence. In order to break the cycle, we need to reduce fear. In our story, both the Hindus and the Muslims found themselves in the same circumstances. Both groups were experiencing a great deal of suffering. If someone in one of the groups could have recognized the fear and suffering on both sides, that person could have broken the cycle of violence. If the groups could have joined together and protected one another so that no one else would die in vain, then a whole different scenario would have emerged. If they could have recognized that they were suffering from the same plight instead of seeing the other as the enemy, and acknowledged them as victims of circumstance just like they were, they could have responded with compassion. That one act could have changed the course of history.

A list of eight things to remember about forgiveness follows. When you get stuck in the idea of seeking revenge, this list will help you remember that forgiveness is ultimately about *your inner healing.*

Eight Things to Remember About Forgiveness

1. **Forgiveness is not mandatory, it is voluntary.** No one can force us to forgive. Only we can decide in our own minds and hearts to forgive. In this sense, we are never required to forgive. Forgiveness is perhaps the most generous gesture we can make, not only to those who have wronged us, but to ourselves as well.

2. **Forgiveness is a state of mind.** In this very sense, forgiveness is forgetting. In so doing, when we forgive, we relieve our memories of the burden of revisiting the wound itself and thus reduce our pain.

3. **Forgiveness is not excusing a wrongdoer.** When someone injures us we are *not* required to make believe the wrong did not take place. Forgiveness is deciding to *not* continue to try and collect the debt of the wrong. If someone owes us money and we forgive the debt, we do not participate in the fiction that the money isn't owed. By forgiving the debt, we mean that we are no longer

going to waste our precious energies in a futile act. This is important when the debt is really uncollectible as, for example, when there has been a wrongful death.

4. **Forgiveness is reflexive.** When we forgive someone who has wronged us, or we forgive the wrong itself, we also benefit from the relief of no longer having to deal with it. We have all known someone who would not forget that he or she was rejected by a lover or by a divorced parent. Often that someone lives his or her whole life making decisions that are colored by the emotional scars left after the perceived wound. This is tantamount to carrying a burden as heavy as the guilt of having committed the wrong in the first place. Often, it is heavier. It is usually wiser to relieve oneself of that burden by forgiving the wrong.

5. **Forgiveness is liberating.** When we are finally able to make the decision to forgive, we feel a lightness as the burden of anger is dropped from our shoulders. Try it. The feeling is almost exhilarating.

6. **Forgiveness does not equate with loving enemies.** No one is ever required to love an enemy. But obsessive hatred costs energy, and, when we nurse a hatred, it is both time- and energy-consuming. Even in war, it is usually more practical to forgive enemies than to nurse the hatred felt during the war. The disastrous consequences of the harsh Treaty of Versailles after World War I proved that it would have been better for the Allies to extend a hand to Germany rather than punish it for making war. Many historians agree if that help had been extended, Hitler would never have gained a foothold.

7. **Forgiveness is never easy, but its efforts are rewarding.** Because forgiveness is a matter of mind more than anything else, it requires understanding. The process of this journey of understanding is not to force ourselves to believe that the debt of wrong is not owed, but that to continue to try and collect the debt would cost us more than simply excusing it.

8. **Forgiveness is self-empowering.** It would be easy to assume that forgiving is an act of weakness. In so assuming, we credit those who have wronged us with power, while disempowering ourselves. But forgiving is an act of strength. Remember that when we are wronged, *only we* can forgive the wrongdoer. We possess tremendous power in that respect. By exercising that power we add to it by demonstrating we have it, and, thus proving we have it, we bulk up our self-esteem in the process.

4

Developing Patience

Learning from the Dalai Lama

"Learning to forgive is much more useful than merely picking up a stone and throwing it at the object of one's anger. For it is under the greatest adversity that there exists the greatest potential for doing good, for oneself and others."

—His Holiness the Dalai Lama

IN THIS CHAPTER, we will meet a very profound and spiritual human being, His Holiness the Dalai Lama. The Dalai Lama is the spiritual and temporal leader of the Tibetan people. He thinks of himself as a simple Buddhist monk, but he is anything but simple. He is one of the few people who practices forgiveness through the eyes of compassion every day of his life. What he symbolizes is the antithesis of revenge. His Holiness the Dalai Lama will show us how to transform the thoughts of revenge to those of compassion by analyzing anger and developing patience. If anyone is justified in wanting revenge, certainly the Dalai Lama would qualify, for he and some Tibetan people have been living in exile while those remaining inside Tibet have been living under Chinese occu-

pation for over fifty years. Yet the Dalai Lama views his situation
through the eyes of compassion and forgiveness. Here is his story.

Traveling to Dharamsala, India

Life sometimes blesses us with an extraordinary experience which
we cherish forever. Meeting His Holiness the Dalai Lama of Tibet
was one of those times. I will never forget that rainy summer day,
dodging puddles of water and hoping to stay as dry as possible as
I made my way toward His Holiness's quarters. Traveling under
difficult and dirty conditions through poverty-stricken India seared
my heart. Images of people living in the streets huddled around
fires to cook and keep warm, with not even the basic comforts a
shelter brings can be shocking to Western eyes. There was nothing
easy about this trip. Being in India made me question so much
about my life and what I valued. This inner and outer exploration
was a difficult one but well worth it. I knew I was going to be in
the presence of a very wise and beautiful human being.

Dharamsala, a beautiful hill town in the Himalayan Mountains
in northern India, is the unofficial home for many Tibetans. These
people have lived in exile since 1949, when the Peoples' Liberation Army of China invaded Tibet. By 1959, many Tibetans,
including His Holiness, had left Tibet and gone to Dharamsala. In
all of its beauty, there is also sadness in Dharamsala, for its very
existence is the result of an occupied Tibet. Although all Tibetans
hope and pray that in their lifetime they will be able to return
home to Tibet, the likelihood is that the Dalai Lama will never see
Tibet again.

In spite of this sadness, it is impossible to visit Dharamsala, talk
to Tibetans and His Holiness, and not feel that this is a very special place. The spiritual qualities of the Tibetan people permeate
the atmosphere. Their determination to survive is not only heard
but can almost be touched. This atmosphere provided the back-
drop for my conversation with His Holiness, an incredible human
being of love and compassion.

Tenzin Gyatso, the XIVth Dalai Lama, is considered by the Tibetan people to be the living Buddha, the earthly manifestation of Avalokiteshvara, the Bodhisattva of compassion. Although this is how Tibetans view him, His Holiness thinks of himself as an ordinary human being, a Tibetan who chooses to be a Buddhist monk. At age three, he was recognized through a traditional process of "discovery" to be the reincarnation of the previous Dalai Lama. He was then taken from his parents and brought up in Lhasa according to a very strict discipline of spiritual and academic study, living in almost total isolation. At age fifteen, three years earlier than what is customary and because of the invasion of Communist China, he was invested with full powers as the head of state of Tibet. He developed relationships with both Chairman Mao and Jawaharlal Nehru in his attempts to maintain autonomy for his people. In 1959, the Dalai Lama was finally forced into exile by escaping over the Himalayan Mountains into northern India. Over one hundred thousand Tibetan refugees later followed him. Since 1959, His Holiness has lived in Dharamsala. He has devoted his life to rebuilding the shattered lives of the Tibetan people, to continuing the struggle for independence, and to promoting world peace through the unwavering policy of compassion and nonviolence.

The Dalai Lama was awarded the Nobel Peace Prize in 1989, which drew the attention of the free world to the desperate plight of his people. He has lived through an appalling sequence of events since the Chinese invasion of his country in 1950. In exile, His Holiness's role as spiritual leader has become far more profound than if he remained isolated in Tibet. The Dalai Lama symbolizes the struggle between power based in dominance and control and nonviolence based on the principle of compassion. He is the embodiment of the hopes and dreams of the Tibetan people. Without him, the Tibetans fear they would lose their struggle. His presence gives the Tibetan people courage to move forward in the way of nonviolence. One listens carefully to his rich sounding voice, which often breaks into chuckles, and is inspired by the wisdom of his words.

When I arrived at His Holiness's quarters, I was brought to a waiting room. Other people were seated there anxiously awaiting their turn to have a private audience. I was also feeling nervous, anticipating what it would be like to be in the presence of such a holy man. When the Dalai Lama's private secretary came for me, I was escorted into a magnificent sitting room where I was greeted by His Holiness. As I looked around the room, I noticed beautiful Tibetan *thankas*, intricate scroll paintings on cloth that depict Buddhist symbols, and religious artifacts, which created an atmosphere of beauty and peace. I tried to calm myself, and His Holiness put me right at ease.

I began our conversation by asking the Dalai Lama his thoughts about forgiveness. I was curious if such an extraordinary Buddhist monk struggles with the issues of anger and revenge in the same way most of us do and, if so, how he handles his struggles. If it is true that we all function within the same system of thinking as part of the human condition, how does a holy man with a Buddhist philosophy step out of this thought system of the human condition to one based in compassion? I asked him if he needed to personally forgive a person or a group who had done something that caused him pain. What His Holiness shared was gripping.

Mysterious Murders

IT WAS DURING the early morning hours on February 4, 1997, when three monks who were sleeping a few hundred yards from my living quarters were stabbed to death. They were cut up in a fashion that resembled an exorcism. One of the monks was my dearest friend and confidant, seventy-year-old Lobsang Gyatso. He was found dead in bed. Two younger monks, Ngawang Lodoe and my Chinese-language interpreter, Lobsang Ngawang, had been stabbed fifteen to twenty times, leaving the walls of the small monks' chamber splattered with blood. I suspect there could have been five to eight attackers. The murderers were sending a very clear message to me.

Who would be capable of committing such a heinous crime? Nothing was stolen. Cash and Buddhist statues were left untouched. Who would want to kill gentle Buddhist monks?

As His Holiness recounted the story, I felt sick to my stomach and faint. In the days following the murders, fourteen more death threats to members of the Dalai Lama's entourage were recorded.

The manner in which the deaths happened and the death threats themselves led the Indian police to believe that the obscure Shugden Tibetan sect may have been responsible for the murders. The Shugden, inspired by the ferocious Tibetan deity, the Dorje Shugden, consider themselves guardians of Tibetan Buddhism, especially their branch known as Gelugs or Yellow Hats. They consider the Dalai Lama a traitor to the Yellow Hats for befriending other branches of Buddhism. The Dalai Lama denounced one Shugden order in particular as a hostile and commercialistic cult. This may have been the motive for the brutal murders against those closest to His Holiness. Since no one saw who committed the murders on that cold night, there are only suspicions and no suspects.

Learning to Forgive by Analyzing Anger

WHEN I HEARD the news I was shocked. My first thoughts were how could people do such horrible things in the name of religion? I became very angry. I needed to deal with this anger by seeing it clearly. Then I realized that without exception every experience, negative as well as positive (including betrayals such as this) could lead to deepening compassion within us. I had to remember that the atrocity already happened. Nothing was going to change that. I needed to focus on how to handle this for the future and on developing a new chapter.

As I began to analyze my anger, I recognized that we think of anger as a friend who helps us in battles or takes revenge against the people who have inflicted harm. Anger and hateful thoughts appear to protect, but in reality this is not so. We even justify responding to violence with revenge, thinking that it would prevent or reduce harm.

Yet the harm has taken place. By reacting negatively instead of in a tolerant way, not only isn't there immediate benefit, but the negative attitude creates the seed for further downfall. In the future, the individual will face the consequences of taking revenge. Therefore, the first step is to develop a clear understanding of what is the root cause of anger. We need to develop a profound understanding of the negative and destructive effects that anger brings. However, if one has been treated very unfairly and if the situation is not addressed, it may have extremely negative consequences not only for the victim but for the perpetrator of the crime as well. Such a situation calls for a strong counter-measure. Under such circumstances, it is possible that one can, out of compassion for the perpetrator of the crime and without generating anger or hatred, actually take a strong stand to stop more crimes from happening.

By analyzing anger, we realize that our anger affects us, and only us, directly. We can choose to remain angry or we can choose something else. The key principle for dealing with our emotions is the recognition of the mind's limitless capacity for improvement. This philosophy of mind emphasizes a detailed analysis of human emotions.

The mind is perceived in terms of a complex, dynamic system where both our thinking and feeling nature are seen as an integrated whole. Part of the process of understanding our emotions is to analyze which thoughts are useful and constructive to us and which are not. In doing so, we will quickly notice that we have two kinds of thoughts, those that make us calmer and give us peace of mind versus those thoughts that create more anger and fear. It is important to make the distinction between beneficial and harmful states of mind so you can fully recognize the values of good states and foster them. Therefore, anger is truly of no use. So the first thing I do is analyze my deeper feelings, especially anger.

Once I have done this I practice compassion, clearly recognizing that others like me desire happiness and have the right to overcome suffering. Forgiveness is about healing suffering for ourselves and others. Until we develop compassion within ourselves and a concern about the welfare of others, we cannot truly forgive.

Karma and Forgiveness

As we continued our conversation, I wanted to share some of my thoughts on forgiveness with His Holiness. I explained to him my understanding that forgiveness is the awareness that there is no practical reason to harbor feelings of revenge or hatred, and that the reasons we think we do have to hold on to these emotions are based in illusion. What greater service is there than knowing this and choosing to let go of our hatred and anger toward those that we believe have wronged us? Forgiveness is a very precious gift. We call upon our wisdom and strength to help us forgive. Love and respect are necessary qualities that will also help keep us from wanting to seek revenge.

I said to His Holiness that my basic meaning of forgiveness is to stop negative karma for myself and, when possible, for others. The Buddhist belief is that all our painful experiences are consequences of our own negative deeds committed in the past. This is the meaning of *karma*, and it is a very active process. For many Tibetans, their ability to forgive is directly related to their belief in karma. Tibetans believe that what befalls them is because of their past negative actions. They are now paying back a karmic debt. Therefore, what happens to them has been brought about because of something they have already done. They cannot blame anyone else.

On the other hand, according to Buddhist philosophy, the person harming others is setting into motion great suffering and torment for themselves in the future as a karmic result of these acts. For the victim, the result ends now. Victims are purifying their negative past actions and while they are paying their karmic debt they are not accumulating any other negative consequences. For those committing acts of violence, they will reap what they sow. Pain and suffering awaits them and, therefore, they are people who need our compassion and forgiveness. They will have to pay back their debt in the future.

Buddhists also believe that when a person inflicts harm, the harm that is inflicted is in some sense out of that person's control. Usually other forces such as negative emotions, delusions, ill feelings, and so on compel that person. If we delve deeper, we find that very negative emotions such as hatred come about as a result of many factors and are the aggregation of many conditions that do not arise out of choice. The law of karma can help people willing to be disciplined and motivated to acknowledge the perceptions that compel them to act the way they do, even against their will, and how to resolve and overcome these forces. This is also true of forgiveness. *Forgiveness is a process of shifting perceptions in which we recognize that these perceptions are only our creations and not fact.* In this regard forgiveness becomes a deeper process for change.

Forgiveness has us take ownership of aspects of ourselves that we feel very guilty about and deny by seeing only in others. When we feel guilty about something we unconsciously believe we should be punished for it. There is no word in Tibetan for "guilt," yet the psychological dynamics that guilt sets up may be similar to the meaning of karma. For Tibetans, their best understanding of guilt is that it is similar to sin, which cannot be eradicated. The underlying guilt sets into motion unconscious behaviors that have negative consequences similar to the laws of karma. Therefore, if someone is attacked and attacks back with malicious intent, negative karma is set into motion. But if one is attacked or violated in any way and chooses not to seek revenge or do anything of malicious intent, then there are no negative consequences. If someone also stops others from negative actions, he or she prevents them from accumulating negative karma, stopping the cycle of guilt.

I suggested to His Holiness that so often when forgiveness is called for it is to heal some form of woundedness. Our fears, anger, pain, hate, and jealousy are some of the many forms of darkness that are often painful to others when acted out. The part of ourselves that we are most uncomfortable with or afraid of is rooted in the perception of what our darkness is. Our hearts cry for love, nurturing, and compassion while our beliefs are driven by judgment, hate, and separation. We are afraid of our shadow, those unacceptable parts of ourselves, but at the same time we are driven by them. The paradox is that only when we experience our darkness can we experience our light. Our darkness provides us with the opportunity to know our highest, most beautiful nature. When we find ourselves in situations where it is justified to hate and we chose love, or where tolerance or patience become a stronger impulse than intolerance or impatience, we are choosing compassion in our lives. *Choosing light—seeing someone through the eyes of love instead of darkness, hate, or fear—is compassion.* When we can watch life's events without judgment, we are living a life of compassion.

In response to my observations, His Holiness began to speak about the qualities, attitudes, and spiritual beliefs in Tibetan culture that strengthen our ability to forgive and may also help people deal with betrayal, abuse, oppression, and torture. This is what he said.

Understanding Forgiveness

WHEN I THINK about the qualities that help us to forgive, I am reminded of a friend of mine. He was the abbot of a monastery and spent twenty years of his life in prison and in Chinese labor camps in Tibet. During that period, conditions were harsh and he suffered a lot. He mentioned that while in prison he faced many dangers. I asked him what kind of dangers. He then said that it wasn't the torture or suffering inflicted in the prison camps that bothered him. He was afraid that with all the suffering and torture he was going through, he was in danger of losing his compassion. This is a very remarkable human being. So I thought how can we develop this kind of compassion and affection, and how does this relate to forgiveness?

Compassion is based on understanding that I, as well as others, have an innate desire to be happy and overcome suffering. We all have a right to fulfill this aspiration. When we internalize this fundamental right, we develop a sense of our oneness. Tapping into our source of wisdom is a complementary factor that will affect the intensity and the depth of our ability to generate compassion and to learn to forgive.

Not only is compassion a wish to put an end to others' suffering, it also implies that we develop a sense of responsibility for those who suffer. This sense of responsibility means that we are committed to finding ways to comfort fellow human beings in their troubles. Forgiveness helps end the suffering of others through the recognition that their actions are based in illusion. Their actions, as harmful as they are to you, are ultimately harmful to them because of the karma and guilt they are accumulating. Their behavior is an indication of their pain. When we come from a place of compassion, we understand this.

We learn about compassion by practicing compassion. Very often in a public talk I am asked what the easiest way to develop compassion is. This kind of question frustrates me. *It takes time and a lot of effort to transform.* Yet in materially based societies where everyone is on the run, we want what is best, cheapest, and easiest. This attitude can not apply in the spiritual realm. When I speak of compassion, people may get the idea that it is something simple. In reality, to practice compassion takes years of training. For most of us, it is actually lifetimes before we truly experience compassion at profound levels of our being, not before. The problem with humanity is that many people are very individualistic and only focus on what is best for them. I think this is very shortsighted. Many people, especially those living in big cities, have an artificial sense of independence. People with money feel they have no need to be one's helper. This artificial sense of independence may be different elsewhere where people such as farmers need to rely on each other. Until we find ourselves in this situation we forget about our most basic human quality or feelings of interconnectedness.

When we understand and feel our interconnectedness at an emotional level we can develop a sense of caring. Sometimes I feel this quality is more alive in young children. Adults, usually through academic education and influences of their environments develop behaviors that separate them from their feelings and from experiencing their humanness. The more isolated we become from one another, the less confident we feel and the more alienated we become. Eventually our health is affected. The reverse is also true. More affectionate persons experience more genuine love and feel less lonely. The more compassionate you are, the more open-minded you are and the better your health is.

From the Buddhist viewpoint there are different varieties of compassion. The basic meaning of compassion is not just a feeling of closeness or pity. Rather, I think that with genuine compassion we not only feel the pain and suffering of others, but we also have a feeling of determination to overcome that suffering. Therefore, another aspect of compassion is determination and responsibility. Compassion also brings us tranquility and inner strength, which is the ultimate source of success.

Why is compassion so important? Someone must take the initiative to move beyond the cycle of old choices and responses that brings more pain and suffering and recognize the opportunity for a healing response to life itself. This is also true of the forgiveness that results from a compassionate heart. Today we face many problems, and the time has come for us to think on a deeper human level where we understand and respect the humanness of everyone. Though we might regard someone as an enemy, this enemy is also a human being who is trapped by his or her own demons and who has a right to happiness.

Anger begets anger. In contrast, if you control anger and impart qualities of compassion, then not only are you at peace with yourself, but the other's anger also diminishes. Anger or hatred cannot resolve problems or painful situations; healing only takes place with compassion and true kindness. The responsibility rests in our thoughts. We can develop a concern for others precisely because they, too, are human beings. Change comes about first within ourselves. Although it is difficult to attempt to bring about peace through this kind of internal transformation, it is the only way to achieve lasting world peace.

Developing Patience

As His Holiness spoke, I realized that compassion is just one ingredient of forgiveness. Whether or not we lead a spiritual life in which forgiveness becomes an important element depends upon success in disciplining our minds. The basic approach for bringing this transformation about is the practice of generating insight or wisdom. To enhance our capacity to forgive, we need to counteract the factors that obstruct our cultivation of these qualities. It is in this context that the practice of tolerance and patience becomes very important. Only through patience are we able to overcome obstacles to compassion. Major religions emphasize the importance of the practice of patience and tolerance for they are the foundation of all spiritual paths.

The Tibetan word *soe-pa*, or "patience," has various connotations. Literally speaking, *soe-pa* means "to withstand" or "to endure something," as in the case of enduring hardships. However, when it is used to describe a person it means "tolerance." Patience according to the Buddhist understanding is a conscious decision not to respond to adversity and to be calm externally and internally. When we engage in the practice of patience and tolerance, we are combating hatred and anger. Because these qualities come from the ability to not be overwhelmed by adverse conditions, they should not be seen as signs of weakness but rather as signs of strength coming from a deep ability to remain steadfast and firm. The person who gains victory over hatred and anger through such an arduous process is a true hero. Forgiveness is the end result of patience and tolerance. When we are truly patient and tolerant, forgiveness comes naturally.

According to Buddhist teachings there are three principle types of patience: patience that (1) absorbs pain, (2) enhances one's capacity for tolerance by reflecting on the nature of reality, and (3) tolerates harm and injuries inflicted by others. All of these aspects of patience are necessary for forgiveness. There are positive aspects in all these qualities. For example, identifying with and absorbing pain opens our hearts and allows us to generate genuine compassion for those who are suffering. When we absorb pain by forgiving, not only can we become more compassionate, we stop the cycle of anger and hatred from being passed down to the next generation.

Understanding the nature of reality or gaining wisdom helps us acknowledge the many factors that may cloud our perceptions. It helps us realize there are many conditions that cause others to act in harmful ways that are in fact out of their control. As Shantideva (1979) states in *A Guide to the Bodhisattva's Way of Life*, "we become ill without wishing to be so. Similarly, we do not intend to be angry, but often find ourselves gripped with anger."

The fundamental Buddhist principle of karma underlies the second aspect of patience, reflecting on the nature of reality. This principle states that nothing arises in isolation, for everything comes into being owing to the aggregation of multiple causes and conditions. This can also be seen in terms of interdependence between our perceptions and the world. These insights into reality give rise to greater tolerance toward events and others' actions. The deeper our appreciation of the complexity of the circumstances giving rise to an event, the greater our ability to respond to that event with a degree of calmness and tolerance. In regard to forgiveness, this principle reminds us that there are many conditions that have led up to causing others to act in harmful ways, some of which are out of their control. If we could think for a moment about the factors in that person's life leading up to the act, it would help us in our ability to forgive.

The third type of patience, developing tolerance toward injuries from others, may be the most important aspect and the most difficult to achieve. Usually the main target of our anger and frustration is another individual, and most often it is someone close to us. Too often we allow our anger to determine the kind of interaction we have with others. If anger rules the situation, no genuine development of patience can take place. Without patience we have cut ourselves off from the place of inner wisdom that is the healing aspect within us. People who harm because of their anger are locked in prisons of pain and illusion. Their illusions restrict what they are able to see and know. For this reason, it is more appropriate to have compassion rather than anger toward those who cause us harm. Shantideva asks us to go further and regard those who harm us as precious, for they alone give us the rare opportunity to practice tolerance. Shantideva (1979) writes:

There are indeed many beggars in this world but scarce are those that inflict harm;

For if I have not injured others, few beings will cause me harm.

Therefore, just like treasure appearing in my house,

Without any effort on my part to obtain it,

I should be happy to have an enemy

For he assists me in my conduct of awakening.

The thinking rooted in such spiritual training provides the basis for the Dalai Lama's statement that our enemy is our greatest teacher. For His Holiness, hatred is poison, and patience is medicine that removes the poisonous toxins from within our mind.

The Power of Our Thoughts

His Holiness commented that when we pass through a difficult period of time we can react by becoming apathetic or feeling hopeless. That of course is very sad. But the difficult situation can also open our eyes to the real situation, the truth. The truth is that each one of us determines the threshold of our anger, hatred, and rage at life's events. We determine the outcome of history by our response to it. Tragedies, wars, and great achievements are records of negative and positive thought. Positive and negative thoughts are always present in the human mind. Therefore, the only worthwhile thing for a human being to do is to try to develop positive thought, to increase the power or force of positive thought, and to reduce negative thinking. If we do that, human love, forgiveness, and kindness will give us more hope and determination, which will then bring us a brighter future. If we give way to anger and hatred, we get lost and live a painful life. No sensible human being wants to live like that, especially in the undertow of such negative emotions.

This is not a spiritual teaching, or a moral injunction. It is a fact that can be verified by today's experience. To have determination, we need hope. To develop hope, we need compassion and forgiveness, the cornerstones of our feelings of interconnectedness and, ultimately, our happiness. This is why every spiritual teaching of the world emphasizes the importance of unconditional love and forgiveness, for they open our hearts to ourselves and to humanity so that we can truly feel good about who we are.

Forgiveness for the Greater Good

His Holiness speaks of developing a greater sense of universal responsibility. He reminds us that we must learn to work not just for our own individual selves, family, or nation but for the benefit of all mankind. Universal responsibility is the best foundation both for our personal happiness and for world peace.

Life is boundless. It has an infinite rise and infinite development, as well as disintegration. There is an ultimate goal for human evolution, and that is an enlightened state. Evolution is not a random cycling around. The development of wisdom, love, and happiness that is beyond our wildest dreams, inconceivable to us at this moment, transcends all dichotomies and is just as powerful in the social realm as it is peaceful in our personal experience. Its core insight is the full embrace of the inextricable relatedness of all of humanity.

On some level, we realize that there is a basic oneness. When someone we are close to is happy, we feel their happiness. When we discover our interconnectedness with every other human being, we suddenly have a different feeling for other people and begin the long, slow process of finding kinship with other people. *Getting over denial of our interconnectedness is the road to peace.* Facing the facts is where we have to begin. We have to be willing to look at the grit in our own mind and clean it up and help our neighbors work on theirs as well. This is what forgiveness is about, and all of this begins at home.

We have a responsibility to prevent catastrophes, and the fundamental way we can all make a difference is to change our way of thinking and become aware of our thoughts, emotions, and feelings. We need to cultivate within ourselves compassion and forgiveness for our survival. What we are talking about is a new way of thinking that helps us step out of the old paradigm of the ego thought system into a new creative process that enables us to embrace our role as caretakers of the earth and our fellow human beings. This process will embrace our awareness of interconnectedness and stem the tides that move us toward depletion and decay.

Finally, I came to understand that the Dalai Lama was correct to insist that all of our actions and choices need to be created from compassion and mutual respect. Within this vision of all beings working together to create shared solutions to globally shared dilemmas, I experienced a surge of hope. Like the Tibetan people, our collective backs are against the wall, and we will succeed in bringing about this great change within ourselves and within this precious world we share because we have to. Our existence depends on this.

5

"Poor Me"

Larry Mathis's Story

"Human misery is more often caused not so much by stupidity as by ignorance, particularly our own ignorance about ourselves."

—CARL SAGAN

WAS LARRY MATHIS the son of a Phoenix mobster? The truth will never be known His father was murdered when Larry was four years old, and, from that time until his early adult years, Larry could not forgive his father for what had happened. Although Larry's story illustrates the different steps of the forgiveness process, it also raises very important issues concerning forgiveness, including being unfairly treated and how this reinforces the victim role and the issue of control, or who is the authority in our lives. Larry ends his story by explaining how forgiveness was able to change his thinking and ability to view the world differently.

Larry's Story

MY FATHER IS dead. Was it murder or suicide? I will never
know. Whatever it was, he brought it on himself. I was only four
when his life was taken, yet it wasn't until I was in my late teens
that I knew the entire story. That didn't matter. I probably could
not have handled it anyway.

My father was only thirty-seven years old when he was shot
to death, leaving behind a wife and seven kids. He owned a hamburger restaurant called "Bills" that once belonged to my grandfather. It was the real McCoy of hamburger joints before
McDonald's and Wendy's ever came to town. Just before my
father died, we lost the place. That was a real shame. My mother,
a stay-at-home mom trying to keep seven kids in check, now had
to face the outside world. She spent the next thirty years of her
life running a post office at Luke Air Force Base.

Sometimes I wonder if I will ever know all the circumstances
about my father's death. What I do know is as a little boy I loved
my dad. In my eyes he was a war hero. He received the Purple
Heart and Bronze Star. He took care of people.

I really don't remember much about my father except for
what my brothers and sisters tell me. I was a "little man" in my
father's eyes, his pride and joy. I idolized him so much that I
wanted to be just like him. If my father had a cigar butt in his
mouth, I had a cigar butt in my mouth. If my father was reading
a newspaper, I was reading the paper. As a three-year-old, I followed him around pretending to be just like him. I loved him,
and he loved me.

My most special memory was when my father took me on a
Boy Scout outing. This is when I caught my first fish. My little
heart pounded as I squealed with joy! I will always cherish that
moment of joy with family, for a time like this never happened
again.

Then my father died. I was told that my father was murdered
because he tried to protect another woman. The woman lived in

our neighborhood, and, according to the story, her husband beat her up all the time. My father went over there to protect her and was shot and killed by this woman's husband in a moment of rage. I felt proud to know that my father was protecting someone. This was the story I believed until my teen years. Only later did I hear the truth.

The real story was too much for me to bear. The truth was that my father was a very unwelcome person in this neighbor's house. As a matter of fact, he was told never to come there again or he would be shot. It was the husband, handicapped and in a wheelchair, who desperately wanted to protect his wife from my father. It was he who shot my father to death. In searching to find the truth, I learned that my father was a gambler who dealt with the seediest people of the underworld and played around with women. I also found out that the abuse was not next door but right at home. My father was brutal to my mother. He continually cheated on her and lied to her. He betrayed us.

When I found out the truth, I nearly exploded. The myth of my father shattered, and I didn't know what to do with the broken pieces. I was in my late teens when I began to boil with anger, but it wasn't until my early thirties that I was forced to do something about it. I had become obsessed with this cauldron of hate. For two years straight, not a day went by without me thinking about how much I hated my father. I couldn't let these thoughts go. My only relief was when I was working in my business. Once I came home, my emotions would come rushing back like the floodgates just broke. I took emotional swipes at everyone at home and was impossible to live with.

Then something very strange happened. When I was about thirty-three I suddenly became obsessed with a very strong fear of my own death. I felt suffocated as though I was literally going to die. At this time my son Trent was the age I was when my father died. I started to think about what would happen to Trent if I were to die. He needed to grow up with a father. His life had to be different from mine. And what would happen to my wife?

How would this affect her? Would she struggle the same way my mother had? An avalanche of emotions overwhelmed me as night after night I trembled from sunset to sunrise in fear. I began waking up at all hours of the night thinking that if there was a God, he was not there and because of that when I died I would be nothing. I had feelings of total annihilation. Now I was having a tug of war with God. As I lay awake at night I remembered how afraid I was to go to sleep even as a child. I would either work or watch TV just so I would not think of my own death. "Why am I having these kinds of thoughts, and why am I so debilitated with fear?" I would ask myself. "Is God really there?" I would have massive anxiety attacks thinking about this.

Uncovering Feelings

Just as I was about to lose it all, I looked for help. The only place I knew to turn to was the church, and so I met with the church elders. I was recounting my story when one of the church elders asked me, "How is your relationship with your father?" I stopped cold in my tracks. "What does that have to do with anything?" Then as though the top of a pressure cooker just blew off, I started to yell, "I hate him, I hate him; he is dead and I am glad that he is dead!" The elders looked at me in disbelief. We prayed, and suddenly I felt great.

As I look back, I realize that a healing took place at that very moment, but as time went on the feelings of doubt and fear came back. How could I have a relationship with God and feel His presence if I couldn't have a relationship with my own father? Because my father was a prototype of God and did terrible things to us, I feared this was what God would also do. My father didn't care about me, my mother, or anyone else for that matter. Therefore, this is what God must be like. And if God was all He was cracked up to be, He could have prevented all this pain and suffering from happening.

I began to look at a lot of things in my life that God could have prevented but didn't. He had a terrible track record. I asked myself how then could He be a good God, not only with things happening in the family, but also around the world? Then I really began to get in touch with the hatred I held toward my father. I realized I hated my father for many things. He betrayed our family by having extramarital affairs. He had other children, adding half brothers and sisters to the family we didn't know about. He drank a lot and gambled away the family's savings. The entire family suffered and dealt with so much hardship because of everything he did. Worst of all he got himself killed. That event changed my life forever and added burdens that should never have been.

—

Before forgiveness was possible, Larry needed to find the true story and experience all those intense emotions bottled up inside him. During this time he began to feel the raw emotions of injury and the deep emotional pain associated with the perceived injustice.

When dealing with trauma, we tend to deny or have difficulty acknowledging painful situations. At first Larry wanted to deny everything that happened, but eventually this denial turned into overwhelming feelings of anger and hatred. Eventually his defenses broke down and Larry saw the injustices that had happened. He began to experience difficult emotions associated with the situation. In the beginning Larry saw his father as a war hero. Only later did he describe his father as being a despicable human being who was murdered because of his own indiscretions. As a result of his father's actions and irresponsible behavior, many other lives were damaged. Acknowledging injustice is an important step in the forgiveness process. This helped Larry experience his anger, hatred, and guilt. As part of his healing process, Larry wrote down a list of all the reasons he hated his father. He discussed adultery and how this caused his mother so much pain, especially when coupled with his father's possible involvement with the underworld. He wrote about what it was like to grow up without a dad.

In confronting his anger, Larry began to uncover a great deal of emotional pain. For a very long time Larry did not want to admit to the raw, excruciating anguish screaming inside of him. He could not speak about it to himself, nor could he share it with others. As Larry became more aware of what he was feeling and began to accept that he had permanently changed, he slowly allowed himself to feel pain. This became evident one day while he watched the movie *Terms of Endearment* and suddenly started crying because his father was gone. "I wasn't crying because of the movie. I was crying because these little boys were watching their mother die. Then I thought of my father." Larry finally admitted to himself that he was in a lot of pain. He needed to share the pain with others. Like a pressure cooker ready to burst, he could not hold the pain inside anymore.

When Larry learned that his father was actually shot to death, he found newspaper clippings on the incident. Emotions began to bubble up to the surface that at times surprised and overwhelmed Larry. Not only was there pain and anger, feelings of being unfairly treated also emerged. The following is Larry's account of what happened:

> I READ THE eulogy and sermon that was given when my father died. I felt like they were talking about a different man. There was the one man that everyone saw, and there was the other man that nobody really knew. In reading the papers I did find out the truth. It was clear that my father was where he didn't belong and was shot by a man in a wheelchair who was actually protecting his wife from my father. My father was having an affair with this woman, and it broke my mother's heart. Only in my later teen years could I take a 180-degree turn from having a great deal of love and admiration for my father as a war hero to seeing someone who cheated on my mother and inflicted pain on the entire family.
>
> I felt hatred toward my father. I resented what he did and the pain it caused my mother. It was tough for her to raise seven kids

on her own, especially during the sixties and seventies when everyone was tuning in and dropping out. After my father's death, my mother began drinking quite heavily and became an alcoholic. She drank every night starting at five o'clock after she got home from work. As she drank, she became extremely abusive. My life began to revolve around my mother's drinking on a daily basis. My brothers and sisters were older than I was so they could leave the house when Mom was drunk. My two younger sisters and I had no escape. When my mother became physically abusive there was no one to protect us. Yet when she was sober she was an angel.

I have forgiven my mother for all of that. I never really held it against her to be perfectly honest because as I got older I started to see that this was not Mom's fault. I started to empathize with her. The hatred I held toward my father came from the pain and suffering that my mother had to endure. And I hated him greatly. I could be talking with a friend of mine about various things and if the subject of my father came up I would say that he was dead. I would continue by saying that he got shot because he was messing around and finish by telling the whole story. If someone would ask me specifically about my father, I would say that he was this stupid SOB who cheated on my mother, gambled away his income, got shot being were he shouldn't have been, and got what he deserved. He made the family suffer. He was dead, and I was glad.

———

As I was talking to Larry, I could feel the changes taking place within him. Larry was beginning to acknowledge all of whom his father was. The pain and anguish surfaced especially when Larry spoke of the suffering he felt his father caused his family. During this phase of the forgiveness process, it is not uncommon for the person who has been terribly hurt to compare his or her pain with the lack of pain the perpetrator felt. As Larry began to ask more questions, he experienced more pain. This served to intensify his hatred. Larry continued with his story.

IF I WAS ever to really forgive, I needed to find out the entire truth. I needed to talk to my brothers and sisters and my mother, who really knew the truth more than anyone else did. In my quest I found out that my father died two years and one day to the date of purchasing a $50,000 life insurance policy. He knew that by going to this person's house he would be killed. Then I found out what was behind it all. I learned from other family members that my father was a well-known businessman, mainly because of my grandfather. This is what led him to the activities of the underworld where he was involved in gambling and a lot of illegal stuff. He knew a lot of high-profile people who were involved in all sorts of criminal activity. Because of his activities, my father realized that his time on earth was going to be very short. He also understood that if he ever wanted to get out of what he was doing, he was going to have to tell the truth about other people. If he did that, he knew he would be killed.

I do not know if the family that lived behind us was part of the "other" family. I do know that my father went to this place knowing that if he saw this woman, he would be killed. It could have been viewed as a suicide or a murder. That is why he waited two years and one day, until the suicide clause in his insurance policy did not apply any more. What I do know is that this man told my father that if he ever came back there again he would kill him.

There were other women my father messed around with. To my great surprise, I found out that I have a stepsister, but I do not know anything about her. Unfortunately, there are a lot of things I will never know about. When I finally got the courage to speak to my mother about the past I made arrangements to see her, but something terrible happened. A few days before the visit she suddenly had an asthmatic attack that left her permanently brain-damaged. For reasons that I would understand later, this experience became a great teacher. All the lessons of forgiveness required a lot of psychological growth on my part. I struggled with the process and how it touched every aspect of my being. Now I can truly say I am sorry my father is gone.

Feeling Unfairly Treated

One of the greatest issues to be faced at this juncture is the issue of fairness. This concept is critical if we want to understand forgiveness at a deep level. Whenever life brings us pain, we feel unfairly treated. Larry and his family felt this way because of his father's actions in life and death. As Larry tells his story, this theme reappears and reinforces his hatred toward his father. Anyone would agree that Larry had a right to feel this way. Our pain and suffering justifies our reason to even the score. The question is what makes the difference between a justified attack and an unfair one. If we perceive something has been done unfairly to us, it is all right for us to be angry, but if we do something vindictive to someone else it is justified in our minds. We have judged certain attacks as appropriate and others as totally unjustified. Larry learned that attacking is senseless when he understood why the man in the wheelchair attacked in the first place. Unfairness and attack are so connected that when we notice one we automatically notice the other. Our physical sight blocks our spiritual vision.

When we hold on to the idea that we are unfairly treated, we allow ourselves to become the victims. Although outside events do occur in which we feel unfairly treated or victimized, they would not have such a great impact on us if we didn't already have these feelings within ourselves. The belief that we are unfairly treated comes from the notion that someone else (but not ourselves) can deprive us. What we haven't recognized is the sacrifice we have made concerning ourselves that is at the root of everything perceived to be unfair. What we have sacrificed is our wholeness by identifying so strongly with the limits we place on ourselves, such as believing that we are victims.

Larry isn't the only one caught in the victim role. Many of us are tempted to perceive ourselves as unfairly treated, holding on to the stance of "poor me." We hold on to this belief to claim our innocence while simultaneously making the other party the guilty one. What we've done is unfairly judge someone else so we don't feel our own pain and guilt. The world becomes a threatening place through our judgments. The truth is that if we bring the light within to injustice and learn to see it differently, the sense of unfairness will be resolved and replaced with true justice and love.

Another issue that arises during this phase of the forgiveness process is the issue of control and who the authority is in our lives. This issue depicts the conflict between the very limited perspective of our ego state and the spiritual vision of our divine nature. Larry, like most of us, identified very strongly with his ego. He believed that he was the creator of his life, the authority on everything that happened to him, and the controller of everything. Larry is no exception in feeling that he was the sole determiner of his life. We all feel like we are the authority on what takes place in our lives. Larry was so caught up in this restricted way of thinking that he lost sight of his true identity. It wasn't a surprise that Larry was riddled with anxiety because of his inability to embrace the totality of who he was. As a result of this inner conflict, Larry was not at peace with himself.

Are we the creators of our existence or is there something our minds can't comprehend that has created us? If so, are we trying to seize this power? These fundamental questions face all of us and how we answer them determines how we live our lives. Larry began to grapple with these questions. Ultimately, these issues served as a catalyst in his psychological and spiritual growth. Larry realized that if he was invested in being right, he would perceive a situation of conflict as one in which he fought for "authorship." He believed that if "I am the author of my experience and others don't see it my way, they must be wrong." It is true that our perceptions give meaning to our world. However, there is one caveat. "Only those who give over all desire to reject can know that their own rejection is impossible" (*A Course in Miracles*, 1975). Whatever power is behind all of creation is also within. We cannot assume it, but we can lose it. "We are free to accept our inheritance, but we are not free to establish what this inheritance is" (*A Course in Miracles*, 1975). A conflict arises when we confuse our egos with the center of creative intelligence. When this happens we do not recognize our divine inheritance and our profound spiritual destiny. In rejecting our divine inheritance, we experience fear. To deny that our authorship is that of a creative intelligence is to deny our own peace and is the cause of our sense of separation from one another.

Larry struggled a great deal with the authority issue and who was really in control. He began to question this very deeply.

AM I IN control of everything?
    Is my father in control?
    Does God know what is going on and is He in control?
    Did God allow things to happen in my father's life so that my life could be improved?

Larry was really asking who is the author of our existence and of everything that happens to us. He believed he was in control until now. Uncertainty crept into his mind along with profound insight. When we deny the function and power of the creative intelligence, we can only see segments of ourselves. We run into trouble when we believe we can assume the power of creative intelligence. We believe that we created ourselves. If people do not believe as we do, the situation becomes like a tug of war over our authorship. This is an underlying error in thinking for all those who believe they have seized the power of God.

Larry kept struggling with this issue. In his soul-searching, Larry realized that there was indeed a force greater than himself that was in control, a force at the helm of all creation with an infinitely greater wisdom than our minds can comprehend. Knowing this, how could Larry control everything happening in his life? Larry understood that because he could not know everything that was going to happen to someone in the future, he could not know what was in their best interest now. If this was the case, then how could Larry be angry with his father, or with God for that matter, for allowing all this stuff to happen? Larry's entire way of thinking shifted as he began to share his innermost thoughts. He continues his story:

I WAS TRYING to take away God's power by saying no, your plan is wrong. My plan would have been a lot better. I did not recognize the wisdom in not knowing. As I began to think about this more, I realized that not only was there a creative force behind all that happened, there was also an infinite wisdom. If this is the case, what about the issue of fairness because what happened to our family seemed so unfair? I don't know if you want to call it divine intervention, but suddenly I understood that the only way things could be fair in life is if we all have and live the same number of days; if we all go through the same pain and joy; if we have the same diseases and the same number of colds; and, if my child dies at two years old, your child must die at two years old. The only way things could be fair is if our life experiences were exactly the same at all points of our lives. If everybody dies at forty-seven years, three months, and two days, that is the only way life can be fair and God can be fair in our lives.

But when we come to realize that we are His, *then we understand that we are His to do with as He sees is appropriate for His reasons even when they do not necessarily seeming to benefit us.* The creative forces are the powers that be. It is not for me to want things done my way according to my time line not just in relationship with my father, but also with my wife, children, coworkers, and employees. I wanted things my way, but that is not necessarily how things work. I am a controller. I probably will always have to deal with that. This is where the importance of psychological growth steps into play. Not until I was really able to deal with issues of control, authorship, and trust in an infinite wisdom that determines when I die and what kinds of experiences are important for me could I begin to experience peace.

Of course we are always tested to see if we have learned our lessons well, and my test concerning issues of control and authorship was not an easy one. Suddenly I was faced with the possibility of my own son's premature death. At a very young age, Trent became ill. We feared he had leukemia. I was shocked. What good could come out of my son having leukemia, I thought? No way, this really can't be happening. This is when I thought I really needed to be in control. I had to work hard at letting go. Then something very startling happened. When I honestly stopped thinking I was in charge and accepted that there was a more powerful force at work here with an infinite wisdom I could not understand, my son regained his health. This was so striking that I could not deny any more that there was a higher wisdom. My son's illness and the incident with my mother made me realize that. What brought this to fruition was my overwhelming fear of death and its sense of nothingness. I realized that all we are is dust in the wind. That's all I thought about. That's right. That is all we are, dust in the wind, swirling around with no control while wanting control. The paradox is that when I learned to finally give up control I embraced a greater power.

There comes a time when we are able to rethink what has happened, especially in terms of how we view the perpetrator. We are able to change our view of the situation based on a new understanding of who the perpetrator is by our willingness to empathize with his or her past and life experiences. We are able to acknowledge his or her woundedness and possibly begin to identify with the offender, or have a sense of compassion toward that person. The greatest sign of our own maturity at this phase is when we choose to accept and absorb the pain that ends the cycle of hatred and revenge and of passing our traumas onto others. For most people this is extremely difficult to do, but in these actions we find profound healing. This is how Larry worked through this step.

I LATER FOUND out that my father was not raised by his own father. My father's mother died when he was very young, four or five years old. His father did not want anything to do with him so his uncle raised him. It became obvious that there were issues my father had to deal with that I knew nothing about. There is no way I could know what he was going through. To this day we all judge others, but I really strive to say Larry, you do not know what that person is going through. You do not know what he or she has gone through in life; how can you hang a title on that person when you have no right to do that?

Once I made the decision to forgive, I realized *that in order to let go of my pain I had to accept it.* I knew I had to accept my father's adultery and the pain he caused my mother. I knew my mother adored my father so much even though it appeared that he didn't care. I had to accept the role he played in causing my mother to become an alcoholic. I also realized that drinking was my mother's choice. I had to accept that my father took my mother away from me as a child because she now had to work. Not only did I lose a father, but I felt as though I lost a mother, too. I look at what my kids have with my wife, and I realize what I missed. I never came home at 3:00 in the afternoon to have cookies and milk waiting for me. Instead, I had to clean the house and help my sister start dinner so my mother did not have to do it all when she finally did come home. I had to accept the fact that my father disrupted the lives of my brothers and sisters, causing them to go through a lot of pain and suffering. I had to accept the fact that I lost so much of my childhood. I had to accept that my children did not have a grandfather because he was dead before they were born. I even had to accept the shame he caused my family. I still wonder to this day what people thought of my family because of my father being shot to death and messing up the lives of another family.

How do we get to the point where we want to let go of our anger and pain? When does enough become enough? When do we make the decision to forgive? The decision to forgive comes when we struggle with our pain and literally can't stand it any more. The pot of fear, anger, and hatred boils over with such intensity that we make ourselves sick. Our emotional pain has worn down our resistance. Our defenses lose their grip. It is at that point that we ask, "Can I look at the situation differently?" By having a little willingness to see the situation differently, we learn to overlook behavior that is the result of someone else's psychological baggage. We have a change of heart because we recognize that what we think we saw may not be the truth of the situation. This realization leads us to the next phase of the forgiveness process—gaining inner peace.

Gaining Inner Peace

Forgiveness is a decision. It is a choice we make so we can move on with our lives. Eventually, after we walk through the doorway of painful memories, we begin to see things in a different light. Larry was no exception. In a conversation with his brother David, Larry talked about very painful memories. Anger and hatred consumed Larry as he told David how much he hated their father, especially for what he did to their mother. As Larry recounted the horrific things his father did, David suddenly looked at him in total disbelief. Then David said, "Larry, if you only knew how much your father loved you and what he did for you." That moment gave Larry pause. Larry then told his brother about his anger and the struggles he was having with his belief in God. David interrupted Larry again. "Have you ever thought that maybe God took our father to protect us so that the pain he was causing other people would stop? He caused a lot of pain while he was here. God finally said enough. We are going to stop that now, and the only way that it can be done was to take his life because dad would not change. He did it to stop dad from hurting mom and from hurting us."

This stopped Larry in his tracks! He never thought about his father's death in this way before. He was also very tired from carrying the burden of his anger. In that moment of wanting to let go, he was able to hear his brother and see the situation differently. This was a turning point in Larry's life. This is also an example of what can happen at this stage of the forgiveness process. If we are open to seeing things differently, we gain new insights that can lead to a change of heart. We realize that our old strategies are not working and begin to consider forgiveness as an option.

The last step in the forgiveness process is when we find deep meaning in what has happened to us. It is a time of self-reflection and seeing the world through spiritual sight. We have grown in compassion and see ourselves extending that compassion to others. This is also a time when we recognize that we, too, have needed or need to receive forgiveness from others. It is a time when we recognize the importance of receiving support from others. The phase may culminate with an inner transformation in which a new sense of direction in life emerges. This is where the paradox of forgiveness can be most evident: *When we unconditionally give forgiveness to others, we ourselves are healed.* This is how Larry ends his journey.

I HAD TO admit there was a lot of pain, and I needed to share that with other people. I couldn't just hold it in. Then I realized all the pain I have caused other people in my life. I needed to ask for forgiveness from my wife and child because of my fits of anger and belittling of my son. I had to understand that in many respects I was no different than my father. When I really understood the amount of love that God had for me, and that He did forgive me, what else could I do but to forgive my father? I had to understand my own forgiveness. If we really believe in the love and grace of God, we must extend that grace to others. That is forgiveness.

It was not only forgiveness with my father that I went through. It was forgiveness with my wife, my mother, and all those types of things. I realized that it was more of the same. I had to grow spiritually. For without that, forgiving someone only on an emotional level would be empty. Now that I can see through the eyes of forgiveness, I have no ill feelings at all about my father. I love him, I miss him, and I would like to have grown up with him. I would like to have had him see my kids and my wife and to see how we all turned out. I would like to have gone fishing with him.

Forgiveness for me is releasing the bitterness or wrath toward an offender even though he may deserve it. My father deserved the anger, hate, and all that stuff just as I deserved the wrath of God and God's forgiveness. It isn't just saying "I am sorry." Forgiveness goes way beyond "I'm sorry." Forgiveness is a state of grace. When people now ask me about my father, I tell them who he was—and I speak very highly of him. As a result of forgiving him, I do not have to tell the whole story. If people ask how he died, I tell them that he was killed. I don't go through the whole thing. I am honest about it but give him his dignity. I honestly believe that the only reason I have not done some of the things that he did is because God has allowed me not to do so. "There but for the grace of God go I." That is true for me.

My father's death taught me important lessons in life. With my father dying at such a young age, I take advantage of every moment, especially with my kids. I think of my own death. I take advantage of my time here and do not take it for granted. I really understand that we are not promised tomorrow and do not know what tomorrow holds. I understand that if my time comes tomorrow, I want my sons and wife to know who I was and that I loved them.

Another important lesson I learned about forgiveness is that if you are unable to forgive others or ask for forgiveness, you will have a difficult time in relating to other people. If you are unable to forgive others, how can you expect others to forgive you for the things you have done? That was a very important part of the process, now that I think about it. I had to go back and write down things that I had done against my children. I became aware of the ways that I had erred against my children, my wife, and other people. Not only did I have to write them down, I also had to go before them and ask for their forgiveness. It was hard. There were times I had to write things out. It was amazing. It really strengthened my relationships, especially my relationship with my wife. When I admitted some feelings I had toward her, including some things I had never really forgiven *her* for, and asked her for her forgiveness—when I went through and listed those things out—only then could I learn to forgive my father. The response I got from my wife was really amazing. She was amazed at what I thought I had done, and at the same time it helped her to understand that I loved her so much I wanted to go back and ask her forgiveness for these things.

Why do we even think about forgiving someone? If we don't forgive, we end up holding something against someone else. That other person may or may not feel it, but you will feel it and you will not be able to have an effective relationship with him or her. It's impossible to have a very close relationship with somebody if you hold something against him or her.

How do we get people to ask for forgiveness? In my life it came down to the fact that we had to be truthful with each other. If we really want to experience a close intimacy with others, nothing can come between us—even in business relationships. We cannot have all the joy and fullness of a relationship if there is anger. We have to tell somebody what we are feeling. Until we do, a wall will be there, and until that wall is dropped the relationship is limited. Saying you're sorry is not enough. We have to humble ourselves. It is really an indication of pride if we don't forgive. The question we may want to ask is would we rather be right or happy? If we say we would rather be right, our pride is talking and having too much pride is not a good thing. Asking someone to forgive us is a step of humility. We are putting ourselves where we need to be. It is humbling to say, "I am sorry, I ask for forgiveness."

Too often we tend to let our emotions rule our actions. We don't step back to think about what the consequences may be. We've been taught to express anger, for example, but we don't stop and ask ourselves what our anger is trying to teach us. *Where do we have to change?* If we can recognize our emotions are signaling to us that change within ourselves is necessary, we might be able to develop a little willingness to forgive. That's all. If that little willingness is heartfelt, a miracle does happen. Call it grace, call it the work of a greater intelligence, call it God—whatever it is we will not be disappointed. The forgiveness process can be difficult, and we get so much help along the way if we are open to it. It is our little willingness, *the action of committing to forgive someone, that starts our healing process.*

Once I was able to ask someone to forgive me, I experienced a weight being lifted off my shoulders. I felt lightness where I once offended someone. Forgiveness opens the doors of under-standing for everyone involved. It gives us a sense of fullness and freeness and deepens feelings of love. When we are able to for-give, we are also able to put ourselves in someone else's shoes. This can open us up to a *wow!* We avoid doing this especially with perpetrators. We don't want to know about the suffering that led them to behave in such horrific ways. We don't want to acknowledge that their twisted minds *are* the result of the per-sonal suffering *they are trapped in.* The paradox is that, when we are willing to enter into their "head space" and allow ourself to feel what is inside without judgment, something very powerful happens. *We* experience a sense of release. When I truly allowed myself to understand where my father was coming from to the very best of my ability, my anger and even my fear of death were released. Now I hold a totally different view of my father.

The person feeling the detriment of not forgiving is the per-son who needs to forgive—not the other person. This must sound very strange and probably creates resistance in some peo-ple. It is another paradox of forgiveness. Holding on to strong emotions indicates to us that we are wounded and are in need of healing. Forgiveness paradoxically is what helps us release our pain and suffering. Only after I was able to let go of my anger and hatred toward my father could I experience him in another way. I am better because of this. I am now able to feel the emo-tion of missing my father, which adds to my life tremendously. I honestly wish he could be here. It also enhances my relationship with my wife and my children. I am capable of being a more lov-ing man. I want to give them experiences I could not have as a child wholeheartedly—it gives me back something. I am so much better off because the foundation of my relationship with my children is based on forgiveness, something I could not give to my dad.

Perhaps the purpose of life is to provide opportunities for us that we consciously have chosen to listen to our higher nature and for us to learn how powerfully healing that is. Only through complete forgiveness can we learn this. Forgiveness teaches us how to make a shift in thinking from a fear-based way of seeing the world to a way that is led by divinity. It is a process that heals our thinking. The result of this healing is the experience of true joy, love, and compassion. Forgiveness is the healing process that helps us to do this.

Forgiveness heals our misperceptions, which in turn releases our past. When we develop spiritual vision we realize there is no need to be defensive. We recognize the inner beauty of others and ourselves. We are able to look past errors and see the truth of who we are. This is one of the greatest gifts of practicing forgiveness. We also realize that when we use our defenses we are engaging in a process that is antithetical to forgiveness. It is impossible to be defensive and be able to forgive at the same time. Forgiveness can only happen when we release our inner light.

Our spiritual vision recognizes our weaknesses and defenses for what they are and looks to the beauty of our inner being. This kind of vision is able to look past the errors to see our inner truth. The way we heal through the forgiveness process is that it opens us to the power of love instead of the power of hate. When we are able to forgive, the barriers of fear toward another person that were once there are now lifted. We can begin to see their humanness in a different light. Unfortunately, we do not understand healing because our fear gets in the way.

The essence of forgiveness is the ability to recognize the holiness that lies within us. Only spiritual sight can recognize this and does so with perfect clarity. Forgiveness is at the center of this inner altar, where it undoes the split in our psyche and restores wholeness in our mind.

Forgiveness is a process that teaches us another way of thinking, a thinking that promotes healing. This type of thinking begins with the reawakening of spirit and a de-emphasis of what our physical sight would lead us to believe. Our experience when we first begin this process is one of fear because we are so afraid of what our spiritual sight might show us. We haven't learned that spiritual sight looks beyond past mistakes to the true essence of who we are. Our fear of healing arises as a defense against the fact we haven't accepted that healing is necessary for ourselves. What our physical eyes tell us is usually not the picture we need to see and will not help us think in a way that promotes healing. Our real vision is obscured because we cannot bear seeing our defiled altar. And we must see this before we can feel truly loved.

Healing rests on giving to others and is a way of perceiving the perfection of another, even if you cannot perceive it in yourself. This kind of charity is basically the weakest form of a more powerful love—compassion—yet it helps set the stage for us to grow in that direction. Forgiveness is a form of this kind of charity and is charity we give ourselves. This is the greatest paradox of all. To give to others we give to ourselves. This was the greatest lesson Larry Mathis learned.

6

Working with Anger

Kate Wilson's Story

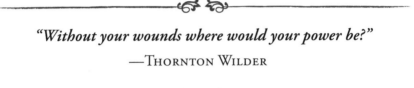

"Without your wounds where would your power be?"
—THORNTON WILDER

ONE OF THE challenges of Step Three is working through anger. It is impossible to forgive until we have faced this powerful emotion and have learned how to deal with it. The difficulty is in understanding what anger is trying to say. Anger may give us a great sense of power. We may even believe that anger will make us feel better but it undermines the happiness of ourselves and others. Other times we feel that anger is lurking under the surface in some repressed form that influences our life.

All of us have a reservoir of anger and resentment that we hold against others. These may be owing to abuse, battery, divorce, or some breach of trust. However, holding on to resentment serves no productive purpose. *We harm only ourselves* when we go over in our minds how someone has hurt us. Repeating what took place just makes us angrier and can result in our taking revenge on others. When people harm us we need to remind ourselves that they do so because of the pain they are in or because of something they lack. They are acting out of a place of limitation and woundedness. Forgiving grudges and resentments simply means that we have stopped tying up our energy by being angry. Forgiveness doesn't mean that we have to like someone's behavior nor does it mean that we ignore the problem. It does mean that if we look at our own behavior we will recognize that at times we have regretted how we have behaved. We would want others to understand our mistakes and hope that they would forgive us as well.

In this chapter we will meet Kate, a woman who knows a lot about anger. Her anger was so detrimental to her health that it would have destroyed her if she didn't do anything about it. Through Kate's story we will get to know the face of anger and how we can harness its energy to help us heal and learn to forgive. We will also learn steps to help us work with our own anger. Here is Kate's story.

The Importance of Anger

I was born into a very dysfunctional family under strange circumstances. My parents were part of a cult. My father in particular was drawn into the beliefs of this obscure religion, perhaps because of his own childhood experiences. As a child he was severely traumatized and sexually abused by his mother. While fighting in the Korean War he participated in some atrocities, which also left their emotional scars. To this day he has flashbacks of the war. There is no question that his very traumatic childhood and the trauma of war made him vulnerable to the persuasion of the cult.

This cult has an odd mixture of religious fanaticism coupled with the notion that certain people are chosen to initiate acts under God's command, including sexually possessing someone if you felt called to do so. When I was about five years old, as far back as I can remember, I guess this was going on in my dad's mind.

I have no idea what led him to this, but my father felt that he was called to carry out certain prescribed rituals of the cult; he would somehow cross through a metaphysical door by doing so. My father somehow got it into his head that God wanted him to make a human sacrifice of me, not by killing me but by raping me. I remember his tying me up and telling me that I was a sacrifice, that God commanded him to rape me and I had to keep it an absolute secret. Fortunately, I repressed it until I was about twenty-eight years old, although I had flashbacks at times. Apparently, I even told friends about it, but I don't remember doing so. It isn't like it is a foggy thing; I have no recollection of these incidents whatsoever. I wouldn't believe it myself if I hadn't been repeatedly told by doctors that I have a lot of scar tissue, as though I had an unassisted labor in which I tore very badly and gave birth without being cleaned up surgically. It is so odd because doctors would tell me these things, and it never seemed unusual to me. I never wondered why it was there. It never struck me as odd. *It did not process for me.* It is just amazing what the mind does to protect itself.

The abuse went on for a number of years. I am not sure how many incidents there were, but by the time I was six years old all I could think about was suicide. I did not have memories of the abuse, but I was absolutely dead set on dying. I remember just feeling like an evil creature that had to die. I was thinking that it was wrong for me to eat, sleep, or do anything that would be life-supporting. I stopped sleeping deeply at that point. From then until I was about eighteen I was clinically depressed. I do not remember a time during this period when I was happy, ever! All I could think about was that some day I would die, and all of this would be over.

Finally, my sister took me to a therapist, who was able to go right to the issue of sexual abuse. I still could not talk about what had happened with my father. Yet the therapist was kind and sweet, and he served as a father figure, which I desperately needed. This was an amazing experience for me. It was the first time I experienced the world as not completely empty and cruel, without any hope whatsoever. I never a went back into a deep clinical depression.

I got married at age twenty-three. I often had flashbacks when I was with my husband without understanding why. It is still hard with my husband. Sometimes he walks into the room and part of me says that it is Peter and everything is fine. Yet there is still a part of me that panics if he walks in suddenly or it's dark or a set of circumstances triggers memories of my father. Before I know it I am across the room screaming and holding my arms up in front of myself. Fortunately, Peter is very sensitive and makes me feel safe, similar to the therapist I saw when I was younger. This is a real gift.

My most profound healing began when I was pregnant. Becoming a mother with a life to take care of changed my belief system. I realized that every child was worthy of being loved, and that, as a mother, I had an awesome responsibility to take care of this child. Therefore, I needed to take care of myself so I could be there for my child. It was when I was pregnant with my daughter that I had some profound spiritual experiences.

Yet I was still very sad. Although I was not clinically depressed anymore, I grieved all the time without knowing why. Each night I waited for everybody to go to sleep, and then I would sit up and cry for hours, like a marathon. It was so difficult to get through the day with a smile on my face, waiting for my daughter and husband to go to sleep so I could cry. I would have cried all the way through my twenties if I had my druthers, but I knew I had to deal with my pain.

When I finally started remembering at age twenty-five, so many things clicked into place. My husband felt relieved because he finally understood all the strange reactions I had to him and the issues I had about sex. It just fit.

My ordeal continued for about three or four more really horrible years but not necessarily from the memories. My pain came from dealing with something very difficult and being retraumatized when I talked with my friends. I would call them and tell them that I was disintegrating, absolutely falling apart. Their universal response was that I wasn't telling the truth. Only one person could acknowledge my pain, which was hardly validation for what really happened. Instead, people would react out of fear, wanting me to be silent. I felt very unsafe.

I finally got into a therapy group, but was afraid to talk about my abuse. I sat there for three years and talked about other people's problems. Then one day I couldn't handle it any more. I finally broke the silence of what I was so ashamed of. I was very shaky, still wondering if I was accusing an innocent man. Even with physical scars to prove what happened, there was part of me that still didn't believe it. I tried to think of other ways to account for what happened to me, but I couldn't. I didn't believe I could fake the intense memories and emotional upheaval that came with the trauma. It is very difficult to hang on to reality, especially when so many people are telling you that you made it up and you denied it as a kid.

When I broke the silence of what was locked inside me and told my story, something very powerful happened. The group made me realize that what had happened was indeed real and that I had to learn how to protect and take care of myself, even if it meant saying goodbye to my family. With their support, I finally got the courage to move away from the area of my childhood. Once I left I began to heal rapidly, and my life began to change.

—

Anger's Message

MY FATHER MANAGED to obliterate almost every instinct of survival in me and the ability to act on my own behalf at the completely vulnerable age of five. What he could not do, though, was extinguish my anger, even at such a young age. The part of me that was angry knew what he was doing. This carried into my teens, when I tried hard to starve myself to death. I ran one hundred miles a week. I remember the many times I collapsed because I would go two weeks without eating. I would fall over and think, oh good, now I can die. I was a wreck. I got to a point where skin rubbed off my bones because it was stretched so thin. Yet part of me did not want to die—my anger. Everything else in me said get out of this place. Yet there was a tiny, but very bright, flame burning in the very center of my soul—pure anger. It was the only thing that kept me alive. In a way this was odd because I never expressed anger and never raised my voice to either of my parents, even when confronting them. I never had a rebellious period, ever. I always tried to be nice and ingratiate myself to people because I figured that I had no other reason for being alive. Because of my feelings of low self-worth, I never expressed anger or even let myself know that I felt it, but it kept me alive. Then I had a white-light experience that connected me consciously to that anger. The first time it happened my husband tried to hug me, and I pushed him away. He kept hugging me and wouldn't let go. I pushed back against him as hard as I could and felt a huge surge of anger. All of a sudden I was five years old again. It was so vivid. It was as though I had all these experiences stored in my nerve impulses that couldn't process in my brain. Twenty-three years after the abuse occurred, my anger lifted the gates that had blocked those memories from my conscious awareness. *My anger was trying to keep me safe.* It was only in the context of wild rage that I was safe enough to remember. I never hurt anybody, *but I had to embrace the anger and let it protect me.*

There was an extremely long, wooden bench in our bedroom. It was kind of worm-eaten and old. Over a three-month period, I kicked it to splinters and cracked its huge boards. There was also a concrete birdbath that we wanted to get rid of. I took a sledgehammer and beat it down to dust because I was so angry. The interesting thing was that when I let my body express my anger, the physical pain that I was carrying began to lessen. Usually whenever I exerted myself physically I would be in incapacitating pain. In this case, the pain let go when I used my body to express anger. This helped me change from being a person who was horrified of anger, terrified of other people's anger, and who didn't allow myself to be angry to someone who was a big fan of anger.

I had oceans of anger. It was what kept me alive to care for my children. It was my safety valve. Anger was part of my experience. If I denied that, I could not handle the pain. I realized that if I was going to get in touch with my feelings of horror, betrayal, violence, and anguish, the feelings of anger would be there, too.

I realized I needed to *listen* to my anger. After all, anger is what got me through this whole thing. My anger made it clear that what my father did was wrong. It was as simple as that. Anger would also say other things that were more complicated. When I felt guilty my anger would say no, the only thing you did wrong was blaming the child for a man's abuse. That was wrong. Anger helped me to tease out those differences.

My healing was a process of learning through anger, strangely enough. Every time my anger said, "You need to make yourself safer," or "You need to stop believing this lie," I would make a change. That's why I left home and stopped keeping what happened to me a secret.

Anger is a messenger. It is a red flag flying in our faces saying something has to change. Very often we resist asking ourselves what our anger says about us. We are so focused on blaming that we don't want to acknowledge something within us needs to change as well. Our unconscious guilt gets in the way, and we don't want to deal with our own issues. The problem is *if you don't change you will be stuck in anger.* You will just sit there boiling in your own juices and never change your life. Anger says make a change so you will not be angry anymore. *The hard work is being painfully honest with yourself about how you need to change.* This honesty is the hardest part about working with anger, but it opens the door for forgiveness.

Anger isn't healing unless we clearly hear its message. If we understand its function, anger serves a very important purpose.

Anger became the compass in healing my pain. It showed me the pain of feeling alone and heartbroken in a universe with an evil God. Anger helped me create a safe place to grieve. It also gave me the courage to change.

In dealing with my anger, I had to face my memories and deal with them. The memories were so horrible and filled me with such adrenaline that I became overwhelmed unless I physically worked it out. Sometimes I went through periods where I just didn't believe that anything had happened. Then I would repeatedly question why I had scar tissue and surgery to correct it. If it were a stranger that did this to me, why didn't my parents know about it? Why didn't I remember ever telling anyone? Why didn't they notice when there was blood all over everything? Why didn't anyone take care of me? I went through this whole process, and friends around me would say, "Oh, Kate, it happened!" Without warning I would have another set of flashbacks. They would be so vivid it felt like it was happening again. I am sure that it will keep processing throughout my life, but it doesn't take up much of my time anymore.

Anger can be a force of destruction or it can be a wise teacher. If you use your anger to make positive changes in your life instead of hurting yourself or other people, it can save you. Anger is the path to true forgiveness, as strange as that sounds. People are so afraid of the destructive power of anger that they block it out. If you are moral and are committed to not hurting people and making every change based on love, the way out of that horrible pain is lit by anger.

I am not a fan of expressing anger through violence. You may work out anger through physical exercise but not through destruction. Accepting my anger and recognizing that it did not make me evil was the biggest stepping stone for me. I was angry about being abused, and it was OK to be angry. That was the biggest lesson I learned. I needed to make a change within myself, one I was responsible for. It had to be a moral and compassionate change. I also had to realize that it wasn't about what kind of change I wanted to make in another person's life. It was not that I needed to change my father but, instead, to recognize that my father made horrible choices. My choice was to not imitate him, to not follow his path, and to not believe what he told me. *Anger's message is to always look inward.*

You can live a life exposed and open, or you can live a life dominated by hatred and great resentment. I chose to live openly so if I died today I would die with a peaceful heart. I got this peaceful heart from the divine spark within me. I was born with it. During my lifetime there was a lot that served to hide my heart from me. I had to uncover it by clearing away a lot of the poison injected by misunderstandings, perceptions, and other people's bad choices. The more you clear away, the more you can hear your real feelings speak to you in a clear voice. Following your inner voice may seem to require bravery. The gift is that you will always be peaceful by listening to your heart.

Healing Anger

There is a process to help us work out our anger. Kate's anger ultimately saved her life. Yet in her early years, Kate was very afraid of expressing anger. In this case, her survival depended on keeping still. Even as she got older, her feelings of low self-worth prevented her from expressing what she felt inside. But to eventually heal anger, you have to know it. This brings us to the first step in healing anger.

Acknowledge Anger

You need to look as honestly as possible at the anger within you as a result of what was done to you. Don't be afraid to get in touch with all the anger within. It will not devastate you. This is a critical step. Underneath your anger you may find other emotions such as guilt and shame, or you may be so afraid of your anger that you have blocked out these feelings. It is important to reconnect with all of this so your emotions can be healed. Ask yourself, "What am I really angry about? What am I accusing that person of?"

Face Your Anger

Look at how you protected yourself from your anger before you began feeling it. All of us want to avoid pain, and we find psychological ways to do so. Some deny that anything happened. Even when Kate had scar tissue to substantiate abuse, she still tried to convince herself nothing happened. Denial is one way to avoid feeling anger. Some of us may also suppress our feelings by pushing our thoughts out of conscious awareness. We create other fantasies that allow us to escape the pain. Repressing the memory of the event is another mechanism we use, especially if what happened to us was very traumatic. As we have seen with Kate, this kind of selective amnesia is more likely to occur when the victim is a child, especially in females who were sexually abused.

There are other ways you can protect yourself such as transferring your angry feelings toward the perpetrator to someone else. This is the "kick-the-dog" syndrome. You are angry with your boss, but you don't show your anger toward him for fear of losing your job, so you go home and "kick" someone else.

In this step it is important to identify how you are running away from your anger to begin to own it. Remember you built these walls to protect yourself, so be gentle as you begin to take those walls down. Look at what your anger is trying to tell you, why you needed to be protected, and how holding on to it may be harming you.

Feel the Depth of Your Rage

We have shields to protect us from dealing with our anger just as anger, in turn, can be a shield to protect ourselves from feelings of guilt and shame that we may experience because we were victimized. It is not uncommon for people who have low self-esteem to find it difficult to express the rage inside of themselves. Kate was no exception. It was only when she got in touch with the depth of her rage that she felt safe enough to remember. As she got deeper into her anger and let her body express anger, the physical pain she carried began to lessen. We have to feel the depth of our rage before we can heal it.

Take Responsibility for Your Own Behavior

What makes anger rise? Anger does not arise from one factor alone, but from a complex set of factors. The greatest cause of anger is our misperception of what we think we see. This misperception has to do with the way we *choose* to see the world. We see the world through our need to place what we don't want to accept within ourselves onto someone else. Anger is a manifestation of this. The problem is not with me; it is with you. That is not to say people can't do awful things to us—they can. What is at stake here is how we choose to interpret what has been done to us and why.

Our need to unconsciously place on others what we don't want to see in ourselves rests heavily on our needs, desires, fears, guilt, and other feelings we want to disown. This dynamic is in operation all the time. Unfortunately, the world we see merely reflects our internal frame of reference, including our thoughts and emotions.

In the thought-provoking book *A Course in Miracles* (1975), the principle "projection makes perception" is fully described. The book states,

> *The world you see is what you gave it, nothing more than that. But though it is no more than that, it is not less. Therefore, to you it is important. It is the witness to your state of mind, the outside picture of an inward condition. As a man thinketh, so does he perceive. Therefore, seek not to change the world, but choose to change your mind about the world. Perception is a result and not a cause.*

When we get stuck in our anger it is an indication of something inside us that we don't want to see. Usually it has to do with feelings of guilt, which is why it is much easier to be angry with others than to look within ourselves. When we can stop blaming others for the shortcomings that are also ours we can recognize the humanness that joins us. This can have a profound healing effect.

Learn Anger's Message

Once we are willing to take responsibility for our behavior, we open up to the possibility of hearing anger's message. Anger tells us that we need to see the world differently and that we need to change. This point is clearly made in Kate's story. We need to look at something within ourselves that we are choosing to avoid, usually because of the pain it brings. A way to help us learn what anger is trying to say is by asking the question, "What am I accusing that person of?" Whatever your answer, that is what you are secretly accusing yourself of. Our minds are very clever so we will have to dig a little bit to discover it. For example, you may be angry with your spouse for being irresponsible and not paying the bills on time. You may ask, "What does this have to do with me, I always pay bills on time," and you probably do. This is where the mind becomes a trickster. You may be responsible in paying bills on time, but are you secretly accusing yourself of being irresponsible in some other area of your life that you haven't forgiven yourself for? It could be something in the past or the present, it doesn't matter. The point is this is a place where *you* need healing. We can always justify our anger, get people to support our innocence, and never look within ourselves, but if we do, we will get stuck and never get beyond this intense emotion.

Look Inward and Make a Change

This last step requires that we look inward and make necessary changes. This was one of the greatest lessons Kate learned through her healing process. She realized that anger doesn't heal unless you hear its message and take necessary action. When you make a change the anger goes away.

The Healing Power of Forgiveness: Kate's Story Continues

FORGIVENESS REQUIRES constantly returning to the center of myself, to my deepest truth of experience, which for me is synonymous with the divine spark. I need to constantly go back there and ask if I am living in accordance with my inner truth. If I'm getting angry, what is it that I need to do in my life so the anger will not be here anymore? I have to live according to that every day.

Once I was able to forgive, everything in my life changed. I lost every friend that I had in my early life except for my husband. I developed a new career and a new way of living my life. I dropped out of college and decided to do more creative writing. I became much more independent and developed an identity separate from my husband. My husband "refathered" me through my twenties and helped me grow up. I developed a totally different set of friends, different place to live, different spiritual place, different everything.

I had to heal before I could forgive, instead of forgiving and then being healed. The beneficial effects of healing brought about forgiveness, not the other way around. As long as you are broken, as long as you are in pain, it is very difficult not to regret that somebody caused you pain. Once the pain heals, as Ernest Hemingway said, you become strong in the broken places; then the breaking itself becomes the gift. You become much stronger than you would have otherwise. For me, one of the most profound lessons was not realizing that I had forgiven my father, but realizing that I was grateful for what he did.

I had to give myself lots of time to heal and not pressure the damaged child within myself. I realized that reliving a loving and nurturing new childhood was a very important part of my healing process, and I was fortunately able to re-create it. I desperately needed "reparenting." My wonderful new friends helped me heal with the unconditional love they showered on me.

What got me through all of this is my overwhelming belief in a creative intelligence. This intense spiritual belief is at the center of my existence and is so wonderful, real, and accessible. I was lucky. At times I have experienced something I call *the grace of God,* which helped enable me to forgive. I think I feel it a lot. It is basically a sense that I am loved by a power so mighty that I am absolutely safe. Yes, I am going to die, and yes, bad things are going to happen to me, but I feel totally loved when I am in connection with this energy. There is not a doubt in my mind that it is there all the time.

I first felt this connection when I was eighteen years old. True to the pattern of many incest survivors, I typically dated men who were much older than I was. The person I was dating at age eighteen was no exception. He was quite sweet, and we were pretty serious. I remember kissing in an art studio. Usually, any kind of sexual situation would trigger my abuse memories. I had been in therapy and wrestled with this, but that day was different. I had a very unusual experience while I was with this guy. I suddenly felt that my whole worldview was being shaken. It was like I was seeing something in my mind's eye that felt like a dream. My whole view of the universe suddenly shifted. I felt like a butterfly in a steel factory. I noticed something flickering, which I began focusing on. Then I saw a vast, barren plain and a knife blade suddenly pierced through it. I realized that it was just a screen and my head projected what I thought on this huge empty nothing. *It was all just a screen and everything projected on this screen was of my own making.* Through this little rip came a brilliant light. It looked like the yellow light that comes through deciduous trees early in spring. It burst through the grayness, and then the whole gray thing ripped. It was a very visual feeling, and it tore right down the center and just peeled back. I realized that this horrible, empty, cold place was, in fact, full of light and love and always had been. I hadn't been able to see this before because part of me had been locked away in this illusory world of pain. I started crying uncontrollably. I just wept and wept and wept. Before, when I had been clinically depressed for twelve years, I never cried. I could not feel anything, I was so numb. As soon as the feelings came back, I felt huge grief—inexpressible grief—and joy. Joy came in the mix. Love came in that mix. I could see that the pain of loss and of being hurt was more than balanced by the ability to experience love and joy.

From that moment on, I vowed to always embrace my feelings. To not be able to feel is the most horrible torture there ever could be. I think this person set the stage for me to feel love, but whatever was happening was in me and between God and me. This other person didn't understand what the hell was going on. He dumped me a week later because he was just so freaked out by the whole thing. Surprisingly, that didn't bother me. I was really sad, but I recognized that I could be happy, too. Yes, I would fall back into depression, but I recognized that I had a conscious choice about that, too. I chose to believe that I was in a bright world. Every time I made that choice, things seemed to work. So I learned to stay there all the time.

I learned that the healing power of forgiveness enables us to encircle the perpetrator in a compassionate world so that no one is left out. I went from a universe with a completely evil God to a universe where nothing—no matter how evil it was—would be forgiven and to a God who forgives everything. God will not judge me harshly because God does not judge anyone harshly. I think forgiveness in that regard comes free. I don't believe Western religion when it says you must suffer and be in agony to be forgiven. I think we are here to learn. Our only punishment, if you want to call it that, is that we have to look inward at the pain that caused *us* to do wrong things. All of this brought a great deal of sadness for me. I hope my father can look inward. The healing process could cause him a lot of pain. Yet there is not a doubt in my mind that when he dies, the biggest surprise of his entire existence will be to realize that he was forgiven long ago. There will be no judgment.

Forgiveness is really just another way of loving one another. Love truly is the one indestructible element in the cosmos. The more you have in your life, the less pain there is and the less it matters that other people have created pain for you. It is such a joyful thing. Forgiveness is just a small part of that. You want all the parts in there because it is so rich.

The gift of forgiveness is about the beauty of change. I see that as pain's gift, as my father's gift, and as God's gift to me. Forgiveness is finding our way back to the pure center within all of us. It is a life-long journey. The path that gets us back to that place is forgiveness. I would define forgiveness as the process of learning to love yourself after you have been hurt. Everyone thinks of forgiveness as loving the perpetrator and forgets about oneself. Once you learn to love yourself, the rest becomes secondary.

—

7

Understanding the Impact of Guilt

"Nothing in life is to be feared. It is only to be understood."
—MADAME MARIE CURIE

SUDDENLY, A BURST of applause erupted out of the depths of silence. I felt a momentary sense of relief. Just when I thought I could sit back and relax, a woman from the audience stood up and shouted, "I must speak, I must speak!" I saw in her face the same kind of intensity I was feeling while speaking to this crowded audience.

"I am very relieved to hear you address the issue of guilt," this woman said. "I am Lebanese and have seen a great deal of fighting in my region of the world. Everyone has blood on their hands, and no one will admit it. How do we admit to our guilt?"

When I heard her question I thought, "Thank God, this woman really understands what is at the heart of the matter of forgiveness." I told this woman that we could not fully understand guilt until we discussed the nature of our perceptions, for it is how we see the world that determines our reaction to it. There was mur-

muring in the audience when someone asked, "What does guilt have to do with how we see the world?"

I asked them to imagine that we were walking movie projectors and that the guilt running through our minds was projected on what we saw through the projector lens. As we saw people moving across the screen we became critical and judgmental when we noticed different kinds of behavior that were actually behaviors buried within ourselves. The more guilt there was in our minds, the more there was on the film and the more fault-finding we became. The problem was that we were totally unaware that what bothered us so much about others was what we found most disturbing in ourselves. Because getting in touch with our guilt was so incredibly difficult and painful, the film projected a picture outside of us that became the focus of our self-hate. This was important to understand because when we were angry with someone, we viewed them through the guilt running through our minds. Nothing appeared as it seemed. The forgiveness process began to undo this guilt so we could see people and circumstances in a different light. We were so quick to blame everyone and everything and so unwilling to look at ourselves.

Guilt, that terrible feeling inside of us that says there is something wrong with us, is the culprit that stops us from going deeper within ourselves to our inherent goodness. We are so afraid to look guilt squarely in the eye because of the sick feeling we get in the pit of our stomach. We haven't realized that once we face our guilt, we can begin to make different choices. Its ugliness dissipates once we realize that holding on to guilt is a choice, too. This is liberating.

"Guilt?" someone yelled. "When I know I am defending my rights and my life, guilt is never an issue! I am angry and have every right to be angry. There is no reason I should feel guilty!"

I gulped, thought for a moment, and said, "We all feel justified in holding on to our anger."

People do appalling things. We could have an ex-spouse who treated us terribly and put as through an ugly divorce. We could have been raped or violated in some other way. It would be very appropriate to be angry at anyone in these circumstances, and all of us could justify our anger. But what really makes us angry? It's never the reason we think. Why is it that when bad things happen to some people they get very angry while others say remarkable statements such as, "That person must have been so tormented inside to do such a horrible thing"? It could be the same incident with two very different responses. The reason for these different responses comes from the way we choose to see the world. Those choices are determined by our mind's contents, which—and here is the hard part—get filtered through our guilt. The fact is that none of us is innocent. We don't want to know this about ourselves but want to keep this truth deeply hidden.

As I was talking to the audience, I remembered a story that happened many years ago to a client of mine. This person, a schoolteacher, was walking down the street when she saw something strange. A man called to a child as though he wanted to play ball with him. They seemed to be enjoying each other's company when suddenly he pushed the child into a busy street. Everyone around them was stunned! How could someone do such a thing to a child? People, including my client, gathered around to help the child and were very angry about what had happened. For the next day or so, people in the neighborhood were talking about the incident in anger and disbelief, but then they went on to other things. My client had a different experience.

As the days went on, her anger grew. She could not stop talking about the incident for weeks. Finally I asked, "What are you accusing this man of?"

"I am accusing this man of inviting this child to play ball while he seemed to have hated the boy in his heart and really wanted to push the child away forever!"

There was a long silence in the room as she thought about what she had just said. After a few minutes she shook her head as tears welled up in her eyes. "How could I be doing this? I am doing something as awful as the man in the street did to the child!"

You could see by the expression on her face that she was overwhelmed by guilt. "I can't believe that I am capable of doing what the man did."

I had no idea what she was talking about and asked what she was referring to.

"I come to school every day, spending my entire time with children. I pretend that I like them when what I really want to do is push them away. I really dislike kids, but I continue to teach them when what I would really like to do is get rid of them!

"Yikes! How can I teach when I don't even like kids? How could I do such a thing? I lure them by being nice when what I really want to do is push them away. I am just like the man on the street."

The audience sat motionless. They were beginning to understand how we use anger as a defense against our guilt. It is so much easier for us to be angry at someone else and not take responsibility for our personal healing. Yes, it was a terrible thing that the man on the street did and anyone who saw it would be angry. The difference is that after a day or so people were able to move on, except for this person. She held on to her anger. Something inside of her needed to be healed. Her guilt inhibited her from looking deeper into her emotions to finally get to the root of what she was really angry about—herself!

I cannot stress enough the tricky dynamics of guilt and what it does to our thinking. We are not consciously aware of most of our guilt feelings. Who wants to be constantly reminded of all the things we feel are inherently wrong with us? Guilt is an all-pervasive sense of failure that looms in the background of our minds waiting to rear its ugly head. To feel guilt hurts. We don't like it so our unconscious mind decides to do something about it. We pretend it doesn't exist. Whatever it is, it is blocked from our awareness. This is why it is so difficult to become aware of our guilt.

Unfortunately, we go one step further by wanting to remove guilt from our minds. We need to dump our psychological waste on something or someone else, relieving us of our responsibilities. We have now become the victims, and the world becomes the victimizer. The way we dump this psychological waste is through anger. Through my anger I tell you how guilty you are. It is my attempt to make you responsible for what I refuse to take responsibility for. This dynamic is clearly illustrated in the incident with the boy, when my client could see that she was acting no differently than the man on the street.

When we can't let go of our anger, holding on justifies our guilt. Our anger is an attempt to make someone else responsible. We believe that someone else has to change, not ourselves. Unconsciously, we believe that by putting our guilt onto someone else, we are better off because we are liberating ourselves. We never look at what really is going on. We don't realize that by fighting with other people we have found the perfect way of holding on to more guilt. On some fundamental level we know that when we attack someone it is because of our own feelings of self-hatred. If I can't change my perception of you, I haven't healed the guilt in my own mind. The more guilt I feel about myself, the more I need to attack someone else, which makes me feel guiltier. My belief is that guilt is not in me or my mind but in the world. In actuality, I have placed my guilt on the stage of my life and what I see being played out is a mirror of what is actually in my mind; the world is a reflection of what is in my mind. The client who witnessed the incident on the street actually witnessed a mirror image of her own guilt. This is not to say that anger isn't an appropriate response to certain situations. What is important to remember is that if we have a negative emotion we can't let go of, it means that the problem is not out there but within ourselves.

Someone in the audience asked, "How do we undo the mess we find ourselves in and where does forgiveness fit into the picture?"

This is where the process of forgiveness becomes so important. If we recognize that when we get angry at someone we attack ourselves, the people who are upsetting us the most are also our greatest gifts. They have served as a mirror reflection, providing an opportunity for us to look at ourselves, see the problems within ourselves, and forgive ourselves.

Forgiveness becomes a process of undoing our guilt. When we are able to see the world in a different way from our faulty perceptions, we are no longer victims of this world because of a shift in our thinking. When we choose to see things differently through the eyes of forgiveness and not listen to the part of ourselves filled with guilt and self-hatred, we are reunited with the truth of who we are, a spiritual essence. This is the path to wholeness.

The Lebanese woman stood up once again shaking her head in agreement. It is so difficult for people who are incredibly angry to be able to step back and be willing to look at what they are truly angry about. It is so much easier to yell at one another and not take responsibility for one's actions. In our defensiveness, we block the role we are playing in perpetuating the conflict from our awareness and believe we are innocent. Instead, we need to ask ourselves whether this fighting or blaming gets us what we really want in the long run. What do we gain? We have to ask ourselves what the *basis* of our anger is and what lenses have we chosen to see our world through. Is it through our desire for revenge, our need to be the innocent victim so we do not have to take responsibility, or because we would rather be right instead of happy? If we can ask ourselves the right questions and do this kind of soul-searching, we may perhaps find peace in our hearts.

I ended the afternoon with these parting words, "When we can understand and uncover our guilt, we are getting to the core of the forgiveness process. Whenever we become so angry that we feel we can't forgive, remember it is guilt that keeps us from moving on."

The next time you become angry and are not able to let your anger go, ask yourself, "What am I accusing this person of? This is what I am secretly accusing myself of." In finding out what you are accusing yourself of, you will uncover your guilt. Once you see your guilt, you have a choice to do things differently. You can let go of your guilt in this healing process.

What Guilt Can Do to Us

Taking our guilt and placing it on others is the meaning of *scape-goat*, a term that originally came from the ritual of purification that took place in ancient times on the Day of Atonement for the children of Israel. On that day the high priest performed a ritualistic sacrifice, selecting a goat, placing his hands on the goat's head, and confessing all the faults of the sons and daughters of Israel. The goat was then sent to the desert, bearing all their faults with it. The sins of the people were transferred to the goat that was driven away.

We see many examples of this psychological dynamic played out in our everyday experiences. We see it in the individual who is humiliated by his boss, feels incapable of doing anything, and comes home to fight with a family member. These dynamics are also apparent in the actions of dictators and oppressors who compensate for their own perceived inadequacies and inferiority by persecuting and even seeking to destroy those judged inferior.

Although we may temporarily feel less guilty by placing our anger and guilt on someone else, we know on an unconscious level we have attacked, which reinforces our guilt. Making others feel guilty always involves attacking someone, and deep inside we know the attack is wrong. This begins a cycle in that *the guiltier we feel, the greater will be our need to deny and project it by attack; the more we attack, the guiltier we will feel.*

The importance of understanding this cycle is twofold. First, as long as we experience guilt, even unconsciously, it reinforces the feeling that we are separate from our spiritual nature. Our guilt cleaves the human psyche. Healing the split within our minds is an important step toward healing the divisions within our world.

The second important point is that this cycle reinforces a tremendous investment in anger, leading to the need for a "we-they" orientation wherein we must find an enemy for our own comfort. This is the foundation for the development of prejudice, stereotyping, and discrimination, for in these situations we choose to project our unconscious sins on scapegoats.

It is so difficult for incredibly angry people to be able to step back and be willing to look at what they are truly angry about. It is so much easier to yell at one another and not take responsibility for one's actions. In our defensiveness, we block the role we are playing in perpetuating the conflict from our awareness and believe we are innocent. We need to ask ourselves if this fighting or blaming is getting us what we really want in the long run. What do we gain?

The perception of a "we-they" orientation ultimately reflects our internal split, with our ego pitted against our spiritual nature. This inner conflict is projected into the world where we attack the enemy outside rather than inside ourselves. In many ways different societies sanction attacks, making them appear socially acceptable without recognizing that the need to find scapegoats to hate is overwhelming. The history of humanity, especially with respect to religious and political persecution, has provided ample witness to the hidden hate concealed behind the language of love and peace. People behave this way not because of basic evils within them but in their *unawareness of guilt that had been successfully denied and projected.* If we could recognize the serious consequences of being afraid to embrace and heal our guilt and recognize and forgive ourselves for our illusions and mistakes, perhaps we could stop the cycle of violence leading to the war on terrorism or to the ethnic violence so prevalent in the world today.

Our perceptions are formed as a result of seeing the world through our "guilt-colored" lenses, which means that our perceptions will always be distorted. We see people the way we want to see them. Perception is a relative phenomenon that does not represent an accurate picture of what is around us but rather an interpretation—our interpretation—of the way we chose to see the world.

Forgiveness of others actually constitutes forgiving ourselves, for it is *our* guilt we see in them. *We are not forgiving others for what we thought they did, we are forgiving ourselves for our negative thoughts and the guilt we have placed on others.* This process reverses projection by undoing the blame we have put on others for our mistaken thoughts. If we hadn't attacked others because of our judgments, there would be no reason to forgive. When we acknowledge and heal our guilt we will have no need to project it and accuse others. As we begin to look at situations through the eyes of forgiveness we recognize woundedness and can respond in love and mercy instead of seeing something despicable.

The Need to Defend Ourselves

The more sensitive we become to feelings of guilt, the more we feel fear. At its deepest level, fear originates in the punishment we feel we deserve as a result of our wrongful acts. We come to such a conclusion because we believe deep within our psyche that we have attacked the part of ourselves linked with divine nature. Our original sin is believing that we have separated from our spiritual essence, turning love to fear. In anticipating punishment, we defend ourselves by attacking others, thereby shifting blame and punishment to someone else. Such an attack merely reinforces our sense of vulnerability, creating an expectation of punishment again.

We get pulled into defending ourselves when we get hooked into the cycle of guilt. This defense cycle is the result of the fear we experience. Fear is the result of our feelings of guilt. Fear signals unconsciously to us that we will have to pay the consequences because we have done something wrong. Therefore, we have to defend ourselves. This begins a cycle in which we project negative feelings about ourselves on others by attacking them through anger and violence. Expecting retaliation from others and believing that their counterattack is fully justified by our unfair actions, we build our defenses and try to convince ourselves that the counterattack is an unjustified one on our innocence. Although defenses are designed to protect us from our guilt and fear, they actually reinforce them because we would not need defenses if there were no guilt and fear. The more we defend our innocence, believing unconsciously that we are guilty, the more we reinforce our guilt, fueling the flames of this cycle. All sides reinforce each other's guilt and fear, resulting in a continual attack-and-defend mode. We see this pattern being played out in our personal lives, especially in relationships with the people closest to us.

In owning our defenses, we begin to take responsibility for our lives, which means accepting life the way it is and recognizing that we cannot look to others to provide change for us. We have to deal with it ourselves. We have to look at our shattered assumptions, the fantasies we once held, and our misbeliefs and accept experience.

The way we view our situation is also our responsibility and what we chose to see is likewise in our minds. If we see the situation in a negative light, it is because we are not willing to see the situation in its entirety. How we interpret the situation will determine how we feel. When we reject something or become too attached to it, we indicate that we are not accepting the situation.

Taking responsibility means being willing to question our perceptions and beliefs, which are not facts although we tend to treat them as such. Perceptions seem so real to us that we can't even imagine how others can view the world differently. Taking responsibility serves as a reminder that, in fact, we don't see things eye to eye, which is OK. Once we become more aware of our feelings and how we use our defense mechanisms, we might begin to see how our emotions, especially fear and desire, influence what we believe and see. The more we understand desire and fear, the more we become free of their compulsions. As we begin to grow in the understanding of forgiveness, we recognize that forgiveness is about seeing through the eyes of love instead of fear. This involves a different, more objective way of looking at the world without being attached to what we see.

How to Heal Guilt

You probably realize by now that you can't get rid of your guilt by wishing it away or placing it on someone else. The only way guilt can be undone is through the opportunities forgiveness offers us. All the relationships we had fueled by guilt can be transformed by this one act. At the very moment we see an opportunity to project, the creative force within us speaks to us as well, gently urging us to see the situation through different eyes. We are asked to shift our perception from projecting guilt and fear to extending love and peace. By choosing to look differently at the person involved and forgiving what we have condemned by going beyond appearances, we make the same choice for ourselves.

There is a spiritual axiom that states, "Ideas leave not their source" (*A Course in Miracles*, 1975), which may seem a bit strange and hard to grasp but is quite simple. We know that if we share anything in the material world, it becomes less for us. On the other hand, when we have thoughts and share them with others, the thoughts still remain with us and become stronger. Therefore, the more love we give to others, the more we receive. The same unfortunately holds true for guilt and fear. The more we place it on others, the more it is reinforced in ourselves. The guilt we thought we got rid of now has a greater grip over us.

If we can't get rid of guilt by giving it away, what are our remaining choices? This is where forgiveness comes in. Learning how to forgive is the function of all of our relationships. Forgiveness is the process that transforms hatred toward someone to feelings of forgiveness and love. Therefore, each person we meet offers the opportunity to either project guilt or practice forgiveness. The reason we think we are in relationships with people around us could be very different than reality. Perhaps people come into our lives who present us the strongest temptation to project whatever our needs or desires are on them, be it guilt or love. We have choice in all our relationships. Are we going to view them through the eyes of self-hatred and condemnation, or will we be able to shift our perception and see the world through the eyes of forgiveness? The only way to undo our guilt is through the latter.

Identify Your Guilt

The process of forgiveness involves identifying our guilt. We need to realize that we secretly condemn in ourselves what we attack and judge in others. Even if there has been abuse or an argument with an ex-spouse, we project what we hate about ourselves. This doesn't mean that we don't take action to protect ourselves. What we are talking about is creating a shift in our mind and owning what is ours. When we can do that we begin to see the situation with more wisdom and clarity; we begin to reverse the process of projection and undo its effects. We begin to realize that the problem isn't outside of ourselves, but within. We do not allow our projections to become a smoke screen by diverting the problem elsewhere.

This is a huge step because our natural tendency is to see abuse only in the abuser. We see the abuser through the lens of our unconscious guilt and self-hatred, which colors what we see, and we become incapable of seeing the abuser as someone who is suffering as well. We don't recognize that, as we attack the abuser with our own thoughts, we add to *our* guilt and self-hatred. While we may temporarily feel better when "justice has been served," those feelings can dissipate, and we sometimes feel even worse. If we can recognize our self-hatred and not place it on the abuser, we can experience the love inside that had been shielded by our guilt. This love dispels what we were so afraid of—our guilt.

Change Your Interpretation of Reality

By taking this another step further, we realize the problem has no reality beyond our belief, and it is our *interpretation* that has caused our suffering. Therefore, our interpretation needs to change.

Make the Choice to Let Go of Guilt

Once we realize that our perceptions of the situation are based on guilt within us and the anger we project as a result of unresolved guilt is a way to avoid that guilt, we are ready to take the next step. This step recognizes that the guilt we feel about ourselves is also a decision that can be changed. Remember that our guilt ultimately comes from a mistaken belief we have about ourselves, and healing our guilt rests on how we experience divine intelligence in our healing process. When something beyond us intervenes, a transformation occurs. This is a key point because it is psychologically impossible to feel as though something is inherently wrong with us and simultaneously feel an incredible spiritual presence within us.

Therefore, in this step we begin to look at relationships differently. Once we recognize that the creative intelligence within us is not going to destroy us but be gentle toward us, the premise of our thinking begins to shatter. What scares us most is that the divine energy within us holds us in great love. This energy reaches down to us, sometimes in the form of grace or overwhelming feelings of love and joy, and our perspective of everything changes. If this weren't true, our ego's thought system would be validated. This has been brought to our awareness so we can now question our guilt. Hearing the words of a higher authority, which we can now identify with, creates a shift within our thinking as we recognize there is something greater within us that we have concealed behind guilt. It is through this experience that we can choose to release our guilt and listen not to the loud voice of the ego but to the gentle voice within.

Listen Within

This opens the way for the last step in the process, which is the work of the divine energy within us. It is precisely because we are so enmeshed in our own thinking that we need something outside of this thought system to enter our world of fear and guilt. All we need to do is to open ourselves up to the possibility of forgiveness. The force within us has been placed there to complete our healing. Our only responsibility at this point is to make the decision to listen not to the dictates of our lower self but to a higher voice within. *This* is the process of forgiveness.

8

Stop Running and Face Your Guilt!

Ed Minami's Story

"If the doors of perception were cleansed, everything would appear to man as it is, infinite."

—WILLIAM BLAKE

Now THAT YOU have some understanding of what guilt is about, I would like to introduce you to Ed Minami. Ed is a Vietnam vet who joined the army on his eighteenth birthday, partly to get away from a very dysfunctional family. Ed felt that the army would give him a sense of pride and prove he wasn't like the rest of his kin. Unfortunately, there was a problem. The scars of home life not only followed him into the army, they continued to follow him until he realized he could not abuse *his own family* any more. Once the victim, now the perpetrator, Ed couldn't stand himself any more. His guilt kept him trapped in a life of misery. Ultimately, Ed needed to learn to forgive himself more than anyone else.

Ed's Story

IT WAS MY eighteenth birthday and I couldn't wait! Most males dreaded this day, but I had something to prove. This was the day I could finally do better for myself. I could leave this dysfunctional bunch of people called family who were filled with "nigger this and spic that" and make something of myself. Free at last! I wanted to stand on my own two feet and be my own man. I wanted to be so different from my family, show everyone I was not like them—that I was a good person. But they were still my family and for some reason I wanted to make them proud of me. So, on my eighteenth birthday I went to Rockaway Beach where the service board was and said, "Listen, I am eighteen years old, here is my birth certificate. I have already registered for the draft. I want to register and volunteer for the army and do not want to wait." I guess that became a hallmark of my personality, especially in the years to follow. I would rather be in control.

In basic training, every waking hour, day and night, was geared to Vietnam. I remember always being one of the last kids straggling up and down hills, way behind, with the drill sergeant yelling at me, "You little fat [so-and-so]. If you don't move, Charlie is going to get you!" Charlie was the Vietcong. Everything was geared to Charlie being the enemy.

As I look back at it now, I see that this was the very beginning of our desensitization training: These were not people; they were the enemy. They would kill you. They would kill your mother. They would kill your sister. (In those days, it was our job to protect the weaker sex.) I remember during hand-grenade training our targets were in the shape of graveyard markers, but they had faces of Asian people on them. It was all those subtle things to dehumanize these people.

When training was over I had lost a lot of weight. It was not about the war in basic training. It was about an eighteen-year-old boy wanting self-esteem and wanting to make his family proud of himself. That's all it was.

After basic training, I became a grunt and was sent to Fort Polk, the hellhole of the South. I somehow lucked out and became the commander-in-chief's driver for most of my time there. I guess it was because I wasn't a little fat guy anymore. One of the major perks, something that changed my life forever, was the fact that the commander liked me. He thought the best thing for me to do to help my self-esteem was to graduate from advanced infantry training and be promoted to private first class. That was the primo reward. Guess what?! I didn't get promoted.

I questioned everything. Why didn't I get promoted? The commander took me aside and said, "You know, Minami, you are really a good kid. I think you have a lot going for you. I am promoting you to an E4, and I am sending you to noncommissioned officer's candidate school, Fort Benning, Georgia, and we are going to make you an NCO, a noncommissioned officer. When you graduate, you can either graduate as a Sergeant E5 or E6. Now, that *is* an honor."

So off I went to what was called "shake-and-bake school." They put us in, shook us up, and threw us out! I became a Sergeant E5 in all of thirteen weeks. It was such a head rush to be so young and have those three gold stripes on my arm. I had power all of a sudden, and I was only eighteen years old! What a head trip! Now we were doing the training ourselves, only being out of school no more than thirteen weeks. We trained those guys, even though I do not know what we trained them at.

It wasn't easy being an eighteen-year-old sergeant. I had men in my unit who were older than me. All the while I was in training, it was drilled into me not to become friends with my subordinates. You have to understand that there were a lot of NCOs in my rank who were in their thirties. They resented us. They didn't want anything to do with us. So in terms of having friends, I didn't have any. I couldn't be friends with men my age, and my peers didn't want to have anything to do with me because I was too young. A lot of time we "shake-and-bakes" were given dangerous assignments just because we were expendable.

When you didn't think about war, Vietnam was a very beautiful country. If you didn't look at the burnt vegetation, scars, and destruction and saw only the lushness of the countryside, you could almost fool yourself. Escaping the war became more difficult when looking into the eyes of the gentle Vietnamese people. They were going through hell themselves. These simple people tried to continue working in the rice paddies. Inside their huts, their homes, was a corner made out of mud that served as a shelter during firefights. Can you imagine living in a one-room hut with a bomb shelter inside of it? They cooked in the middle of the floor. There was no furniture to speak of. It was third world.

The Vietnamese were friendly and loving people and forgiving in spite of what was going on. People would always give me tea. To be on the outside receiving their kindness and then to turn around and kill them was an unspeakable conflict. I remember a new lieutenant who was assigned to our platoon fresh out of school. I had been in the country four or five months and had a cynical attitude. We walked into an area that had just been napalmed. It was next to a river. We could smell the freshly burnt vegetation. We looked into the river to see swollen bodies floating, decaying. They were Vietnamese people. They were non-people. They were pieces of meat. This lieutenant yelled in disbelief, "Oh my God, are those bodies in the river?"

"No," I said, "they are goddamn frogs. What do you think they are? Come on, let's go. You are supposed to be my leader, so get your act together." Later on, the lieutenant was killed.

I remember one time when we did an ambush. Sometimes we would walk for miles and miles. It wasn't like walking down a mountain preserve or something. We walked through rice paddies where we worried about stepping on mines and wire and losing our legs. Even worse, we worried about stepping on bungee sticks that were dipped and soaked in feces so we would get an infection when we stepped on them and they penetrated our feet. That was the type of walking we did. We were so tired. The mosquitoes would draw blood but worse of all were those goddamn leeches. They would attach themselves to our skin and suck our blood dry. If we were lucky, we would run into a nest of red ants as we walked through a banana grove. The Vietcong would take banana leaves and make nests out of them. If we touched them, creepy crawlers would jump on us in multitudes and eat us alive! Swarms of red ants all over! We'd scream, strip, and pray that other guys could brush them off before we got eaten up. That was living hell.

I will never forget one particular night, the night my innocence was lost. My life has never been the same. We were planning an ambush. It was not my turn to be awake, although to this day I haven't forgiven myself for sleeping. That night everybody fell asleep. It was the one out of ten times that an entire squad of VC walked right in front of us. They came out of nowhere. I was the first to wake up. Initially I couldn't see. Only when I looked up did I see all these figures. The VC didn't know we were there. They were walking in between us. I realized right away that my men had to be asleep; otherwise someone would have blown the ambush. There were about twenty men in a small area, and everyone would be shooting if they realized that people were all around.

Suddenly all hell broke loose. Only moments before I was praying, "God, let them walk through so I can go ahead and blow the ambush." It didn't happen. The Vietnamese were shocked. They didn't know what they were firing at. My men didn't know what they were firing at. A couple of my men were wounded, but the Vietnamese got the worst of it. Then I realized my point man, Charlie, was killed.

Dawn was approaching. We stood motionless, barely breathing, and afraid to move. The sun began to creep up over the horizon. The smell of death also crept up. There were dead bodies all around us. We slowly kicked them away to make sure they were really dead. We didn't know how many more were out there. There were so many dead bodies except for one who tried to drag himself but was not very far away. They dragged him back to me. Vietnam was such a political war. One week you didn't shoot anybody. The next week you only took prisoners.

This kid had to be no more than twenty years old and was really thin. I think he was wearing khaki-colored clothes. He was shot in his legs, dragging himself on one elbow. He was trembling out of control, pleading with us in Vietnamese. I remember my men and I were standing around him. We had our rifles down at our sides, and my men asked me what I wanted them to do.

"Check him for his papers," I said. "Take him to the commander to be a POW." Then I was overcome by an ugly stranger inside of me.

—

After what felt like an endless silence, Ed continued in a trembling voice.

I TOLD MY men that I would take care of it because we were not taking prisoners that week. We had eighteen bullets in our magazine. I put my rifle to his head and just let it linger there for awhile. I listened to him get more desperate. Then I said, "This is for Charlie. This is for everybody." I emptied the full magazine in his head. His brains were spattered all over the place!

How could I not feel anything? I did not feel anything. Nobody cared, nobody. We walked away like we had just stepped on a bug. He had a mother, father, girlfriend, or wife. I don't know. . . . What kind of a horrible person would do something like that? Anyhow, I have to tell you about Charlie. I was not paying attention, figuring that it would be an ordinary day. We would not make contact with anybody. We would do the clips, the distance, and then go back to base camp. Charlie got on my side. He was my point man. He was a neat guy. I was a little jealous of him. He was a little older than I was and what I lacked in maturity he made up for. He had left a newborn baby back with his wife in Alabama. He should have been the leader, the sergeant. He was older. He knew that I was younger and he respected me as his leader, but I was also like his little brother. We weren't friends; I was his squad leader. I was the man who was responsible for his safety. He wanted to be point man, and I was against it. I didn't want someone with a kid and family to be up front. That was the most dangerous position to have in a squad. But he insisted. I think it was his way of protecting everybody else. I was walking down an open field and on the side of us there were scrubs. We finally got to an area where there were some trees and stuff. He went behind the trees and got out of sight. I never saw him again alive. It took years before I could talk about this. Eventually, I wrote Charlie a letter to help me deal with my guilt and grief.

Dear Charlie,

Thirty years have gone by and I find myself writing you again for the second time. The first time I wrote to you was a very difficult time for me. I was on my way to Washington, D.C., to commemorate Veterans Day by visiting the "Wall" and paying respect to you and 58,000 others who sacrificed their lives in the Vietnam War. You see Charlie, this is 1998 and the war is now history.

I found it difficult to form images in my mind of that fatal day without bringing up immense pain within my soul. I was fearful that those images would become real for me again and that I might react to them by acting out my emotions of the past while in that plane in 1996. I had entertained hopes that my second letter to you would be less laborious. However, this was not to be the case. I imagine my first letter to you was wholly an impulsive act. I was caught up with the day and the emotions accompanying the fear I felt at that moment. This letter comes from a more settled soul, however, yet one still not lacking the guilt and tremendous burden of anger that I carry with me daily. I remember the anticipation I experienced on that plane, speculating what it would be like for me to finally run my fingers across the finely-etched engraving in the marble panel that identified you by name. I felt somewhat distraught that I could imagine no clear-cut reasons for the war. I think that, even until this day, those reasons are murky and indefinable for me, as well as for innumerable other peoples of the world. In many ways, I yearn for all those lives and sacrifices to count for something. I wish for your personal sacrifice to count, Charlie. I do not wish for your loss of life to be in vain.

As my mind, full of visions and memories, travels back to that day, I find myself welling up with tears and pain. I want you to know that I think about you every day in one form or another. When I see children, I wonder how your son has prospered without you. When I see someone in a uniform, I imagine you there with a grin on your round, cherublike face, bragging about your son and wife. When I hear someone talk with a southern accent, I wonder how life was for you in the deep forests of Alabama before the war. When I see a family, I focus on the wife and speculate how your wife is faring today and wonder whether she remarried or remained widowed. When I look in the mirror, I ruminate about my feelings of guilt and how things could have been if only I had done something different. "If only," the two most powerful words that traverse my soul continuously with no discernable destination in mind. If only I had taken those bullets instead of you. If only I had appointed another point man. If only I had paid more attention in military strategies classes. If only I had been more alert and less tired that day. My head abounds with "if only," and no respite is in sight.

In many ways when I regard it, I believe you received the easy way out, as opposed to what I have endured. But that is a rather selfish and angry position to take, is it not? I have to believe that you are at peace and in a better place than I am. I want to believe that you are happy and reconciled to the action that day in April 1969. As you probably have already recognized, I am in great pain. I agonize over that day and have not been able to reconcile it to any degree of comfort. My dreams have assimilated current events and the horrors of that day and year. My sleep is sporadic and my dreams are nonsensical. Half of those dreams I do not recall, but I carry the emotions they create into the fabric of my everyday experiences.

I remember the night well. I remember the sweltering heat, humid air, and smell of fresh napalm from the acres of rice paddies and vegetation around us. I remember being very tired, wishing desperately to just sit down and alleviate the great weight I felt on my back as well in my heart. I remember daydreaming and not really paying attention to our surroundings. I remember hearing the shots jolt me back to the sense of responsibility that prevailed for me, your squad leader. People say your life flashes before you when faced with a life-threatening situation. I agree with them, as in that moment—that flash of a second—I was flooded with a plethora of thoughts and visions. I saw the open field and remembered the chalkboards in training stressing the dangers of traversing an open field. I envisioned the ambush and spider traps as my location prevented me from seeing where you were and what you were up against. I knew that something terrible had happened. I felt your soul take flight, but I ignored the feeling. I wanted you to be alive, healthy. I remember yelling orders. I hear the echoes of my yells to this very day. I yelled for my RTO to stay behind and monitor transmissions from the company commander. I wanted him safe and out of harm's way. I yelled for a medic even as I knew instinctively that "Doc" would not remain behind regardless of my orders. I remember ordering the rest of the squad to stay back and provide cover for us. "Where the hell are you, Charlie? Where did you go down? God help me, I have to find you!"

How impotent I felt when calling out your name and you did not answer. Then I saw blackness raised out of the earth, with rifles firing down at Doc and me. I saw you dead with the bullet hole to your head. I cried with rage; I heard Doc scream. Charlie, nothing mattered anymore but revenge, anger, hate, and the safety of the other guys.

They tell me I stormed the gooks' position and lobbed several grenades into their bunker. They were only fifteen feet in front of me. Many shots were fired at us. Doc was hit eleven times but he survived. I am so ashamed that I only received powder burns. The shrapnel I felt pierce my thigh was from our own side. Wilson, the FNG, was trying to help and threw a grenade. But it fell short and hit me from behind. Humorously enough, he got a Bronze Star for that. They say I killed them all. I do not remember, Charlie. I remember all the guys around me, protecting me. I remember them hauling off Doc on a stretcher. I remember feeling intense grief, hopelessness, horror, and relief—relief that I was alive. I remember heaving and racking with bursts of sobs and laughter. I remember the warm fluids trailing across my legs, the mixture of blood and urine escaping from myself. I did not want to leave you, Charlie. I fought with them to allow me to stay with you and the men. But they forced me on the medevac and took me away. I never saw you again, except for in my dreams. They gave me a Purple Heart and a Silver Star, Charlie. Is that not the epitome of justice, a medal for a life?

I can see your proud face while showing us the picture of your newborn son. I wanted to be proud like that some day. In just a few short seconds that was all circumvented. Gone. And I remained marked till this very day.

My therapist tells me it is not my fault. He reminds me that I was only eighteen years old, with responsibilities that no eighteen-year-old should have had. My psychiatrist tells me that I will never recover but will learn how to manage this disorder with lifelong medication and therapy. In short, it does not seem likely that the scars in my mind will ever heal. The memories, terror, guilt, depression, and all the other dragons that entered my soul on that day prevent me from functioning in a fashion that would enable me to carry on a normal life. They diagnosed me with severe, chronic post-traumatic stress syndrome. I guess you could say I carry the events of that day on my sleeve, and I have never being able to change that shirt. I firmly believe that it should have been my life that day rather than yours. Please forgive me, Charlie. God help me, I feel so racked with guilt thirty years later.

I tried to call your family and introduce myself two years ago. I was too afraid and I chickened out. I am sorry. I keep looking forward to the day that I can tell your son that you died quickly, with no pain, and that you were a good man. I want to tell him that you loved him and spoke of him often. I would wish no less for myself. But I am still afraid and the dragons hold me back. Maybe some day they will loosen their hold on me, and I will be able to take flight to Alabama and fulfill my mission. Maybe . . .

Charlie, I pray fervently that you do not mind my sharing this letter with others. I was challenged to write about something I believe in that is controversial today. And I was further challenged to write deeper, to challenge my soul. This is as deep as it gets. So the purpose of this letter is twofold. I have satisfied that challenge, and I have opened my heart and soul to you and to myself. This is a good thing.

By the way Charlie, I am gay. I did not think it was an important factor at the time. They say that people like me should not be in the military, that we do not have the mettle. They say we present a security risk to operations. If that is the case, I am glad I fooled them because if I had not been there, it would be difficult for me to fathom the letters others would be writing now. I love you, Charlie. Rest well my friend. God grant you peace.

Eternally sincere and remembering,

Ed Minami/ SSG US Army/US52755497

When it was all over, I felt so painfully helpless. There has never been a day in my life when I have felt so helpless. I was in such a state of mind that I didn't care if the whole world blew up. My emotions were very intense. They were all lumped together, the anger, hurt, frustration, disgust, guilt—everything—so intense. Charlie wasn't a "gook." He wasn't Vietnamese. I wasn't trained to be insensitive to this. He was a dad. He wasn't going to see his son any more. He wasn't breathing. God, where was I? He wasn't real anymore. I wasn't paying attention because I was really tired. Perhaps I didn't take my job seriously enough or maybe I didn't make the right choice of a point man. I wished now I could have done something differently.

Maybe I had too big of a head in training and now as a sergeant I was trying to prove things to my family and myself. What was this for? Why was I there? Why was he dead? Why was Doc shot?

Why do people do this to each other? After all, when years go by, it is just history. It doesn't mean much to most people. Why do people hurt people over little things? Why don't they understand how horrible things can be for us as human beings and how we can make things horrible for each other? Don't they understand? I am not talking about clean dying in a hospital in a clean bed. I am not talking about dying in an accident and being cleaned up and picked up by a clean ambulance. I am talking about being somewhere in a strange country with nobody that you know, no support systems, and dying on a dirty battle-ground. It just haunts me. It makes no sense. When I killed those people who killed Charlie, I killed them with such a vengeance, with emotion exploding everywhere. Vietnam was a war where you didn't see whom you killed. It was either long distance fighting or the VC dragged their bodies away. This was the first time that I saw the consequences of my actions.

There was no reason for me to kill that man. I don't think it would have mattered if it was me on the ground at that point. I felt total indifference.

The Pain of Guilt

SOMETHING HAPPENED to me in Vietnam that changed everything. The lenses I viewed the world through when I went into Vietnam were shattered, and I have never been able to find a pair of glasses that color again. I firmly believe my experiences in Vietnam dictated the way I lived my life thereafter. I realize now that shortly after I returned home I was hiding so much anger and guilt for what had happened. I had no emotional support. My family acted like I had just taken a weekend trip to camp and had a bad experience. I was very angry. After three months, I went back into the military and lasted for about three years.

By the time I left the army for the second time, I had already met Kathy, my now ex-wife. She had two sons and by the time I was twenty-three years old, we had two daughters. I didn't know how I was going to raise my family or structure the upbringing of my children. I had no skills, couldn't hold a job, and had terrible role models as a child. I also had a lot of guilt. So I did what was most familiar to me: I became an abusive father.

I did terrible things. If I had a bad day, all of a sudden hell would break loose in my mind. I raged inside not understanding why. Anything could set me off. I could open the refrigerator and see a half-eaten hot dog sitting on a saucer and go into a rage. I would line up all four kids and no one would say anything. I would tell them that I was going to get the belt and hit each one of them until someone told me who ate the hot dog. Still, everyone kept quiet. I would get through the second child and realize that I was getting out of control. I would say, "Screw this," and tell them I was going to find flour, dust it on the refrigerator, find whose fingerprints were on it, and hit that person twice as hard. My oldest daughter started rubbing her fingers because she was the culprit. Then all of a sudden she started screaming, "I did it, I did it! Not the flour test!" It was so sad. It really scared her. This is how my children lived. The diet was intimidation, yelling, and screaming at them.

I look back now and wish they could have understood that I was a very sick person. In my heart I didn't want to put them through such things. I didn't know how to be a parent, and I didn't know how to control my anger or give myself good things. I was wracked and living with so much guilt over things that happened before them but took it out on them.

I have something else to share, which is the most difficult of all. My father had five daughters. Unbeknownst to me, my father sexually molested every one of them. The youngest was molested at a very early age. The oldest son was married and out of the house by the time this happened. He tried to take my father to court and have him put in jail or institutionalized. By the time of the court hearing, my mother talked my sister out of testifying. So everything was dropped.

Two days before my mother died, my father sexually molested me. I was so scared and so alone. I was between seven and eight years old and only in the second grade. My father's method was to berate me and yell at me to the point that he made me cry and shake. Then he would hold and hug me, start tickling me, and then sexually molest me. He would make me have oral sex. He tried penetration. That was the only affection my father ever showed me. As an adult I realized that it was anger. But I was a little boy and he was my daddy. Maybe this was the way daddies and little boys acted. I didn't know. How could I?

The night before my mother died, I sneaked up to her hospital room. I got to see her all by herself and I remember her saying, "Eddie, if anything happens to me, go live with your sister Louise or Georgette." That just blew my mind. I was only an eight-year-old boy.

When she died, my father became very bitter. The beatings became worse. We lived in rundown tenements and he actually threw me through a wall once, the walls were so thin. We lived in Mexico for awhile with common showers and children speaking a different language. The beatings and the sexual molestation became more regular. He then got a graveyard job in Florida, and the little cottage we lived in had rats. I was afraid the rats would come in my bed. I had a choice: I could stay where I was or I could go up to the big bed where they couldn't get me. I went to the big bed to fall asleep and then Dad would come home. Everything would start up again in the morning. To this day, I am terrified of rats.

The worst thing is that I repeated the cycle with my oldest son. I had found out that when he was in junior high school he played sexually with my daughters. Right away I saw my father. I guess the healthy response would have been to get us both into counseling. I felt so alone and so ashamed, but I was angry with him. I started sexually abusing him. It was my anger. I don't know why, but I finally looked at him and said, "You know this is very wrong. We need to tell your mother." He begged me not to tell Kathy, which was convenient for me. Kathy and I were having marital problems at the time, and we didn't need more stuff to rock the boat. We didn't even deal with the gay issue because at that time I really didn't know I was gay; I just knew that I was different. One day Kathy and I drove up the driveway, and she said, "I think it is too late."

"Why?" I answered.

"David told me what you had been doing."

She then asked if it were true. All I could do was nod and say, "Yes." I remember saying that although it hadn't happened in a long time, a couple of years, I think he should move out of the house. He was seventeen years old then.

My other son became angry because David was moving out. He said, "You always loved David and didn't pay any attention to me. You think that I am ugly and you don't love me."

I screamed, "It is not that I love David more, it is because I am guilty! Do you know what I have been doing to your brother all these years? This is what I did to him, and I am trying to make up for it *because I am guilty*! So don't say that I don't love you. Don't ever say that I don't love anyone."

The turning point for me was that day in the driveway when I looked at Kathy and said, "Yes, that is what happened." I realized so much had to stop. There was so much madness and bitterness and people I had hurt. It seemed as though everyone I touched became spoiled like ruined meat. I was losing myself quickly.

I realized that in order to get out of this madness I had to break the silence, as painful as that was. I had to tell the truth and take responsibility for what I had done. That is how I began to heal from guilt. You can't be responsible and guilty at the same time. One has to go. The more responsible I became to myself and others, the more guilt I could let go. Part of becoming responsible was learning how to forgive, beginning with myself. I am working on these issues. I am working on my guilt and on forgiveness, learning to forgive myself and others. That is a full-time job. It is also the most difficult job I have ever done.

Removing Guilt

How does one heal guilt from the horrifying events of the past? This was the primary issue facing Ed, who recognized that, in order to forgive himself, he needed to take responsibility for what he had done. As we will witness in Ed's story, healing guilt requires unlocking the layers of hurt, wounds, and numbness that feel akin to a never-ending spiral. This is what Ed went through. He cycled through the issues of guilt at many different levels. Even Ed wasn't aware of this until he realized how closely connected his personal issues to guilt. The paradox is that one becomes liberated in owning one's guilt and taking responsibility. Here is the rest of Ed's story:

UNTIL THE DAY I die, I will experience a sense of great responsibility, overwhelming sadness, and feeling of senselessness over my early life. I also carry a lot of grief and, to a lesser degree, I still have feelings of guilt. There has been a lot of processing between the guilt I feel and my other emotions. All of this is not so much from killing the young Vietcong or Charlie's death. It's that I feel so intensely upset over the state of world affairs and they're leading any individual to do something like that. I feel very intensely about the things we do as parents, what we teach our children, and what we do that would make an eighteen-year-old man like myself feel that it was OK to do what I did in Vietnam.

I can't remember if it was Ralph Waldo Emerson who said behind every behavior is the ancestor of thought. I believe this is true. This is why uncovering guilt becomes so important. Those hidden thoughts run by guilt can turn us into monsters. Where do we get our thoughts from? Of all the millions of things we can think about, why do we choose what we choose? I believe guilt is behind most of our thoughts. All the bad stuff we think about ourselves motivates us to do some pretty awful things. The tragedy is that we don't even know what is going on. We choose our thoughts, and we really need to start sprucing ourselves up as a species. We need to discipline our thoughts and our minds. We manifest what we think.

I have come to recognize my guilt and my self-hatred, calling them my "dragons." I have learned that using metaphors has helped me understand how to step out of myself and look at myself differently. Sometimes when I felt as though I was falling apart I would say, "You know, I have my dragon Anger sitting in the parking lot and my dragon Guilt sitting on top of Camelback Mountain." My goal is to diminish their size and to lessen their strength because my life decays when I am busy fighting with them.

Beyond what happened in Vietnam and my experience with Charlie, I am most ashamed of my actions with my son David. I look at it this way: if I turned into a child abuser, my guilt feelings alone would probably make me want to kill myself. This would be the only atonement for my crime. I could choose to live a miserable life. I could hate myself and everyone else for the rest of my life and die a lonely and bitter man. These aren't very good options for me. Something else has to happen.

I realize that by holding on to guilt I was able to play the "poor-me" and "innocent-victim" game. Luckily, the pain became so great that I realized the only way out was to accept responsibility for what I had done. That is what I chose to do. I was able to say, "Yes, I did that. There is no acceptable moral excuse for what I have done. I have to look at who I was, what my life was about, and what led me to do those things." I think this is where knowledge and lots of support seeps in. For me, that was the point where I started saying, "Oh God, it hurts, I feel sorry for Eddie when he was a little boy. That was a horrible thing he had to go through. I feel really bad for Eddie that he had nobody to tell and nobody to support him or get him the help he needed." I had to feel pain and accept those circumstances. That was hard! Believe me, I went kicking and screaming, and the odd thing was a lot of the pain was gone after all my crying.

Then there was Vietnam. I remember saying to myself, "I feel really sorry for that guy in Vietnam. To have seemingly no feelings, no remorse, no emotions, to blow that man's brains away, what a terrible place that man must have been in, the Ed that did that." Guilt made a prisoner of my heart. By owning what I was once afraid to see, by bringing darkness to light, I could begin to see things differently. That was the key.

To hurt what I love most in life, my son, how could I have done that?! I realize now that I did it out of anger, as a way of retribution and punishment. Oh, yes, I deserve to be punished. That is what guilt is all about. You know you have done something wrong, and now the wrath of God will descend upon you. The truth is guilt does demand punishment. Either we set it up that someone will give us our just desserts or we will do it to ourselves. That's the deal. What I have come to learn is that the specific reasons we feel guilty reflect a deeper sense of unworthiness and inadequacy too painful to acknowledge.

I started asking myself more questions and began to say, "You know, Ed, you will never forget this. You will never flippantly just throw this around like it doesn't bother you or wasn't an important thing. The truth is you have to start forgiving yourself because if you can't, you are going to have blackness inside you. Not only will you continue to be that hateful, angry, guilty person that you were, how do you expect other people to see you differently and be able to forgive you? It just won't work."

Some of my friends may read this book. Maybe I will use my real name and maybe I won't. I wondered if I would to tell the story about David, yet all of it is linked. As painful as it is to share what feels like incredible darkness in me, there is nothing hidden anymore. I truly am an open book right now, and I feel free because of that. This gives me courage to go on, to know who I am on the inside. What I have learned is that there are higher forces than just myself. By taking responsibility for what I have done and owning my feelings of insecurity, self-hatred, and the sense that I may be defective goods, I don't have to hide behind a mask. I don't have to bury guilt within the recesses of my unconscious mind that ultimately became the *cause* of my doing terrible things. I can see now that how I treated my ex-wife and family was directly related to the way I felt about myself. I hated myself for what happened in Vietnam, and I took out my guilt on everyone else. What is most important is that we understand what guilt really does to us. If we don't allow ourselves to feel the pain of guilt, take responsibility for what we have done, and choose to move on, we will destroy everything that has meaning in our lives. Guilt separates us from knowing the real truth of who we are. How can we know the wellspring of love and joy within ourselves when we feel sick about ourselves and what we have done? How can we love others?

I guess for many years guilt was *my* higher power. I worshipped guilt in an insane way. I felt more comfortable operating with guilt. Now I see how I used guilt to manipulate others and get them to do what I wanted. What I know now is that guilt has a very negative taste to it. It will rear its ugly head unless we take action. If we choose not to and remain unaware of our negative feelings and the pain guilt brings, we have to find someone to place our negative feelings on. We may feel better momentarily but what we have actually done is push more guilt underground, out of our awareness. Then we see everyone through the eyes of even more guilt.

Guilt doesn't have a good effect on other people, either. When I can let some of my guilt go, something really neat happens inside of me. I can actually look in the mirror and smile at myself a little bit. I can like myself. I can say, "You had a great day and did some good things today. You really touched people." I feel in sync. My higher power is not God per se, but being in sync with the universe. Truthfully, I had never thought of myself as a part of the universe until now. I see my life as a string. This string and trillions of other strings make up the very fabric of our world, our universe, and I have a very definite part in that. So part of my string got beat up a little bit. I didn't take care of it. Part of the string got frayed, but that doesn't detract from the whole string. I am still part of the universe, the human race, the goodness that is definitely there. I hope I can be a really great string and add to the betterment of the rest of the universe, the rest of the strings. If we realize that we are responsible to everything and connected to everything, we become alive, vibrant, and all that is good. The only thing that I know how to do is to be responsible and acknowledge the horrible things I did, cut myself a little slack, and forgive myself. We can't shuck responsibility, because *taking responsibility is about healing.* If I can be a better person and fix that frayed end of the string, maybe I can even interweave with other strings, the people around me, other souls. Maybe I can have a healing effect on them, too. You see, I don't have to stay a frayed string all my life. I can help others. I am an integral part of this universe. I have a purpose, and all these pieces tie in.

Until I could start forgiving myself and realize that there is a place for me in the grand scheme of things, I wasn't able to work on my other emotional issues. I deal with post-traumatic stress disorder (PTSD). I think the things I talked about in terms of changing behaviors and working on self-forgiveness, which is difficult for any person, become more challenging when you also deal with trauma. This work takes a lot of guts, internal gutsy stuff, to go against the face of society. Our society attempts to cover the guilt with a face of innocence that says I suffer at your hands, yet underneath the innocence is hate. That is the pain of facing guilt because we don't want to deal with those terrible feelings. *The paradox is that when we begin to deal with pain and yucky feelings they go away.* That is when we become free. I think that is what you have to do first before you can forgive yourself. You don't feel worthy enough to move on if you don't get in touch with guilt and deal with pain.

I hope that I have made a good choice in the people I have chosen as friends and as a support system. That is scary. But when you get all of that stuff out of the way, including the guilt and the trauma of acknowledging what you have done and what has been done to you, the pain does subside. This is when you can start working on forgiveness. You start with forgiving yourself. Forgiving yourself is the hardest. *The truth is you have forgiven everyone else if you have forgiven one person completely.* After honestly forgiving myself, I could forgive others, including the government, my ex-wife, everyone!

Being able to forgive has helped me understand my daughters and not be angry with them for cutting me out of their lives. I can see there are other options that would be better for all of us, but I certainly understand where they are. It is all about stepping aside and honoring other people. My whole life now is focusing on being calm even if there is a hurricane going on around me. I want to keep exercising my heart and my understanding of people around me and try to love them, not hate them. That is what forgiveness has taught me.

Forgiveness has let me experience peace. I've got a body that was ravaged by guilt on the inside. So, to experience peace is a blessing. I am not saying that I have completely forgiven. I think I am 75 percent of the way there. Every once in a while I come up against the curtain that blocks my feelings. At least now I know what the drill is. I recognize that I have choices to make. Do I want to be the sort of person with an attitude problem or do I want joy and peace of mind? I remind myself I want to be able to do something with my life. I want to make sense out of everything that has happened in the past—the things I have done—and maybe make sense out of everybody in my life. I just want to go there. Life is to be enjoyed, which is the feeling of being free. I never took time to think of everyday things like the fragileness of a bird or the fresh smell of morning. That is what forgiveness does to me.

Hidden Treasure

I thought the interview was about to end when Ed wanted to share a few more thoughts on forgiveness. His love for metaphors surfaced one more time as his eyes became fixated on an old Tibetan trunk that was against a wall opposite from where he sat. Ed talked about the trunk in terms of forgiveness.

YOU HAVE A beautiful trunk over there. It is detailed with a lot of different designs and paintings. It tells a life story that I have not yet heard. We are like that trunk. We paint ourselves and present ourselves a certain way. Inside that trunk is its true meaning, if only we could unlock it.

If we did open that trunk it could possibly say, "I feel so good. I am open and everyone can see me. Look at these people coming up to me; they want to talk to me, they like me, they want to see my pictures, they want to hear my story." But what if the trunk has chains around it and can't open? The chains are also part of the trunk's story but they keep it closed. All that people can see are the chains, and they know that the ornamental painting on the outside doesn't really tell the whole story. You miss the greatest value of the trunk by not going inside it. Forgiveness is like a hatchet that opens the trunk. Once you start forgiving yourself and others, it breaks the chains right off. The trunk opens with many surprises inside. The trunk actually feels good inside. You feel good as a person looking at that trunk. You get to see more of it and learn from some of the stories or things that are inside it. There might even be some seeds that get planted. Maybe some seeds are from generations past that want to take flight and end up in your yard. Perhaps a beautiful tree grows from it. There are so many possibilities once those chains are gone. The problem is you can't pull those chains apart except with the tool of forgiveness. If you want to open the trunk to see the beauty inside of it and want to see the effect it has on its environment, the only way the chains will come off is through forgiveness. That's pretty much it!

If somebody takes an active stance, has an awareness of what the problem is, and understands how he or she contributes to it, you have all the tools you need to forgive. Sometimes the hard part is getting the power to put things into motion. Something was nagging me; something very spiritual inside of me gave me that power, that strength, to move forward. I tend to stay away from thinking that a higher power has one meaning, one person, one entity, but I have to speak in those terms. Having that entity inside of me constantly telling me, "I made you, you are intrinsically good," has a transformative, healing effect. To hear that you have the ability and power to change things, that you are empowered through this creative energy to make changes, and that all you need to do is pick up the chip and acknowledge your responsibility for who you are in this world is incredibly awesome. So I decided to pick up the chip and do what I have been guided to do.

—

Sensing that there was more that needed to be said, I asked Ed, "Are you aware of a time when you heard the voice say to you that you are intrinsically good, that you can move forward?" Ed only needed to think for a moment.

Yes, I remember a time when I felt as if I had an out-of-body experience, when you are not so wrapped up in yourself or so caught up inside your body and trapped inside yourself. You let yourself out. You are over here or over there looking at yourself and the people around you. When you do that you detach yourself from all the turmoil going on, and you are in a peaceful place able to look at things much more clearly. That is when I heard, "Edward, you know you are intrinsically good. If we can motivate you and focus you in the right direction and you feel our support, you will be able to do something really good for this world." Then I drifted back into myself. The experience was so profound that just the memory of what happened helps me to support myself and makes me more aware. Something shifted inside. For example, if someone made me angry, I used to very willingly counterattack in some way. This was second nature. Now I don't do that. I try to understand where he or she is coming from, smiling inwardly and saying, "It's OK, you are probably right where you need to be and that is good."

In telling my story, I was afraid of how my family and friends would react if they read this. What I have come to realize is that if they read it and cannot deal with it or me as a person, that is OK. That is a road I will have to travel. It has taken a lot of courage for me to share all of these things, but in learning how to forgive I have gained an inner strength that will help me deal with anything. I know I will be OK. That is what I have gotten from this experience, which was really great. My hope is that by sharing all that I have been through and letting people know that *forgiveness has a profound effect on ourselves*, someone in need may remember my story. I hope my story gives them hope, even if it is just a glimmer. Then everything I have been through has done some good.

9

Releasing Our Pain

Azim Khamisa's Story

*"From the onset I saw victims on both ends of the gun.
My only son a victim of his assailant—the assailant a victim of
society—a society you and I created. Therefore, I take my share
of this responsibility for the bullet that took my son's life
and so should every caring American."*

—AZIM KHAMISA

How do we heal our pain and grief that results from unspeakable tragedy? When someone dies or something in us dies, we grieve because of the lost possibilities and a future that never will be. Step Six is about grieving. We have to learn how to deal constructively with our pain in order to forgive. This requires grieving. During the forgiveness process, victims of violence may cry for the first time. As we give ourselves permission to grieve, we begin to release our pain and sorrow. As we cry, we "absorb" the pain, slowly dissipating it until the cleansing is over. The truth is that as you stop running from your pain, you discover that you can handle it. The more you face your pain the more it lessens. By doing this, you have broken the cycles of violence and need for revenge and have become the initiator of positive change.

In our next story, we will meet someone who, in spite of the heartbreaking loss of his son, found his way to forgiveness that changed his life. He did this through the grieving process. As he grieved, he realized that what he called spiritual currency was a very powerful and transformational healing agent. For him, doing something for others was developing spiritual currency. This tragic yet amazing story began in San Diego, California, on the tragic evening of January 21, 1995. Twenty-year-old Tariq Khamisa, a San Diego State University student, was shot to death while delivering pizzas. The assailant, Tony Hicks, a fourteen-year-old boy, was on his first night out as a gang recruit. He fired the fatal bullet on orders from an eighteen-year-old gang leader.

What makes this story so remarkable is that Azim Khamisa, Tariq's father, responded in an extraordinary fashion. It wasn't the knee-jerk reaction of, "I want to get my hands on who ever did this and kill that son of a bitch." Instead, Azim felt there were two victims, his son and the assailant. Although Azim will mourn Tariq's death for the rest of his life, his grief has been transformed into a powerful commitment to help change society. As Azim said, "Change is urgently needed in a society where children kill children." Here is Azim's story.

Azim's Story

I WAS BORN in Kenya. My ancestry is both Persian and East Indian. I went to England when I was fifteen as a student and returned to Kenya six years later when I took over the family business. Then Idi Amin came to power in neighboring Uganda and kicked all the Asians out of Uganda. So at twenty-five I immigrated to Canada. That was in 1974. I have lived in the United States for the last thirty years. The irony is that I left a region of the world where there was so much violence only to come to the U.S. to experience violence firsthand.

I am a Muslim, an Ismaili. This is the Sufi faith. It is the mystical part of Islam. I share this with you because it is my background that laid the foundation for what was to come, especially my reactions to my son's death. It also laid the groundwork for me to ultimately forgive, although a lot of emotional healing had to take place.

I will never forget the morning I found out about my son's death. I had just returned from a trip to Mexico the night before. My friends Dan and Kit picked me up and we went to a fiftieth birthday party. We partied until around two o'clock in the morning. Then they took me home. Someone came to my door around four or five in the morning and rang the bell. I didn't hear it as I was sound asleep and on the second floor of a two-story townhouse. So they left a card.

Fortunately for me, my maid came in that particular Sunday morning and saw the card stuck in the door. If she hadn't come, I probably would not have seen the note until much later. It was about eight in the morning when I came downstairs and saw the card left by Sergeant Lampert, of the Police Homicide Division. On the back of the card was a message that said, "We are trying to reach Tariq Khamisa's family." So I made the call.

Sergeant Lampert was not there, but a woman spoke to me. "Your son has been shot to death by a gang member." I was in total disbelief! They must have made a mistake. I was in such a state of despair that I frantically rang Tariq's number. He had just moved in with his girlfriend, Jennifer, three weeks before he was killed. When Jennifer finally picked up the phone she was crying. She knew about it.

That moment felt like a nuclear bomb had exploded inside of me. It was like being blown into a million pieces that can never come back together. I was devastated. Life drained out of me. Facing the loss of a child is unbearable. Our bodies are not structured to take that kind of shock.

I immediately called my family, who were living in Vancouver, Canada. Then I called Dan. He told me not to do anything. "Kit and I will be right there." These two very dear friends of mine stayed at my house and essentially took over what needed to be done. Kit went to get Jennifer so she wouldn't be by herself. When Dan and I were alone one of the first things he said to me was, "Whoever did this, I hope they fry in hell." When Dan was speaking to me I was in such a state of shock that I think I left my body. Suddenly it felt as though I went into the loving hands of my Maker. It was an out-of-the-body experience, an experience of light where I felt safe, loved, and secure. I knew everything would be all right. When I came back into my body, I came back with the wisdom that both boys were victims. That's when I said to Dan, "I don't feel that way, there were victims at both ends of the gun."

Dan broke down and cried. He said, "I couldn't respond that way if Adam my fourteen-year-old son was killed." Although Dan is a mediator and a very spiritual man, his thinking about this was different from mine. His reaction was what people expected of me. I often get asked why and how was I able to respond differently. I think there are two possible reasons. One is that I grew up in Africa in a very loving family with a lot of spiritual values. I also feel fortunate to come from Eastern roots, where spirituality was a fundamental part of my upbringing. This set the foundation for my thinking and for my beliefs in which I found great comfort. My education and the rest of my life have taken place in the West, which has given me the best of all worlds. I always feel that my mission in life is to capture the soul of Africa, the spiritual wisdom of the East, and the material wisdom of the West. I think that would be a great combination to have as a mindset and lifestyle. My upbringing contributed greatly to how I handled my son's death because I grew up with love, peace, forgiveness, and all the good values those religions can teach.

I felt paralyzed for the next several days. Then my family flew in from Vancouver, and with each arrival I felt more anxious and overwhelmed. The intensity of my grief kept me awake all night, and during the day I felt like a zombie. We had a memorial service on Tuesday and then flew him to Vancouver on Wednesday. The funeral was on Thursday.

During the days leading up to the funeral I spent quite a bit of time talking to the religious people of my faith. I did a lot of praying, meditating, and got out in nature when I could. This gave me time to think about such questions as, "why am I here and what is the purpose of my life?" This helped me orient to the future, not the past. I got in touch with my own spiritual philosophy that gave me hope. At the same time, I was introduced to *The Tibetan Book of the Living and Dying.* This book is filled with the priceless wisdom of Tibetan Buddhism and gives practical instruction and spiritual guidance on how to live when dealing with the pain of death. This book helped me to understand the true meaning of life, how to accept death, and how to help the dying and the dead. I was just finishing the chapter on the Bardo, those states of consciousness after death, when I heard that my father was having open-heart surgery. He had seven bypasses so we were concerned about telling him what had happened to Tariq. My sister was the first to see him so she took the book with her to the hospital and read to him. She spoke of things such as the immortality of the soul and that we were created by a divine intelligence and this is where we go back to. This intelligence is within all of us and resonates with his direction. Some of the Hindu sages speak of the soul as being born one thousand times to learn all the lessons that are needed to achieve enlightenment. My sister comforted him with this information and then told him about Tariq.

The day after the funeral my mind started to come back. I felt really angry, but it wasn't directed at my son's assailant. Society at large was the object of my rage. America was the only superpower in the world. We can do anything we wanted to, yet we have failed in our responsibility to our children, at least to the children who are at risk. They join these gangs because they need substitute families. Their parents and the communities have thrown them out.

You and I have created this society. It just doesn't happen that these kids are born gangsters. They were born with the potential of being heroes. Seeds of disappointment turn them into gang members. Their parents and their communities could have behaved like family. But whatever the reason, the growth of gangs is now like a deadly cancer that is spreading as a result of a lack in societal responsibility.

I was very mad at my country, especially since I left Africa to escape from Idi Amin. I came here to protect my family. So I said to myself, what a fatal mistake. My first reaction was to leave this country. I could have gone to any place in this world, to England, to India, to Canada. Why here? I thought about this a lot. Then I remembered my goose bumps when I took my oath of allegiance. I was so proud to be a citizen of this country. I thought, "My God, I am so lucky to leave Africa because it is so much easier here. I have lived here for thirty years and have fallen in love with my adopted country." Even if I left this country I would still have to deal with this life. I cannot sweep what just happened under the rug. So, I have to stay and fight, but I did not know how. I had no clue as to how I was going to get through the rest of my life. One thing I did know was that expressing my anger was an important step in my recovery process.

We come into this world in self-chosen roles to learn, to teach, but mostly to serve. When we complete what we are here to do, then it is time to move on to our next journey toward enlightenment. Tariq had finished his mission in this world and was now moving forward to his next journey. My belief is that we made an agreement before we were both born to go through this because of the essential lessons that we needed to complete. This tragedy put me in touch with my life's mission. As an investment banker, I was very busy. I never knew that delivering pizzas was dangerous. I never knew that we had youth gangs and that we lose a child to a gun every ninety minutes. This entire arena of teen violence needs to be addressed so we can begin to heal our society.

Unfortunately, grief takes a long time to heal. Those important days come and go when your heart feels heavy. Even when I am asked to speak in public I feel tears well up in my eyes. I think that in the bigger context though, you can't avoid grieving. Only after you deal with your anger and grief can you forgive. *Something inside of you lets you know when it is time to let go. And when the time comes, you will know.* But before we can forgive we have to deal directly with our pain. You can't escape it. Eventually, if you make the effort, you will stop hurting because of your willingness to deal with it. The main thing is not to rush into something, to think that by distraction you can get away from it. Even today I have to work on forgiving.

At the end of our forty-day mourning period I went to see one of my spiritual teachers. He told me that according to our faith, the soul of the departed remains in close proximity to his family and his loved ones during the forty days that are allocated for grieving. He said, "After the forty days, the soul goes to a new consciousness. Continuous grieving by family and friends impedes the soul's journey. *While it is human for you to grieve, my recommendation to you is that in moments of grief you do good spiritual deeds.* Good spiritual deeds are spiritual currency; they transfer to the departed soul and help fuel it on its journey."

That was very powerful and comforting for me to hear and to know that when we are in a great deal of emotional pain, doing something for others will not only help our deceased loved ones but it will also help ourselves. This kept repeating itself in my mind for five months after I lost my son. I spent a week in the mountains thinking about how and why I should go on with my life. Feeling uplifted and comforted by the thought of spiritual currency inspired me. I wanted to do something in honor of my son, something meaningful and something that may help prevent this kind of tragedy from happening to others. I kept asking myself, "What can I do for you, my son, that will make a difference? I couldn't help you that fatal night in January 1995; what can I do for you now?" I heard his answer, and this served as an inspiration to begin a foundation to help prevent teen violence. I wanted to name the foundation after my son, the Tariq Khamisa Foundation. The foundation would give me a sense of purpose and a reason to live again. I realized that with the foundation great things could be done with lots of good deeds. I felt excitement for the first time. Thinking about doing something for others, spiritual currency, does help to heal grief. I knew it would also have a healing effect on my family.

Forgiveness is not a one-time event. It is a process that happens over time, and for some that process may never be completed. There are really two journeys here: one is an outer journey and one is an inner journey. My outer journey is the work of the foundation. There is comfort in helping people who need it. It could be as simple as helping an older person across the road or smiling at someone. A good deed is heartwarming to you and a good antidote for grief. But that is an outside activity.

The more difficult journey is the inner one. You have to dive deeply within yourself and look at the circumstances that led to your loss. Violence in any form is a societal cancer that must be fought. One of the Sufi masters wrote a poem that says we are the limbs of a large body. If we cause pain to one part of our body we can't think that another part of the body is not getting affected. If we do cause pain, we can't be human. By becoming aware of this, I realized that I must carry a message of peace, of nonviolence, and also of forgiveness, whenever and wherever I can.

Going inside is very personal. As I began to look within, I did feel anger. Anger screams out for a need to change. The other side of anger is that it can be more corrosive than the event. Anger that is totally unabated is very destructive to you and to the people around you. It has to be channeled or else it will burn you. You have to take that anger and figure out what can come out of it that is positive. There are always two faces of anger. With one face we become very defensive and want to lash out. With the other face we can learn something that will help us. Thank goodness I was able to choose the latter.

An inner journey cannot be forced, but if you are willing and go down deep enough, you will find an inner voice. That inner voice is what tells you when to let go. Meditation and prayer helped me connect with my inner self, but if you don't have these you can still hear that inner voice if you are open to it. If you do your inner work, you will eventually come to terms with your pain and loss. When your spirit is ready to hear that voice, it becomes possible to let go. When you feel the release, a powerful shift takes place setting the stage for forgiveness. Forgiveness is a bonus. You do that because you need to forgive, not for the perpetrator, but for yourself. Until you are able to forgive, you will not complete the grieving process. This is one of life's paradoxes.

For the victim to be totally at peace, the perpetrator needs forgiveness. This is one of the most difficult things to do because it is extremely human to experience a lot of anger and have a need for revenge. Remember that unabated anger is harmful to the one feeling the anger. If it goes on too long, it manifests in illness. This is another one of nature's strange twists. This is where forgiveness steps in for it may be the only option left for the person suffering. If you don't forgive, then the anger becomes so corrosive that it will consume you and eat you alive. Forgiveness becomes *your* salvation. You cannot force forgiveness, but you can do things to help yourself heal. It is a lot better to go hiking and start looking at your life then being consumed with anger.

Meeting Ples Felix

ANOTHER VERY IMPORTANT person in my healing process was Ples Felix, Tony's grandfather. As soon as he heard that his grandson was responsible for the death of Tariq, he felt a sense of obligation to reach out to my family and express his sympathies. Ples also wanted me to know that he would commit himself to doing anything he could to help me with my loss. He kept assuring me of that commitment. When overtures were made on my part through the district attorney's office, Ples was relieved. Ples had heard about my comments about seeing victims at both ends of the gun. This gave him a level of comfort knowing that our first meeting would not be fraught with finger pointing and animosity.

When we finally met in Tony's lawyer's office, the initial handshake was one filled with a great deal of powerful positive emotion. Ples initiated the handshake by verbalizing his heartfelt sympathy and condolences concerning the lost of my son. We both sat down next to each other, and I began to tell Ples about my desire to establish a foundation in the name of my son. I wanted to focus on eradicating youth violence. Ples repeated his desire to help, especially in the work of the foundation, which he saw as a way to prevent other teens from suffering Tony's and Tariq's fate.

Souls have the same source. I can feel that with Ples and myself. Ples is a very strong and very spiritual man. I invited him to my house a week after I met him. This was for the second meeting of the foundation. Ples's spiritual nature had a healing effect on me. It was very important for me to meet with Tony's family and understand that even he was suffering from this tragedy. I am not sure which is harder, to be the father of the victim or the father of a murderer. It has to be very tough. Ples's offer to help me became part of my healing. There was restoration there. I knew that Ples was going to be here to support me and would be part of my team on this journey. We hope that eventually Tony will join us too.

My forgiveness for Tony came early because of my ability to see him as a victim as well. He certainly pulled the trigger on my son but beyond that there are issues that made Tony who he was. My hope is for Tony to have the support he needs to heal and be restored. I think he is on that path. He reads a lot and has asked for my forgiveness. I am hoping that when he leaves prison he will spend his life working with teens. I hope that Tony and, in spirit, Tariq can work together to prevent teens from ending up in jail or dead. I think that would be very healing for Tony and give him a sense of purpose and something to feel good about.

There are people today who still suffer because they are so caught up in the emotion of revenge that they can't forgive. They want "an eye for an eye and a tooth for a tooth." They want someone to pay. Unfortunately, these same people cannot find peace. They can't find comfort because their energies are so tied up in seeking retribution despite the fact that revenge will not bring their loved one back. I understand through my own experiences in life that by forgiving the person who has harmed me I can find peace. It is also true that forgiveness is an ongoing process and because of this we experience forgiveness at various levels, always creating residual responses to help us find some peace. Finding peace is part of the healing force of forgiveness. It is this peace that supports an environment to strengthen our love. And the more love we have, the greater our capacity to forgive and the more peace we can anticipate.

All imprisoned criminals eventually reenter society. When they return to society, if they have not been restored, then they will commit another crime. As soon as they do that, they lose and the new victim loses. We all lose. So you just can't put them away and ignore them. You have to take the time and include them in the healing circle. All of us have some very special attributes that are given to us. Even criminals have good aspects. Sometimes it's harder to find those qualities. Sometimes you have to dig deep to find those precious gems, and you must remove all the dirt, then cut them, and polish them to reveal their value. This is the same work you have to do with criminals. They are part of this community, and, unless they are restored and healed, our community will not be healed. We will always have violence, hatred, and anger.

For us to have a peaceful society and a meaningful life, we have to restore all human beings because they are part of our society. The last piece is the forgiveness piece. Criminals cannot become whole until they recognize that for their own healing, they need to ask for forgiveness, and, in order for victims to be healed, they need to be able to see the situation with spiritual sight. Victims become victims twice over if they stay stuck in their own anger. Part of Tony's healing is not only to ask for forgiveness but he also must commit his life's work to helping others. He has to go out and say, "I am going to save somebody like Tariq. Because I took somebody's life, my life will not be complete until I know that I can save someone else's life." He has a journey too. His healing is to also gain some spiritual currency. This will make him whole. He can become a productive member of our community in which everyone benefits. He has the power within him to be a precious gem.

To forgive is to be healed. It is to connect your inner self with your heart. Although I have mentioned this earlier, I would like to repeat something I wrote in my journal in 1996. "The pain of losing a son, the pain of losing an only son is devastating. It is spiritually ungodly, emotionally unloving, and viscerally paralyzing. It is like a nuclear bomb detonating inside of you. However, if you survive the devastation, among the debris you see many new paths. I chose the path closest to my heart. As a result of this choice, I am at a meaningful place. I am closer to my heart than I ever remembering being. It is also the way I communicate with my son."

Forgiveness is not only a harbinger of healing; it also serves to motivate us further, to do all that we can to develop more of a repository of forgiveness and love. As a result of the work of the foundation, teenagers hear, "It is important for you to develop your tool kit with knowledge, skill, and education so you can take those tools and go out and create positive outcomes in the world." Just as I was taught and experienced beautiful spiritual values, I tell the teenagers that it is very important for them, too, to develop a repository of love and forgiveness so that when they go through life those occurrences that set you back won't destroy you. Because you have compassion in your heart you will be able to move forward under any circumstances.

This is the power of forgiveness. You can find it in yourself, but it's hard without going through the work to prepare yourself for it. You have to find a place to be quiet, be peaceful, and be still to hear the spirit within you become louder and louder until you are much more responsive to it than to outside forces. I think the inner journey I was talking about earlier is to prepare you to get to that point, and if you continue the preparation, your spirit will know the time to let go. When you can finally let go, it is not only healing, but you are in a different place, one where you will be a thousand times more powerful than you were before the event. The release is so transformative that it puts you in touch with a bigger mission, a bigger picture of life. I feel so thankful that I was able to get to that place.

Forgiveness is the ability to use something that was very destructive and detrimental to you or to someone you love and not to redirect it back, causing more destruction, but to turn it into something very powerfully positive both for the person who was hurt as well as the perpetrator. This is what I was fortunately able to do with the foundation. The programs that have been developed have had a huge positive impact on some school-children in San Diego County. I hope this will spread across the nation and the globe because the issues of violence and forgiveness are issues that affect people all over the world. Potentially what we have begun will have great implications for a world increasingly in conflict. We will need more substantial ways to create peace and forgiveness in environments where they happen to be very lacking. I look forward to expanding this work that I hope will save more of our children.

There is one more thing I would like to add. I feel that forgiveness and restorative attitudes are going to be very effective in terms of helping our children. I would like all adults to take that to heart and find themselves unlearning some of the behaviors and attitudes that affect our children in a negative way. We need to stop being so mean-spirited and learn to be more mindful of the need, within each of us, to have more love, compassion, and forgiveness in our lives. We need to develop restorative kinds of attitudes, behaviors, and programs for people who require that in our society. We need to develop compassionate environments such as compassionate schools so that children can be brought up in and nourished by them. This way each generation can find itself being a little bit more compassionate, a little bit more loving, and certainly a little bit more giving so that future societies can be a lot healthier than the society we live in now. This is my prayer. This is what I hope to leave behind in the name of my son, Tariq Khamisa.

10

Listening Within

Irene Laure's Story

*"I think of the ruins I have seen—French ruins,
German ruins. Whose victory was it? There was no victory;
we were all defeated, defeated by evil."*

—JACQUELINE PIGUET, WRITER

WE ARE SO enmeshed in our own thinking that sometimes we need
an outside factor to enter our world of fear and guilt to enable us
to forgive. Step Seven of the forgiveness program calls on us to
view our situations differently, through spiritual sight. This is when
some of us have spiritual experiences that are so transformative
that they change our lives. It begins by our calling upon something
outside of us, term it prayer or a yearning for something greater
than ourselves. The willingness to call on a "third factor" and the
experience that results in the process of forgiveness is a change in
perception that enables us to release the pain. This "third factor"
may be characterized as the transcending and contingent element
in the relationship of persons, that mystery that opens our hearts
making forgiveness possible. Although forgiveness is probably the

most difficult thing asked of us, if it is something that our heart
truly wants even if it seems that a much larger part of ourselves
wants something else, we will be able to forgive. Irene Laure's story
is a beautiful illustration of that.

Irene's Story

I remember it very well, that cold dreary day in Montreal during
the winter of 1989. I was preparing to walk up to the podium to
give my first presentation on forgiveness and international affairs.
I was to talk about the Franco-German reconciliation after World
War II, which was one of the greatest achievements of modern
statecraft. The presentation was highlighting the experiences of
one French woman, Irene Laure, who had the courage to forgive
and by this one act was able to change the face of Europe.

As I was approaching the lectern, I couldn't help but wonder
what Irene Laure must have been feeling some forty years earlier
in Caux, Switzerland, when she too needed to address the assembly. How did she become such a remarkable woman?

My mind drifted back to the Mountain House, the hotel in
Caux that was built at the turn of the century with such elegance
and splendor. It was as though I was now sitting in the audience
of this spectacular hall waiting in anticipation for Irene to tell her
story. All eyes were on her as this young woman of great strength
began to walk onto the stage. There was a sense that something
very significant was about to happen.

Irene was a rebel against injustice from her earliest days. She
was also taught to be a German hater having grown up in France
during World War I and later suffered at the hands of the Nazis
during World War II. I could hear Irene's voice as she told her story
to the beat in the background of marching boots shattering the
quietness of night. Suddenly Irene is surrounded by a German
patrol, with their torchlight blinding her and their harsh orders
deafening her ears. She was pointing to her nursing bag hoping it

would save her. Instead, she was propelled forward by the muzzle of a machine gun in the small of her back, wondering if this meant her death.

Anger had been fermenting inside of her since that day in May of 1940 when the Germans entered Paris. She had vowed that no matter what happened she would never surrender. Irene became part of the resistance movement. But as this dark night was slipping into dawn Irene had no regrets, not even if the journey of her life was about to end. This night became one of many close encounters.

As I looked into the eyes of my audience, years later, I couldn't help but ask myself how many of them had ever experienced living in a war zone. I knew there were diplomats and foreign service officers in the audience, but how many of them understood firsthand why and how we can hate so much. We speak of conflict so antiseptically. So often we think that once we have a treaty or policy in place, peace will follow. Governments usually don't go further than that and certainly not to the core of the pain and suffering that is at the root of all wars.

Irene was a poignant example of a human being wounded by the atrocities of violence and war. Yes, she and her family suffered in so many ways. Just surviving was an extremely painful ordeal. Standing in queues for food, Irene would wait one hour, two hours, perhaps three or four hoping that something would be given to her before she heard the fateful words "no more." Never mind the times when she would finally make it to the front of the line and into her outstretched hands she would receive just two sardines. She would leave with her basket cruelly light in her hands (Piguet, 1985). That was not the typical focus for an audience of historians and political scientists.

Emotions run deep and if they are not expressed they fester like a blister ready to burst open at any time. They follow *their own* logic often defying any rationality. If we try to short-circuit the process, the blister will reappear elsewhere becoming very infectious. We cannot ignore this fact, especially when building a peace.

How do these emotions get played out? Anger when not dealt with appropriately turns into hatred. When you hate you want to see your enemy destroyed. Anger builds and if there is no healing mechanism available, hatred intensifies. In situations of intense conflict and war, we recycle these emotions over and over again becoming blinded by our anger and heartless by our fear. This was Irene's experience. She rejoiced when she heard Allied bombers flying overhead, knowing that there would be more destruction to Germany. After the war, she witnessed the opening of a mass grave containing the mutilated bodies of some of her comrades. This experience served to reinforce her longing for the total destruction of Germany. Her heart now frozen, Irene never held out the possibility that there could be an understanding where the Germans were concerned.

No one is immune to the toxins of anger and hatred. It is like falling into quicksand with seemingly no way of getting out unless someone else who is not caught up in the quagmire of debris can extend a helping hand.

Irene Laure received an extended hand, although at the time she did not recognize it. During the summer of 1947, she received an invitation to attend a conference in Caux, Switzerland. Irene was under the assumption that no Germans would be there and accepted the offer. She found the Mountain House and the surroundings to be magnificent, but to her horror 150 Germans were also invited. This group was the first to be permitted to leave the country after the war. It did not matter that they might have suffered too during the war. After all, they were Germans.

During the conference if any German spoke to the assembly, Irene and mostly anyone who was French got up and walked out of the assembly hall. At one point when Irene was getting up to leave, an American Lutheran minister, Frank Buchman, posed a question to her asking how could there be a united Europe without Germany. She was at first shocked that anyone would ask her such a question but then something inside of her made her question the possibility of doing something different.

When we open ourselves to the possibility of wanting to do something different, we are also allowing a shift to take place within ourselves. We might not understand what is taking place but just that willingness to do or see things differently allows the doors of forgiveness to gently open. The struggle within us is what moves us forward and, for some, it can be the beginning of a profound healing and inner transformation.

When Irene began to question the possibility of seeing things differently, she unknowingly made a commitment to look deeper within herself. Irene went to her room and for two-and-a-half days wrestled with the question of whether she would be willing to give up her hatred for the sake of a new Europe. She revisited all the reasons why she should hate the Germans and felt extremely justified in holding on to her anger. Sweet revenge felt so good—momentarily. Then the battle within Irene became more intense. Was hatred and revenge going to give her what she really wanted? Irene then realized that "hatred, whatever the reasons for it, is always a factor that creates new wars."

Irene did a great deal of soul searching during those few days. This is a requirement for anyone who is sincere in the quest for emotional freedom. Irene finally left her room to have lunch and rejoin the conference to share with the participants what had happened to her while in her room. During lunch, a German woman sat with her. There was a long silence while they were eating. Finally, Irene broke the silence.

"You represent what I hate most in the world. You cannot imagine what my country has suffered because of you. Our women and our children are nothing but skeletons. Our best men were tortured and killed. Do you know how my son, Louis, suffered? They tried everything. He never talked. But the state we found him in! He was a wreck, a wreck. And the walking corpses who come back from your camps! I have to receive them at the Lutetia Hotel . . ." (Piguet, 1985).

As Irene spoke, the German woman's hands trembled. Irene spoke for a long time sifting through her terrible memories of the resistance. When she was finally finished, there was a long silence. Only then did Irene look at the woman she was addressing. Irene made one more comment.

"The reason I am telling you this, Madame, is that I want to be free of this hate" (Henderson, 1994).

There was another long pause as though time stood still. It was now the German woman's turn.

"I would like to talk to you about myself, if I may," said the woman at last. "My husband was part of a plot to assassinate Hitler. The plot failed, and he was arrested. He was hanged. While I was in prison, my two children were taken away from our family and put in an orphanage under false names. I have managed to find them again, but it is very difficult bringing them up under such difficult circumstances. I realize that we did not resist enough, that we did not resist early enough and on a scale that was big enough, and we brought on you and ourselves and the world endless agony and suffering. Because of this you have suffered terribly. I want to say I am sorry" (Henderson, 1994, and Piguet, 1985).

That afternoon Irene asked to address the assembly. Many knew her background, but no one really knew what happened in her room or the effect the conversation with Frau von Trott had on her attitude. Speaking to six hundred people in the assembly hall, Irene spoke honestly about her experiences with the Germans and what she felt. She went on to say:

"I have so hated Germany that I wanted to see her erased from the map of Europe. But I have seen here that my hatred is wrong. I am sorry and I wish to ask the forgiveness of all the Germans present. One cannot forget, but one can forgive" (Henderson, 1994).

After those words, it became so quiet in the hall that you could hear a pin drop. Unexpectedly, a German woman got up from her seat and walked onto the stage where Irene was standing. She wanted to shake Irene's hand in gratitude for what was just said. Irene hesitated. For a moment she felt hatred rearing its ugly head again. Her hand was paralyzed. She prayed to herself that she could forgive and be healed from this hatred. Then suddenly a miracle happened, a moment of grace. Irene took this woman's hand and was overcome by such feelings of liberation it was as though a great weight had been lifted from her shoulders. Irene finally felt free. *Her ability to see things differently was the miracle.* There was a total transformation in Irene's thinking. By being able to see the world through the eyes of forgiveness, Irene's life took on new meaning. She made the commitment to take the message of forgiveness and reconciliation to Germany and to the world.

The entire assembly was electrified. The guilt-ridden Germans in the room were dumbfounded and everyone knew that Irene had shown the only way open to Germany if its people wanted to join in the reconstruction of Europe.

In 1948, Irene Laure went to Germany with her husband and son. For more than two months, they toured the country addressing the majority of the state parliaments. Irene received apologies from generals and other officers, politicians, and former Nazis after they heard her speak. Irene traveled with some of her compatriots who had lost families in the gas chambers, as well as men and women from other countries who had fought against the Germans. All of them had found a willingness to forgive the past.

Irene felt that it was important to see the destruction of Berlin and went on an airlift with her family. It had such an impact on her that she commented:

"When you have seen with your own eyes the ruins of Berlin, you have a suffering in your heart that vows that those things shall never happen again" (Henderson, 1994).

While in Berlin Irene spoke to a group of women who were cleaning away rubble from the streets. She vowed to them, "I swear to you that I will give the rest of my life so that what you are going through will never again be possible in the world" (Henderson, 1994).

At times this was not easy, especially when there was a solemn reminder of the brutality of the war. There were moments when Irene felt that she was going out of her mind. Was she betraying those who had suffered and died at the hands of the Nazis? Then she would hear her still small voice reassure her: "You are on the right path."

Irene died near Marseilles on July 16, 1987. She was eighty-eight years of age. Her obituary in the *London Times* read, "Resistance heroine and healer of wounds . . . she went to work tirelessly to reconcile France and Germany." Irene Laure's biographer, Swiss writer Jacqueline Piguet, sums up Irene's life, "Irene was committed to help those who suffer, living socialism of heart and generosity but never bound by doctrinal or political points of view, with the turning point in her life the discovery of the power of forgiveness" (Piguet, 1985).

The Power of Grace

Irene's story exemplifies the possibility and potential that a change in perception and transformation in thinking can bring. This is the miracle that only forgiveness and its processes can bring to life. Irene was willing to look into her heart, acknowledge her weakness, and say she was sorry for her hateful thoughts toward the Germans. The results of her actions were profound. In saying, yes, this is what I have done, she was able to change her thinking, grow in compassion, and build a new relationship. This process of self-inquiry, self-responsibility, and letting go of the past renews and deepens self-respect. This is the process and meaning of forgiveness. Forgiveness creates a shift in perception that permits us to see our mistakes and to view them as an opportunity to learn rather than as proof of how "bad" we are. Recognizing that we can release guilt and pain, we deepen our self-knowledge, compassion, empathy, and spiritual growth.

If we were to define forgiveness simply, it would describe a situation where one who is deeply hurt by another eventually stops holding negative thoughts and feelings and gives the other the gift of unconditional acceptance. Irene accomplished this when she let go of her hatred and later worked toward building the morale of the German people. Yet Irene did more than that. She overcame her deep feelings of anger and hatred *not by denying her feelings*, but by endeavoring to view the offender with compassion while recognizing that she had chosen to release her negative feelings. Irene experienced a shift in consciousness when she allowed herself to see that the German people also were suffering from the recognition of being misguided, from their own guilt and fear, and from the effect war had on their lives.

Irene has shown us that forgiveness is more than the "turning of the cheek," or a sign of weakness. It took courage on Irene's part to experience her hatred and anger and to admit that it was wrong to hate her mortal enemy, thus demonstrating that forgiveness was a conscious decision. She chose to see not only her pain but was able too understand that the Germans had suffered too. With the new knowledge she had gained about herself and about other Germans, her perceptions began to change. Irene was becoming more sensitive to the human condition. She became more aware of similarities in all of us, which made it easier for her to let go of her long-held resentments. She then could open herself up to the forgiveness that resulted in adding joy and richness to her life.

There is one more thing I would like to say about this story. It is about the moment Irene was freed from hate. This happened because of the power of grace. Grace is that inexplicable power which comes from God or somewhere beyond ourselves that gives us the ability to forgive when we feel within our hearts that forgiveness is humanly impossible. In an instant, we are moved from a heart of bondage to experiencing a wellspring of love for our enemy. Grace is experiencing the power of God or an unknown source giving love and working in us and through us. In those moments, we are able to accept someone for who they are, not for what they have done or what we attribute to them. When it happens, one feels the power and presence of a higher intervention that transforms our relationships as we experience an outpouring of inexplicable love. As great as Irene's struggle was to forgive, so was her commitment to the forgiveness process. Until the very end of that afternoon in Caux, Irene struggled to take the German woman's hand. Then in a surprising moment, an incredible energy propelled Irene's hand, and a profound change took place within Irene's inward being. There was something new being created inside of Irene, an interior renovation that healed her so Irene could move forward to new relationships with the Germans. Something was written upon her inner self where she had no need of outer instruction. Divine initiative came to pass. This was the miracle Irene recognized. This is the power of grace.

The transformational power of forgiveness moves us from being helpless victims of our circumstances to becoming powerful co-creators of our reality. We learn how to see people with fresh eyes, seeing them anew every day. In becoming more loving, compassionate, and understanding human beings, we gain the ability to have a deeper relationship with ourselves and with the significant people in our lives. Our lives become so much richer. Irene's story is a testament to this. She gave so much to this world. To her, the only thing that was important now was to teach about forgiveness.

11

Breaking Cycles of Violence

A New Beginning

"The holiest of all spots on Earth is where an ancient hatred has become a present love."

—A COURSE IN MIRACLES

IF WE LOOK upon the world as a global family, we would see that it is highly dysfunctional. There is pathology everywhere. Clearly the violent behavior needs to stop, but this must be done in a way that does not reinforce the dynamics that will lead to more violence. To meet insanity with more insanity does nothing except reinforce insanity.

Is it possible under the weight of our anger and fear to see not only the commonality of needs but also the commonality of frailties, such as the perceived need for retribution and the desire for revenge, and to recognize that we are more alike than different? Perhaps by understanding these commonalities we can recognize the human condition that comprises human culture. The way to bring us together and heal these frailties is through the healing power of forgiveness.

Beverly Eckert is one of the people who has the ability to see beyond the destructive behavior of others and recognize what unites us instead of what divides us. She is able to see past her pain to what is more important for greater humanity. On August 8, 2003, Beverly spoke in New York's Battery Park of the importance of not responding to violence with more violence but from a place of understanding and compassion. She was speaking to Japanese *Peace Boat* delegates, including Nagasaki atomic bomb survivors, before the group walked to the nearby World Trade Center site. Beverly's husband had called her on the morning of September 11 from where he was trapped on the 105th floor of the World Trade Center. She spoke of feeling blessed that they had enough time to say what they needed to say to each other before the building's collapse carried him to his death. These are her words.

> *We are here today because we are the ones who hear the voices of the dead calling for an end to violence and hatred—voices that are telling us to rise above our fear in order to have a coherent and compassionate dialogue about the root causes of murderous strife; telling us that we need to shed our doubts about what a mere handful of believers can do; telling us that amid the ashes that covered this city two years ago and Hiroshima and Nagasaki fifty-eight years ago, and amid the blood-soaked killing fields in countless nations overseas, we will find the wisdom, grace, unity, and strength we need so that on some future September 11 we will see a better world when we look around us (Eckert, 2003).*

When Beverly tells the story of what happened on 9/11, she speaks about not only her husband becoming a civilian casualty but about how she, too, became a member of a worldwide community numbering in the millions, "whose lives have been torn apart by the effects of man's inhumanity to man."

Beverly believed that "America was thrust into sisterhood with countries and peoples she had once helped, as well as countries and peoples she had once hurt. And so September 11 is a beginning. My husband died because he was an American and I'm here today so I can help ensure that when history looks back in judgment on this new century, the word *American* will have stood for something righteous and good."

There was hope in Beverly's heart because she had seen the events of September 11 mobilize many to further the cause of peace. She told the crowd, "Someday there will be a memorial at the place nearby that we call "Ground Zero"—an unholy name that resurrects the horrors of another act of unspeakable barbarity those in attendance from Japan know all too well. And that future memorial will be a reminder to people everywhere that we must, above all, demand integrity from those who govern us politically and tolerance from those who lead us spiritually." What Beverly was demonstrating was an act of forgiveness. She was asking all of us to look within ourselves and instead of reacting from a place of weakness—namely, our fear—come from a place of compassion so we can begin to understand the cry from humanity. She asks us not to judge but to come from a place of wisdom so we can truly see the world differently.

Forces of Forgiveness

Unfortunately, life brings pain and suffering. There is no escaping this, particularly on a personal level. Yet pain and suffering are also brought about to groups of people, such as in the World War II holocaust and the genocide that took place in Rwanda in the 1990s. If we can forgive on a personal level can we also learn how to forgive and coexist among enemies?

I read a story about an American physician traveling in Bosnia who witnessed an unspeakable act. Her translator, an ethnic Albanian Kosovar with whom she had traveled for weeks, pulled out a gun in a medical clinic and fatally shot a surgeon. It turned out that the surgeon, a Serb, had committed a crime against the translator and his family, and it was payback time (Bole et al., 2004).

The spirit of revenge is one of the most destructive forces in society. It creates a spiral of violence that can only be broken when our pain becomes so great that someone finally says "Enough!" Such acts of violence demonstrate the need for healing memories and a willingness to transform our hearts, which can happen when we open ourselves to the possibility of forgiveness.

What drives our need for revenge? The first thing we think about when we have experienced deep pain and suffering is how to get the perpetrator to pay for what he or she has done. We keep score, a tabulation of who did what, so we know how to balance the scales. All of us have adapted to this way of thinking. It is the same kind of thinking that leads us to believe in an eye for an eye. But as Gandhi told us, "An eye for an eye will only make the whole world go blind." Herein lies our struggle.

Yet once in awhile we hear other stories that are just as amazing because they don't speak of revenge. In one story, a Croatian woman saw her husband murdered in her home by Serbian attackers. Instead of pleading with the aggressors to spare her life and the lives of her children, she got their attention and let them know that she would strive to forgive them. She told them that she would not seek revenge and that she believed her boys would learn about forgiveness as future priests and teach her how to forgive. With her words, the surprised attackers ended the killing in her home (Bole et al., 2004).

This and the earlier story are snapshots of the forces of unforgiveness and forgiveness. They illustrate opposing forces in human relationships—colliding elements such as truth and myth, forbearance and revenge, empathy and dehumanization. The shooting at the clinic revealed a rejection not just of forgiveness but of forbearance from revenge, along with any thought of eventual reconciliation. One cannot help but wonder what kind of mythological history or distortion of truth the translator indulged in before becoming mentally prepared to slaughter his former neighbor, the surgeon. In contrast, the Croatian mother's vow of forgiveness offered a glimpse into the power of forbearance and the element of surprise often built into such an act, which can lead to forgiveness. How was she, in those horrendous moments, able not to become a vengeful woman but instead envision and articulate a future of coexistence and reconciliation? By her actions, this woman closed the doors of revenge and broke the cycle of retribution.

The path toward the freedom of forgiveness requires us to open our minds and hearts completely to the reality of circumstances, including the fact there are many people who do not share our worldview and even fundamentally oppose it. Yet opposition to one's view and failure to share one's values does not an enemy make. This must be realized and absorbed by any person to truly achieve full freedom and live one's life without anger and all that it entails.

Anxiety is the most agonizing problem confronting human beings taken by such unexpected and overwhelming events. *Anxiety* can be defined as a confusion of emotions dominated by a combination of fear and anger. Individually, each of these emotions has the potential to paralyze a person if it is felt strongly enough. The combination of both can have nearly deadly consequences, out of stress and the loss of a person's desire to go on with life. In such situations forgiveness can be the greatest, if not the only, saving grace.

How does a person forgive being scarred by war, genocide, sexual abuse, or physical violence? Confusion has to be first unraveled like a knot that binds the human spirit to the tragedy. Only that limited freedom, a mere step in the process, will allow the human mind to process the emotions through reason and care to ultimate freedom so that life can continue as before, unhindered by paralyzing anxiety.

The first step in untying the knot of confusion is to separate fear from anger. Of the two, fear is the easier to recognize. Identifying specifically what you fear, making a list of the factors, and even saying them aloud will put your mind on the right track. Identifying anger is more difficult. There is a feature of anger, however, that is fairly easy to recognize: the desire for revenge.

As we have said before, there is nothing fundamentally inhumane about the desire for revenge. Even the Christian admonition "Vengeance is mine, sayeth the Lord" does not negate the idea that the desire for vengeance is purely human. If anything, that statement recognizes and affirms the existence of the desire to take revenge on those who have wronged us. But what it also takes into account is the desire for revenge can itself be a terrible consuming passion, capable of robbing us of the good energies in life by redirecting them toward a goal established *outside* ourselves, by our enemies in fact. In this way, the desire for revenge *binds* a person to those who have wronged him or her and, worse, to their actions. Vengeance can freeze time, compelling a person to dedicate himself or herself to a goal that may prove ultimately nonproductive, possibly for an entire lifetime. After revenge has been achieved, what is left is like a deflated balloon, not the triumphant feeling of having lived a full life.

Another popular phrase, shaped in the form of a promise, tells it best: "Living well is the best revenge." After 9/11 and the subsequent bombings in London and Madrid, for example, people were urged not to give up their regular lives but to go on as before, going to work and pursuing other fulfilling activities, as though the enemies who perpetrated the horrible warlike crime had never existed. This, it was reasoned, would prove that people were much too strong to be intimidated and paralyzed by fear.

Note that I don't say these acts of violence were anything but an act of extreme aggression, perpetrated to hurt us and shut down our society. Nor do I say the desire to punish the perpetrators is in any way not human. It *is* human. But is it the most productive use of our time, resources, emotions, and energy?

There is so much fear generated in our world because of so many horrific acts of violence that it's hard to talk about how forgiveness can prevail in the face of a feverish pitch for revenge. This is part of the human condition, our human nature. When we are afraid, we erect walls around our hearts and minds. In the throes of terror, our thinking becomes constricted and the lens we see the world through is one of hate. Fear fueled by hate becomes a cancerous growth that permeates our consciousness and spreads at veraciously accelerated rates, turning many fair-minded people into seekers of retribution. No one is immune to this kind of thinking.

It is during times when our hearts are filled with anger and call for revenge that it is extraordinarily important to remember the prophetic words of Ghandi concerning the eye-for-an-eye mentality. If we forget this truth, stay locked in fear, and become blind to rage, the evil committed in this world has won. We have lost our perspective and have fallen prey to destructive decisions. What is really called for is a long, slow breath and the restoration of our mental clarity so we can respond effectively and wisely.

Crisis brings danger as well as opportunity. From a psychological perspective, crisis is symbolic on many levels. It asks us to stop and look from a deeper psychological and spiritual perspective at what has happened so we don't perpetuate the cycle of escalating violence and revenge. Just as individuals can learn to forgive one another so, too, can collective evil be turned to good by tapping into the choice to focus on compassion and healing. People can heal relationships by consciously evaluating the long-term impact of their choices and by choosing to live by principles that serve a greater good than one's own. This requires a willingness to see things differently and an openness to develop an inclusive view of humanity that includes a commitment to principles of a high moral standard. Just as individuals can tap into their highest good so, too, can groups fulfill a higher purpose including self-transcendence and identification with the larger community.

A natural reaction to an attack, especially one of great magnitude, is a cry for revenge and painting the face of a monster on those responsible for horrific acts. We see this pattern repeated in history, most recently with the war in Iraq, where aggression and attacks are the mechanisms for revenge. Yet does this give us what we want? What is really called for seems more connected to social and psychological processes that can heal and release deep emotional anguish, the sense of powerlessness, and collective loss than to military might. The question becomes how do we break the cycle of violence and bring groups of people together who hold hatred and animosity toward one another? What role can forgiveness play in healing relationships between groups?

When we react out of fear and hatred, it is an indication that we do not yet have a deep understanding of the situation. Our actions will only be a quick and superficial way of responding to the situation and not much true healing will occur. Yet if we wait and follow the process of calming our anger, looking deeply into the situation, and listening with great will to understand the roots of suffering that are the cause of violent actions, only then will we have sufficient insight to respond in such a way that healing and reconciliation can be realized for everyone involved. We need to develop appropriately acceptable ways for dealing with our group anger in a healing way. One of the gifts democracy brings is freedom of expression but expression in and of itself is not necessarily healing. To ask soul-searching questions about our anger *is* healing. Why did this happen and, more important, how have we contributed to the event? If we truly have *not* contributed to the event, our anger will dissipate after an appropriate amount of time. It is when anger becomes a part of our identity that a red flag is waved in our face telling us there is something *we* need to change. If we can honestly look at this and own our part in what happened, we set the stage for a healing transformation to take place. If we are able to create change, we create a new path that can reverse the cycle of violence and begin to build trust.

Although it is very challenging to maintain openness, it is crucial that we not respond in any way until we have calmness and clarity to view the reality of the situation. Responding with violence and hatred will only damage ourselves and those around us. We need to look deeply into the suffering of the people inflicting violence on us, understand them more deeply, and understand ourselves more deeply. We can respond more compassionately when we have achieved this kind of understanding, relieving not only our suffering but also the other side's suffering as well.

There is an incredible story that illustrates this point. It took place in the small east African country of Rwanda, where 800,000 people were slaughtered by their own government. These were ordinary men and women murdered because they were Tutsi. Virtually the entire world turned away and did nothing to stop the genocide. What took place in Rwanda was perhaps the darkest and most brutal tragedy of our time. This is a story of Violette, one of the victims, and how the power of forgiveness dispelled her fear. Violette realized that she had to change her thinking if she wanted to heal fear. Forgiveness helped her do that, which is true healing.

Violette's Courageous Story

MY STORY BEGINS with the tragedy in Rwanda on April 7, 1994. That was the day after a plane crash killed our president and the president of Burundi. We were sure that something would happen because there was a war going on and there was a lot of tension in the country, but we didn't know what to expect. Early in the morning the following day there was a lot of shooting in the town. We said, "My God, it is the end!"

We turned on the radio, which gave instructions not to go out but to remain in our houses and so on. Then we got a call from a friend who said, "The military is going from house to house. We do not know what they are doing in those houses." Others called us and asked us to call the UN because people were being shot and killed in their homes. The whole day was filled with horrific news. This was the last we heard from anyone. The telephone wires and power were cut soon after the announcement came to stay home.

Around eleven o'clock I opened the curtain a little bit and saw the military trying to cut our fence. I thought they were going to shoot at our house so I called everybody and told them to lie down. Everyone hid under the bed. The house felt so small. Then the soldiers came in and started to break everything. They began yelling and opening windows. I was under my bed. I don't even remember who was with me. When I looked up I saw a gun. I started laughing! He was going to shoot when I said, "I am coming, and I am coming out quickly!" So I came out and went to close the curtains for them. The soldiers asked why I did that. I said we were very frightened and did not know what was happening. "You were breaking everything, and I was afraid. I didn't know what you wanted to do."

The soldier said, "Oh, you must be enemies because you don't open your door." Soldiers started to beat the children. Some were bleeding. They brought us all into the sitting room and asked us where we hid our guns. The soldiers said, "We are going to kill you. You are our enemies, and you are rejoicing because our president is dead!"

"We are Christians. We do not rejoice because our president is dead," I said in disbelief!

"You are collaborators—look, you are the ones who allowed those Tutsis to come here to the country and now you can see they have killed the president," the soldiers yelled back.

At one point my thirteen-year-old daughter innocently asked if the soldiers were going to kill us.

"Yes," they said.

She replied, "Let us pray."

They were shocked. "What kind of children are you?"

"Before dying, Christians must pray."

This broke a little of the tension. Then I said, "If you are looking for weapons in this house, the only weapon we have is our Bible. This is our weapon."

One soldier wanted to shoot the Bible. Another soldier kicked it aside so a bullet hole could not go through it.

The soldiers asked for money so we gave it to them. Then they said they didn't want our blood on their hands so they weren't going to kill us. They knew that another group of soldiers would be coming around who would finish the job.

Then something striking happened. While the soldiers were furious with us, one wanted to throw a grenade and kill us. This soldier was not kidding. Just one word was sufficient for him to do it. I was trembling so much I became paralyzed with fear. The only thing I could do was go quietly within myself and ask for help to see the situation differently. In prayer, I suddenly detached myself from the fear I felt. I became peaceful and calm. I said to God, "I am coming to You, I am coming to You." At that moment I was enveloped with a peace I never thought possible. The fear was released. Surprisingly, my family was no longer fearful as well. Everyone's fear evaporated. I felt like I was going to jump from the fearful present to a peaceful unknown. When they said they were not ready to kill us, that another group would do it, I was a little disappointed. I was so ready to die in that moment of peace. I thought to myself—am I going to have to go through all of this again?

Another group did come, and then another. There were a total of five groups who came by the house. They didn't enter because everything looked so broken. They believed that other soldiers had already killed us, and they continued on. I knew that the soldiers themselves were nervous. Even the army protecting the president came by. That day we stayed quietly in our house waiting to die. The next day it was the same. Finally, the killing stopped because the army was facing war. Rebels were now inside the cities. The army was fully engaged. Bombs were set off and could be heard all over the place.

Now I want to share something about forgiveness. Even if their intent was to kill us, I never considered the soldiers our enemies. Actually, the one who protected the Bible came the third day to see if we were still alive. He was amazed when he found that we had survived.

He said, "Surely your God is alive. Do you need something?"

"We don't have water," I replied with amazement.

He looked for water for us. He brought many things for us. Then he said he could do no more.

I asked him one more favor. I knew that our neighbors, a man and wife, were dead. I asked, "Instead of just leaving those bodies in the house, can you do something to bury them?" He went to look for people who were able to bury the bodies. We couldn't because we were in hiding, yet it was important to us that they were buried.

Every day for us was a miracle: we saw God's protection, and He protected us in a wonderful way. Three weeks had gone by and it still was too dangerous to go out. We couldn't survive much longer and needed to find a street boy to help us. We cared about the boys, and we gave them food when we could. Then one day one of the street boys told us that someone was organizing a group to come and kill us. He wanted to warn us because the boys in the street liked us. Some of them came with tears and said, "Madam, we were trying our best to protect you but now we can't. It is beyond us. They are planning your death and are waiting for new army members to come. It will be those soldiers who will kill you. Please leave this place now."

The street boys finally told us that it was our neighbor, a person we knew well who had worked with my husband, who reported us to the army. We had no problems with him, yet he was the one who was planning to kill us. I couldn't believe it. I was so angry.

Evening came, and we were about to pray at six o'clock. As we began, I felt very bad. I felt as though I was cheating on God because of my anger and what I had said about our neighbor. Then I said, "Now we are in front of You. We can die at any time, and I am still joking with sins." After that I started to understand my neighbor. He was vice president of the political party involved in the killings. If he was requested by his superior to kill people who fit in a certain category and we fit that category, he considered us enemies. I asked myself, if I was in his place playing the role he played, and not being aware of my divinity, maybe I would have done the same to protect myself. What they did was try to protect themselves by excluding others. I could forgive him seeing it that way.

My family and I escaped. Eventually, I met my neighbor in a refugee camp. I held no anger toward him. He, too, was a refugee. He was not surprised to see me. I do not know what he felt, but I felt warmth in my heart when I greeted him. I also felt in my heart that I had truly forgiven him. After all, he was my neighbor, not my enemy.

The Loss of Alicia

All of us have heroes in our lives whom we admire and want to emulate. They could be spiritual leaders or ordinary people doing extraordinary things. Tragedy can bring out the best or worst in people. In such situations heroes can and usually do arise. One such person is John Titus. His daughter, Alicia, flew out of Boston the morning of September 11 and was killed when her plane struck the World Trade Center. His words reflect his ongoing struggle to come to terms with his loss (Titus, 2003).

GRIEF IS SUCH an all-encompassing, personal process. Although there are similarities in the actual process of grief, many factors come into play as it unfolds. Initially, shock and disbelief help protect you from the searing pain, a pain that has the power to destroy, a pain that reduces your life-force and energy; destroys joy, laughter, innocence, and trust; and causes you to question everything that you heretofore held sacred. Sadness and pain of this magnitude can send a person into a downward spiral of depression and desolation—into a deep abyss whose walls seem impossible to scale. Many times you find yourself on the precipice and feel the powerful pull of the dark abyss that longs to consume. Yet even in the midst of all of this, even in my deepest moment of despair, I could feel the presence of goodness and truth, the love that so many people were sending us, the power of God, and a glimmer of hope flickered like a candle in the wind. I was not alone!

Through it all, I was absolutely certain I would not want to be responsible for another father's grief of losing an innocent child to the political machinery of war and destruction. Compassion had found its way into my heart and I could feel a new hope coming out of the rubble, a hope that goodness and truth would overcome hate and deception, a hope that would arise because of what had happened! I could feel it all around. I had been given a precious gift, and I could see beyond the hateful act of angry terrorists, beyond the need for revenge, beyond the fear and anger that seemed so prevalent, beyond my own pain of the worst loss imaginable. I had somehow been given a glimpse into the divine, and I could feel it in my soul. My purpose in life had now shone forth and made itself manifest. Alicia had passed me the torch of truth, and love would give me strength to travel the road less traveled.

My daughter, Alicia, lived in peace with God's creation. She longed for a world in which we could all get along. She openly embraced diversity and saw the world as a rich tapestry of people of differing shapes and colors woven into one big, beautiful creation. She never stood in judgment of others but looked beyond appearances into their very souls and touched their hearts. She could see the presence of the divine in others. Many people told us that she would light up a room with her mere presence, and her smile was one to measure all others smiles against. Her joy was effervescent, her smile contagious. Her sense of peace was pervasive.

I am not a pacifist. I have sought to understand the principles of nonviolence and have tremendous respect for those heroes who have used this means to overcome oppression and war, but I have a hard time letting others run over me and have struck back rather than turn the other cheek in the past. As I've grow in understanding and love, I've learned there are very effective nonviolent solutions to conflict, and I fully support that approach. I believe the perpetrators of the heinous act of murder that killed my Alicia and three thousand others should be made accountable and brought to justice. Yet I am opposed to killing innocent children and families to achieve this. We must find a better way of resolving conflict and stop the senseless killing!

Throughout my grieving process, it has become abundantly clear that the cycle of violence must stop. Hate only produces more hate, and violence begets more violence. In this age of advanced technology, we have the capability to destroy each other and decimate our planet. But do we have the strength, will, and spiritual understanding to overcome violence? If we believe that we are a part of God's creation, is it not possible to grow in love and wisdom to a place that seeks out nonviolent means for overcoming our ideological differences? As the late, great Dr. Martin Luther King Jr. stated, "Only love can overcome hate." From my experience as the grieving father of a beautiful, loving, peaceful, gentle soul whose life was taken by forces of hate and violence, love guided by wisdom is the only solution.

Compassion is a gift that comes out of tragedy. Yet, not all people are ready to receive it. Anger, a natural response to the pain of loss, often consumes people and drives them obsessively. During my grief, well-meaning people would tell me that I needed to get angry. But all I could feel was sadness and pain. I couldn't see how anger would help me heal and revenge seemed so pointless. It would not bring Alicia back or make me feel better. I had searched my heart and looked to God to find forgiveness. I realized that forgiveness was not about condoning the actions of another, it was about my letting go of a cancerous growth that would soon destroy me if I let it run its course. But forgiveness was the miracle that allowed me to feel peace in my heart.

There is so much we can learn from John Titus. Through his willingness to mourn and feel pain and sorrow, he found his way to forgiveness. By being willing to feel the magnitude of despair, John experienced the power of God's love. If only for a moment, he experienced the divine presence where the purpose of his life became clear. This is the transformative power of forgiveness. By not letting anger and hate devour him, John grew in understanding and love. He had the courage to grieve and commit to inner healing. As a result, John knew that hatred and violence must be stopped to stop the suffering of all people and love was the only solution to ending violence.

Reaching into the Depth of Our Soul

All violence is a form of injustice. The fire of hatred and violence cannot be extinguished by adding more hatred and violence to the fire; it can only be extinguished with understanding and compassion. Without understanding, how can we feel compassion and begin to relieve great suffering? How do we gain understanding and insight to guide us through such incredibly challenging moments? To understand, we must find paths of communication that enable us to listen to those who desperately call for understanding—because such acts of violence are a desperate call for attention and help.

How can we listen in a calm and clear way so we don't immediately kill the chance for understanding to develop? We need to explore how to create the environment for deep listening to occur so that our response to the situation may arise out of calm and clear minds, just as Alicia's father and Violette did. Clarity is a great offering; to have compassion in such a situation is to perform a great act of forgiveness.

In order to change our perception of others we need to be willing to listen to and try to understand the "other." We have to be willing to hear pain and fear and to accept each other for who we are. Violette demonstrated this beautifully when she thought about the neighbor who wanted her and her family killed; she realized that if she were in his place, playing his role, and not aware of her divinity, she would have done the same thing. With this understanding, Violette was able to forgive. Only when we come together committed to understanding the psychological landscape of others and breaking down stereotypes and misperceptions, can healing take place. Only when we put ourselves in someone else's shoes can we open our heart to compassion and forgiveness. If we can think in terms of spiritual currency, of doing something for others, we will build trust with one another and a reconciliation process can begin that breaks the cycle of violence.

Being willing to see things differently is a gift we can give one another, but it can only happen if we have the courage to do our own soul-searching. This requires a willingness to put down our defenses and take a long, hard look at the guilt lying in the pit of our stomach instead of denying its existence. Healing guilt gives us the ability to see the situation clearly without distortions. Healing from traumatic wounds is not easy; we would much rather leave that work to someone else. *But our struggle to heal is itself healing.*

When we have done the hard work of reaching into the depths of our soul, speaking our truths, and hearing what needs to be said to one another, we need to ask ourselves whether we have the *willingness* to forgive. Violette had the willingness to forgive because she realized she would probably have responded very much like those who wanted her dead had if she were in a similar situation. John Titus had the willingness to forgive because he could feel the presence of goodness, truth, and love of so many people around him. With such love he did not want to be responsible for another father's grief in losing an innocent child. Compassion gave John new hope, which helped him see beyond the hateful act that took his daughter's life.

Are we committed to a healing process that recognizes our greater humanity—the good and bad in all of us—and allows us to move forward in an appropriate way to create mutual respect and understanding? If the answer is *no*, we have to see if those obstacles can be removed. If the answer is *yes*, we have willingness in our heart to move forward, we will be given what we need to keep us going in a positive direction. We will develop concrete responses that will be effective in healing the situation we face.

In healing the pain and suffering caused by another group, we need to look deeply and honestly at the circumstances that caused so much pain. If we are able to see the source of the suffering within ourselves and others, we can begin to unravel the cycle of hatred and violence. Without understanding, compassion is impossible. When you understand the suffering of others, you do not have to force yourself to feel compassion; the door of your heart naturally opens. We will have begun to create true national security when we define the greatness of our civilization not by military capability or the ability to inflict massive punishment, but by the ability to bring out the best in others and ourselves and by the quality of life we leave our children. We will have begun to create a better world when we commit ourselves and our resources to building a peaceful world with as much dedication as we have committed ourselves to war. We uphold humanity when we use our power to heal rather than conquer and when we measure success in terms of reverence for life. We will have created a safer world when we look out not for our self-interest but for the greater good of humanity.

12

The Power of Love

Yusuf Al-Azhari's Story

"Another opportunity was given you—as a favor and as a burden. The question is not: why did it happen this way, or where is it going to lead you, or what is the price you will have to pay. It is simply: **how** *are you making use of it. And about that there is only* **one** *who can judge."*

—DAG HAMMARSKJOLD, NOBEL PEACE PRIZE RECIPIENT

My Road to Forgiveness

THERE WAS ONE thing I knew, and that was that I was going to marry the best girl in town. I did find her. Her name was Kadija, and she was the Prime Minister's daughter. That's when it all began.

One would have never thought that such a happy occasion would be the setting for a very dark stage. After all, I came from a wealthy family and at the time my country got its independence in the early sixties, I was graduating from Mogadishu University with a degree in international law. I wanted to establish a secure life for myself, and soon I was married and leading a wonderful life.

As I look back on those days, and what was to come, I can't help but to wonder what was the deeper meaning in all of this. Being the son-in-law of the head of Somalia opened many doors for me. Eventually I was appointed senior diplomat in Bonn and then ambassador to Washington. One day, suddenly my world began to change. It was a Saturday morning when someone rang my office.

"Mr. Al-Azhari, I am very sorry to be telling you this," a stranger's voice said. "Did you receive any word from Mogadishu?"

"No?" I said, puzzled by the question.

"Your father-in-law has been shot!"

"What did you say?" I asked in total disbelief. "Did you say that the head of state has been shot?"

The stranger continued, "I think the bullet that hit him was a fatal one, and it has ended his life."

I was totally stunned. What was I to do? I called Prime Minister Mohammed Agi Ibrim Egal, who happened to be in Miami. We talked and realized that there would be a coup. We needed to get to Mogadishu immediately. Unfortunately, the state department was reluctant to help us and instead booked us on a Pan American flight to Rome. From there we flew to Mogadishu.

As Yusuf was telling me this story, the pain in his voice struck me. I could see in his eyes the anguish of losing his father-in-law and his beloved country and the fear he must have felt on his journey back to Somalia. I also saw a tenderness that I would come to understand only later in his story.

WHEN I ARRIVED in Mogadishu, I saw an entire city in chaos. Everywhere I looked I saw people roaming around the streets in shock, mourning the tragic death of a president. I, too, felt numbed. The funeral occurred on Monday. Tuesday morning, without warning, Mohammed Siad Barre came to power in a

Soviet-backed coup. Life as we knew it changed forever. Siad Barre suspended our constitution, the parliament, and all democratic systems and adopted scientific socialism, a form of communism found in the former Soviet Union. Our country was now facing one of the world's most oppressive regimes.

As soon as Siad Barre came into power, he declared emergency rule. Two weeks later, during the darkest time of the night, soldiers broke into my home, handcuffed and blindfolded me, and hauled me to prison. I was there for four months and seventeen days. Then one night while I was sleeping, the cell door suddenly opened. Totally startled, I realized soldiers were ordering me to collect my belongings. In a very rough manner they hurried me into a Land Rover. That night I was taken to a military camp to be trained for military combat and "reeducated" in the new system of scientific socialism.

Yusuf spent nine months in that military camp. After placing number one on the final exam, the army chief of staff boasted that communist ideology could change people from capitalists to socialists, on the assumption that "reeducation" exams could indicate that. Yet the military still felt the need to intimidate capitalistic ideologists, and therefore sent Yusuf to a labor farm. He spent nearly five months there before he was appointed Director General of the Ministry of Information and National Guidance. Yusuf held this post for two-and-a-half years, and when he did not produce what the government had expected, they transferred him to the diplomatic service of Nigeria. This set into motion a whole series of events that eventually would lead to his darkest night.

I WAS IN Nigeria when a delegation from the Soviet Union came to trade with the Nigerian government. The Soviet ambassador to Nigeria invited me to a reception to honor the delegation from the Soviet Union. During my conversation with some of the delegates, I became curious and asked:

"Why do you tell us that dealing with capitalism is evil, and you, yourself, come to the most capitalistic country in Africa?"

"We are coming here in order to sell our equipment to the Nigerians and to show them that our equipment is better than theirs," the ambassador replied curtly.

Recognizing the hypocrisy I asked, "Would you allow any African country that is under scientific socialism to trade with the capitalists?"

The ambassador gave a look of dismay and did not answer.

I was surprised two weeks later to receive a fax from my own government telling me to go back to Mogadishu for consultation. When I returned, the president told me that I was not allowed to return to Lagos. Instead, I was being transferred to the Ministry of Communication. I asked to at least go back and get my wife and children, close my accounts, and take leave from the head of state of Nigeria. I realized that something very strange was going on when my request was denied. The president finished by saying, "We will bring your wife and your children here, and we will write an apology to the head of state."

As instructed, Yusuf began his tenure as the Director General of Telecommunications. Immediately he noticed that the telephone system was very old and passed through Italy. Italy was relaying all calls from Somalia to the rest of the world. Yusuf wanted to modernize the system by establishing an earth station to link with a satellite with sixty lines coming in and sixty lines going out. He developed the idea and presented it to the president. The president seemed at that time to be very pleased with it and encouraged Yusuf to go ahead. A sound feasibility study was conducted, and Yusuf consulted with some Western countries that helped finance the project. Both England and Italy accepted the offer and earmarked a substantial amount of money. Yusuf consulted again with the president who was then ready to publish a tender to construct the earth station. He authorized Yusuf to draft a letter to be signed for the go-ahead.

Yusuf told me that during the time these plans were being made Russian experts were in the ministry. After they heard that Italy and England would link Somalia with the American satellite, they went to the minister of defense, a devoted Communist. They told him that the CIA had infiltrated the ministry of telecommunications and posted a man, the director general, whom they were using as a spy. They construed that the CIA wanted to monitor the conversations of Breshnev and Siad Barre, the head of state.

I RECEIVED A call late at night from the president. He seemed vague about the project. I had to remind him about our conversation. Then the president asked:

"Oh, is this the one linking us up with the American satellites?"

I was perplexed by his question and answered, "Yes because there is no other satellite. Although it belongs to the Americans the whole world uses it, even the Russians."

There was silence for a moment and then he said, "OK, come back tomorrow."

"All right," I murmured.

Yusuf went back early the next morning. The president was sleeping because of a fitful night. So Yusuf met with him later. The president again asked Yusuf to draft a letter authorizing him to develop the tender for the earth station. Yusuf was very pleased. The president asked Yusuf to bring him the letter around 9 P.M. He went home quickly. By 5 P.M., Yusuf was in his office trying to draft the letter. An hour later, two soldiers knocked at his door. Yusuf told them to sit down and continued to write the letter. After a few moments, Yusuf asked them what they wanted.

"We were sent by the party officials at the ministry who would like to ask you some questions."

A bit annoyed, Yusuf answered, "Tonight I have an appointment with the head of state. Can't this wait until tomorrow?"

"No," they insisted. "It will only take five minutes and we were told that you should go to the office now."

Hesitantly, Yusuf agreed. "You go ahead and I will take my car."

"Why spend money on petrol, we have a car, come with us," they argued.

When they insisted, Yusuf said OK. He locked the door, left the air conditioning on, and went with them. When they reached the office of the party, Yusuf was taken to a sitting room. When the soldiers left, they locked the door from the outside. First Yusuf thought that maybe they didn't want anyone to see him. The hour ticked up. It was seven, then eight, then almost nine o'clock. Yusuf knocked at the door very strongly because he was concerned about the meeting with the president. At 9:30, the door opened. There were six soldiers holding handcuffs. Finally, the head of the party also appeared. He ushered Yusuf into another room and told him that the meeting with the president was postponed until 9 A.M. tomorrow. Then he said to go home.

Yusuf half-suspected something and decided to speak to the president. The president told him that there was a delegation with him and that he was sorry to cancel the meeting. He asked if Yusuf would come back in the morning, so Yusuf went home. With a chill in his voice, Yusuf continued his story.

AROUND 3 A.M. while sleeping with my loved ones, soldiers busted into my home. They broke down the front door, and they came into my bedroom. I was stunned. I was yelling, "What's wrong, what's wrong?" My children were crying. There were eight soldiers and a sergeant. They immediately handcuffed me, blindfolded me, and put me into a Land Rover. Off they went without saying anything to my wife or children. They drove me 378 kilometers. Finally they stopped. I was taken from the car and led by two soldiers holding my arms. I was thrown into a small cell four by three meters with two doors. They uncovered my eyes but kept the handcuffs on. I was left like that for the remainder of the night.

In the morning, the soldiers returned with something to eat. Yusuf was so bewildered and outraged that he started demanding answers to his many questions.

"Why did you put me here? Why did you handcuff me?"

They would not answer.

Yusuf was filled with contempt and anger. What he really wanted was revenge. After Yusuf ate, they handcuffed him again. He was kept this way for three days. Every time Yusuf saw the soldiers he was so angry he spit on them. They too spit on Yusuf, beat him, insulted him, and physically and mentally tortured him. For forty-eight days he was handcuffed. During this time, the tight handcuffs scarred and infected his left hand. The infection was growing day by day. The swelling became so bad that Yusuf's front arm was as big as his thigh. He developed a high fever. Not knowing what to do, the soldiers poured cold water all over him. When Yusuf woke up the so-called doctor had arrived. He said to Yusuf:

"You are finished! The infection went too far. We have to amputate your left arm."

Yusuf shouted back, "If I am dying, I will die with my whole body. No one is amputating anything. Just take this handcuff off."

The cuff was completely covered with blood and pus.

The doctor shrugged and said, "You will die anyway."

He pulled off the cuff in such a painful way that everything spattered out until there was only red blood. By the grace of God the infection was squeezed out of Yusuf's arm. Yusuf fainted.

Later the doctor refused to give Yusuf medication to help heal the infection. It was clear to him that the authorities wanted him dead, disabled, or insane. Every day he tried to wash and move his wounded arm, but there was a more terrible disease growing inside of him. It was the disease of hatred and contempt. Yusuf wanted to kill anyone who came into his room. Then in a gentle voice Yusuf began to describe a mystical experience.

ONE NIGHT AFTER saying my prayers, I felt something that I cannot explain. Something inside me was saying that if I continued this way I might really die, become disabled, or even insane. What I felt was so strong that I fell to my knees and prayed from the depths of my heart sincerely wanting to reconcile with almighty God. I asked that if I was misled to please forgive me and help me make peace with my captors. I recognized that I must have done something very terrible to be in a situation like this and prayed for forgiveness. I asked to be granted inner peace and to be released from the torment of hate and depression. And, I prayed that if this was God's will that I be in this situation, I accept this too. I read verses from the Koran with conviction and commitment, wanting to receive him through his messages and visions.

As though suspended in time, Yusuf thought he was somewhere else and not in that cell. Physically he may have been there, but spiritually he was in a different place. Yusuf glanced at his watch and to his amazement it was 4 A.M. Then very quietly Yusuf continued his amazing story.

I FELT AS though a cool breeze was passing through my heart, washing away the strong negative emotions. Everything seemed to be evaporating as though something was leaving my body. I felt like a light being, filled with joy and mercy. I immediately repented for acting so arrogantly toward the soldiers and the guards who came in to torture and insulted me. I asked myself, "Why did I ever react like this? They were only being sent by someone to do a job. There was nothing between them and me." I understood that to fulfill what they had to do for survival, they were ordered to do this by the authorities who had put me in these circumstances. This idea repeatedly came into my mind and made me repent for provoking them and reacting that way.

Yusuf's mystical experience filled him with an all-encompassing love that had a profound healing effect. He was beginning to walk down the road of forgiveness and of inner peace. Yusuf realized that much of his pain came from his mistaken interpretation of reality. Yusuf was able to say to himself that these soldiers had a job to do. They too were part of a sick system. The soldiers' survival was dependent on their doing what they were told to do and had nothing to do with who Yusuf was as a person. When Yusuf could acknowledge this, his behavior toward the soldiers changed, and the soldiers' behavior changed as well.

THE NEXT MORNING when my tormentors came, I was filled with joy and feeling very light. When they opened the door, I saluted them with a peace greeting. I called them my brothers. They looked at me and immediately ran away to report to their superior that I might be crazy. The soldiers came back to see me two hours later. Again I saluted and told them not to be afraid. I told them that I knew and understood in order not to be punished that they had to do what they had been ordered to do. They were surprised and deeply touched. The torture that day was lighter than on the previous day.

From that day forward, Yusuf structured his days. He developed a program that began with early morning prayers. Following his prayers, Yusuf exercised by jogging in place for a half-hour to regain his health. Then he took a shower followed by breakfast. After breakfast, Yusuf reviewed the wrongs he felt he did going back to the earliest times he could remember. He asked, "Was I loyal and good to my family and my wife? Was I a devoted and faithful person in my moral values? Did I infringe on any person's prerogatives and rights? Did I embezzle money from my government or cheat my government." He truthfully looked at all aspects of his life regardless of how painful the issues were. This continued until lunch came. Then Yusuf rested for an hour and a half. He became friends with all of God's creatures in his room such as the ants and cockroaches. He learned to appreciate how a spider moves and creates its web. Yusuf's love for animals began in this room.

Then Yusuf looked at himself again. This time he would acknowledge the good things he had done. Yusuf would check his motivations to see if he was acting from the bottom of his heart or for his own glory and benefit. He looked at every situation very carefully and with complete honesty. Some of it was very ugly and very bitter.

Yusuf agonized over some of his issues. Yet it is only with openness and honesty that we come to know and forgive ourselves. When we can do that we no longer need others to become victims to our ugliness and pain. Working through our guilt is the essence of the forgiveness process. *To forgive we need to deeply know ourselves.* Unless we know ourselves, we will never understand others. Everything starts with us. We criticize and see the wrongs of others, but it is very difficult to examine ourselves and see our faults and difficulties.

Yusuf ate dinner around 5 P.M. Then he spent the evening in prayer. He prayed about many things with all his heart, especially to know God. Only when we are so lonely and feeling so helpless are we so desirous of Him. When we experience God, the mystical quality of our experience cannot be explained. Yusuf experienced this primordial essence, and the awesome power of all its glory and purity. It helped him to accept his circumstances, for he was filled with His love. Yusuf was granted inner peace in knowing that his wife and children were in good hands. He knew God was taking care of them. He had no illusion about that. Yusuf also knew that God was preparing him for something far greater than he could imagine. There was an important and good purpose for why he needed to be placed in this circumstance. From the day Yusuf heard God's voice, he vowed that he would dedicate the rest of his life to the spirit of God's guidance.

This shift in consciousness can come only when we have profoundly experienced our spiritual nature. Yusuf's mystical experience brought him to a different realm of experience and "knowing." His spiritual vision was being reawakened.

Finally, after six years and seventeen days, Yusuf's captors released him. Siad Barre virtually lost all his power and soon after was evicted from his own country. The army was in disarray with a civil war on the horizon. The first thing Yusuf did upon being released was to find his family. He went to the house he used to live in only to find out that it had been sold by the government. Yusuf asked his neighbors if they knew what had happened to his family and eventually found out where they were. He shared with me those anxious moments.

I LOCATED THE house and knocked at the front door. After a few minutes, my beloved wife answered the door. I remember that moment so vividly for my heart was racing with so much excitement. As my wife laid her eyes upon me, she fainted. She was so shocked to see me. She barely recognized me. Kadija had never seen me so thin with such a long beard and clothes torn to pieces. I nursed her for a week to help her overcome the shock. When she could finally pull herself together, she explained that years ago she was told I was dead. She explained that when I was taken away and put in prison she tried to find me and went to every police station in the city. A week after the arrest two military men came to my house and told my wife I was killed while escaping.

As I think about this now, I look upon this event as a blessing in disguise. If my family had known that for six years I was being held in a place where I had been tortured daily—not dead, yet barely alive—the psychological impact would have lead to anger and hate. My wife and children would have suffered greatly. Their lives would have been frozen in time. Instead they mourned. They expressed their pain and suffering with the support of loved ones. They accepted their fate and then were able to continue their life without me.

After the family was reunited, Yusuf committed himself to being a positive force in his country. Civil war broke out, and Siad Barre went into exile. Yusuf began working with other compatriots in mediating and establishing peace among the warring class. Once again soldiers apprehended him, and his compatriots and took them all to a mass grave outside of Mogadishu to murder them. Three survived. Yusuf was shot four times in his leg, and the other two survivors were severely wounded in their stomachs and shoulders. Once their assailants left them for dead they dragged themselves out of the pit and struggled to safety.

After two weeks of medical treatment, Yusuf continued his work. The bullets lodged in his thigh gave him problems in walking, but somehow he managed. Yusuf decided to send his family to Canada to prevent them from being caught between the fires of war. Yusuf chose to stay for he felt it was his calling to help his people.

A year later while in prayer, Yusuf heard an inner voice telling him that he had an unfinished job to do. Yusuf said that his first reaction was disbelief and then recounted the next part of the story.

WHILE IN PRAYER I clearly heard, "Why don't you forgive that man?" I thought this was just my imagination and pushed it out of my mind. Yet the thought kept coming back. I said to myself to forgive whom? Was I to forgive the person who assassinated my father-in-law and who put me in that prison to see me rot, die, or become insane? Is this the devil putting ideas in my head or is this something else? The idea continued to torment me and became most intense after prayers. I needed to ask for guidance and so one morning I got up at five o'clock, started to pray, and sat for one hour in silence asking for help from almighty God. It became clear to me that I was to forgive that man. I accepted.

Siad Barre was now living in Nigeria. It was a seven-hour flight from Mogadishu to Nigeria. He had confiscated all Yusuf's money in the banks, auctioned his property, and made him the poorest man in Somalia. Yusuf was left with nothing. How could Yusuf go and tell Siad Barre that *he forgave him*! God certainly does work in mysterious ways. When Yusuf finally in his heart forgave Siad Barre, something miraculous happened. Within a few days Yusuf received a call from the United Nations office in Mogadishu. He was told that three compatriots and he were chosen to represent Somalia at the Organization of African Unity Summit Conference that was being held in Dakar, Senegal. There was the ticket he was looking for. All he would have to do would be to break the journey in Lagos and contact the ministry of foreign affairs concerning the location of the former president of Somalia. Yusuf continued his story.

WHEN I ARRIVED in Lagos, I discovered that the former president was under house arrest. There were several policemen at his front door, not allowing him to come out. I showed them that I was sent by the ministry of foreign affairs and was allowed in. When he saw me he asked me if I was not Dr. Yusuf Al-Azhari.

"Yes, I am," surprised that he recognized me.

"What brought you here?" he responded.

"I came all the way from Mogadishu to see you and for nothing else except to *forgive you* before you or I die."

As I spoke, I could see the astonishment in his eyes. He was so tormented inside. Eventually I could see the tears of remorse running down his face. Then I thanked the almighty God who had helped me to reach this holy place in my heart. When he finally got hold of himself he said, "Thank you, you have cured me. I can sleep tonight knowing that people like you still exist among the Somalis."

Now I am a self-appointed peacemaker and reconciler in Somalia. The vision and guidance of the almighty God enables me to be where I am needed, where the helpless need courage, and where love can dispel the darkness. Love has been planted in my heart. I vowed in prison to serve my fellow countrymen and women. I vowed to reconcile their differences with compassion and forgiveness. I am finally in a position where I can help my people.

Justice Through the Eye of Forgiveness

After Yusuf finished telling me his entire story, I was particularly struck by his sense of justice. After all, so many horrific events had occurred in his life that caused him a great deal of suffering. Yusuf grieved over his father-in-law's death, which led to him being imprisoned twice where he was tortured and beaten. He lost a highly respected position that, literally overnight, almost cost him his life. Yusuf escaped death again, being left for dead in a pit filled with dead bodies. He ultimately asked his loved ones to leave the country for their own protection while he stayed on to help rebuild it out of the dust of civil war. And never once did he speak of revenge. What Yusuf saw was that we all needed healing, and he chose to see the issue of justice through those eyes.

Many of us would probably not have survived this ordeal, and we would have certainly struggled with the idea of forgiveness. Yet through his ordeal, Yusuf not only learned about forgiveness but he also learned about justice in a way most of us are incapable of thinking about. He was able to see justice through the eyes of forgiveness because of his experiences. These are some of the thoughts Yusuf shared with me.

> JUSTICE IN TERMS of human beings can never prevail and have honest roots unless it is coupled with the knowledge of our spiritual essence. Most of the people in this world, especially leaders in Africa, do not know the meaning of justice. They think justice is a dictatorship and obedience. It is only through the reinstitution of moral values and the faith in our primordial essence that a person could know the true meaning of justice. Justice is based on true honesty, love, and forgiveness, because if we worked in accordance with spiritual laws, then we would know the meaning of love in accordance to the spirit of God and could forgive. If we know the rewards of forgiveness in accordance of the spirit of the almighty creator then we could care. If we cared then we could make this world a better place to live in. Unless you have the commitment and conviction of the guidance of the spiritual essence deep within your heart you will never know what justice means, *never!*

I was very touched by his words, and I thought hard about the true meaning of justice. What does justice look like through the eyes of forgiveness, and was Yusuf right? If for a moment we consider that true forgiveness is the dispelling of illusions that then enable us to recognize the indwelling spirit in all of us, then it follows that true justice permits us to see situations that we would normally judge as having victims and victimizers as situations that provide opportunities to learn of our greater humanity. As Yusuf realized, people would not oppress, victimize, or even murder unless they felt impoverished, guilty, or vulnerable within themselves. Outer acts of violence and injustices are the projections of interior guilt and fear. True justice recognizes that all people must be looked upon as the same because of this. Therefore, the arms of justice must embrace each one in forgiveness, not for the seemingly terrible things that we have done, but to undo the fear and guilt that underlies them. Justice does not punish one because another might feel justified. This is revenge.

True justice enables us to perceive acts of violence as frightening calls for help. When we understand this we can no longer see the perpetrator of injustice as evil or sinful. Indeed, many of the individuals in this book have recognized that when we experience the unconditional love of the source of our creation, we realize that the perpetrator is also loved by God and deserves this love, regardless of his or her actions. When we feel the love coming from within the depths of our being, we only want to demonstrate this love to those who do not know it. This does not mean that we necessarily approve of the actions of the perpetrator or oppressor, but merely that we expand the circle of help to include among those who suffer, the ones who seem to bring it about. This is the meaning of true justice. Yusuf continued.

WE SHOULD NEVER wait for any reciprocation. An honest man and pure man never waits for any reward or reciprocation of anything. We are all the images of God—and God is glory, merciful, compassionate, peaceful, loving, forgiving, and caring. Still there are those who do not believe in Him. He doesn't expect anything from them. His glory will not be diminished because someone doesn't believe in Him. A pure man should meditate and be at the footsteps of God. No one should expect any rewards or reciprocity from another human being. He has to do what he is committed to do and that is the essence of forgiveness itself. So many people have asked me what to do when they argue with their friends. I tell them that they will be doubly glorified if they can forgive because the hatred that was in you has left and you are now a free person. They will be the prisoners, but you will never be the prison because you have opened the door and God will reward you even better.

Forgiveness has become a part of my life. I can't live without it. We are all human beings and have weaknesses. To help one another heal those weaknesses is what forgiveness is about. Once forgiveness is planted in your heart, it is there forever. By living a life of forgiveness, hatred will never come to your mind. If you don't hold hatred in your heart, you can begin to grow in compassion. Forgiveness should be part and parcel of everyone's life. It is for me. It is a sacred moment when we can truly forgive one another.

13

A Justice That Heals

"The mark of your ignorance is the depth of your belief in injustice and tragedy. What the caterpillar calls the end of the world, the master calls a butterfly."

—RICHARD BACH, WRITER

So OFTEN WHEN we hear the word "justice" or the phrase "justice is served" we assume that something rightful has taken place. But is handing down a death sentence for a murder always rightful? Many people think so and consider it justice, but is this the true meaning of justice? If an individual's definition of justice is predicated upon his or her perception and beliefs about the world, and if each of us has different perceptions, how accurate can that definition of justice be?

A justice that heals is based on the premise that when we perceive evil in others we recognize that whatever act is committed "in the name of that evil" is done out of woundedness and/or fear and is a call for help. *As one learns to forgive and cleanse perceptions from guilt, true justice becomes possible.* Many of our storytellers have demonstrated this. A prime example is Azim Khamisa who, instead of seeking revenge, created the Tariq Khamisa Foundation. Azim understood that his son's assailant, Tony, was a troubled soul who needed help. Yes, Tony needed to be held accountable for his crime and is serving time for it, but he also needed the opportunity to heal his pain and guilt.

What do we need to do to base our decisions on true justice? First we need to recognize that much of our thinking is based in illusion that clouds our judgment. For example, many of us believe that our problems are caused because of something outside of ourselves, such as another person. We are hard-pressed to recognize that our own fears, needs, guilt, and so on are what give meaning to the outside event. We focus on what is happening *outside* of us so we can deny what is really going on *inside* of us. By focusing outside of ourselves, we obscure the true source of the problem, which involves our thinking. We are now stuck in a thought process that keeps us very restricted in the way we see the world. It is a thought process based on our perceptions that we believe are fact. This is how we begin to judge the world and determines how we view justice.

How does this relate to issues of justice? We tend to judge problems that we see in the world as awful rather than recognizing that those problems are cries for help. There would not be abuse or violence if people were healthy and whole within themselves. We also view this world through our personal lenses that are colored by our personal traumatic experiences. Yet as the psychological axiom states, *all that is too painful for us to see and acknowledge about ourselves we see in others.* This is true on an individual level as well as with groups. In our pain, we become blind, and we can't see ourselves or what we do to others. Or, we split ourselves in half, seeing only what we want to see about ourselves and dumping what we don't want to see on someone else. We now have created a dichotomy in the world of "good guys" and "bad guys," "victims" and "victimizers," the former group being the innocent ones subjected to harmful words or actions by the latter group.

This kind of thinking is represented by what Jungian psychology calls the "false" self. We see the world through very limited vision based on whatever is negative within ourselves. When we are able to step out of this kind of thinking, and that is what being able to forgive teaches us, then we can begin to see with a wiser and more mature vision. Only then are we able to see that expressions of anger and violence are actually cries for help. There is a shift in our thinking and a change in consciousness; we now have the ability to step out of this thought system and see the world through different, more compassionate lenses.

Our view of injustice changes as we transform our thinking. We realize that what we see in this world is a question of perception, not the situation itself. We can choose to see the world through the eyes of anger, guilt, and fear, or through the eyes of compassion and understanding. For Yusuf Al-Azhari, this shift happened when the soldiers entered his cell and began torturing him. When the shift in his thinking occurred, Yusuf first asked himself, "Why did I ever react like this? They were only being sent to do a job. There was nothing between them and me." Instead of seeing these soldiers through the eyes of anger and despair, Yusuf understood that the soldiers needed to obey orders to survive and that they were put there by the authorities. When Yusuf could acknowledge his different perception of the soldiers' actions toward him, his behavior toward the soldiers changed and the soldiers' behavior changed toward him as well. The severity of Yusuf's torture was lessened.

To understand true justice more fully, we need to understand the elements of injustice. The first element deals with how we use our anger. Anger directed toward others often indicates our attempt to change someone else's behavior so we do not have to deal with our own shortcomings. We can make someone feel guilty through our anger to try to stop or change their behavior as well. Very often we use our anger in the name of justice because we are unwilling to look at the situation differently or we want to control the situation believing our judgment is right. We use our anger toward the perpetrator in the name of justice because we automatically believe that the perpetrator is bad and should be punished.

If on the other hand we recognize that the injustice that was done comes from fear we can recognize that the person committing the act needs our help. Azim Khamisa demonstrated this when he spoke of victims at both ends of the gun when his son was murdered. What is important here is the way we think about the situation. We do not refrain from taking action to stop an injustice or approve the actions of a victimizer. We recognize that what is happening is a call for help. The help includes expanding your understanding of those in need of help to include those who suffer, and those causing the suffering. If we are unwilling to include the perpetrator in the circle of healing for those needing help, then perhaps there still exists an unconscious need to find a scapegoat to place our own guilt.

The Meaning of Injustice

Our understanding of injustice changes when we experience forgiveness at deeper levels. There is a shift in our thinking because we recognize how we have been defending ourselves at the expense of others. We realize that we aren't so "innocent" either and that through *our* healing we come to understand that if we lived under circumstances similar to those of our perpetrators, we might have behaved similarly. We learn to respect the humanness that connects all of us to each other. Forgiveness at a transformational level serves as a catalyst that helps us break through our personal barriers and lifts the veil of illusions. The depth of wisdom gained by our self-examination enables us to see beyond our personal pain to include the suffering of others who may have offended us. This is the miracle we talked about earlier when there is a shift in our thinking from condemning someone to seeing through the eyes of compassion. When we are able to embrace the suffering of our enemy, a shift in our thinking about injustice takes place. The more we are willing to acknowledge and understand why we and others behave the way we do, and open up our hearts to the human condition, the more likely we will understand the meaning of true justice.

When we hear of injustice, whether it involves ourselves, significant others, or people living in foreign countries, we judge the person or situations negatively and in the name of justice demand some form of punishment. What we actually are saying is that people should not hurt others because it makes *us* angry, and we do not approve of it or them. Because the actions are "evil," the people committing them also must be evil. They can be accepted only if they stop what they are doing. Therefore, once the perception of injustice is made, no alternative can follow but that of a judgment that subtly sets up the conditions of what they, the "evildoers," must do to be accepted. Either people behave in accordance with our values, or they are denied acceptance. This is an example of the arrogance of the ego. We presume to absolutely know what is right and best.

If, on the other hand, we understand and acknowledge that acts of injustice arise from woundedness and/or fear, we will recognize that injustice is not necessarily coming from a place of evil. Rather it is the result of things done to others, whether on an individual or societal level, that have created frustration and anger or pain leading perhaps to twisted thinking and acting out. If we can come from a place of wholeness within ourselves, then we also can realize that all people are worthy of being loved, regardless of their actions. A loving person would *especially* want to demonstrate love to those deprived of it. This kind of thinking, motivated by compassion and not anger, will help us determine what kind of action to take. The actions we take might be the same in either case, but those motivated by compassion will have a greater impact. Again, this is not about whether to act or not but about the kind of thinking that is motivating our behavior. We have choices when it comes to thinking about any given situation. When our actions are motivated by revenge then what follows may be equally as unjust. When our actions are motivated by compassion we are recognizing the importance of expanding the circle of help to include not only those who suffer but also those who seem to have caused the suffering.

Irene Laure is an example of someone who was able to see beyond her pain and acknowledge the suffering of others. She was able to extend healing not only to the victims but also to whom she once saw as the perpetrators of unthinkable crimes. Instead of wanting to destroy the German people, she wanted to build up the morale of those same Germans. Irene dedicated the rest of her life to building bridges between the French and Germans. She made frequent trips to Germany especially to help build the morale of the German women with whom she now felt a special bond.

The Meaning of True Justice

What is the meaning of true justice? True justice is remembering that there is a creative intelligence within all of us, despite the negative acts dictated by our egos, and acting accordingly. True justice can separate out where the woundedness is and what would be most healing for all parties concerned. The face of true justice looks on all people as the same and recognizes that each of the many forms of fear conceals the same meaning. The arms of justice extend to embrace everyone in forgiveness—not for the seemingly terrible things that were done but to undo the fear and guilt that underlie them. When we see the world in terms of injustice, we are labeling situations in terms of innocent victims and evil perpetrators. In following the path of true justice, we can see the same situation as an opportunity to learn of our greater humanity. The more we are able to respond from our higher nature, the more capable we will be to move beyond *our* fears. If we have the courage to face our pain and learn what it has to teach us, then it can guide us to heal the most fragile segments of our society and the most devastated wounds in our soul. When we come from a place of spiritual strength, then we can address the more practical questions of what we are to do in the face of attack and suffering. The answer will always be based upon a desire to help all those concerned. The focus is not on what we do, but why. What motivates us becomes fundamental.

For example, you are home alone at night when suddenly a stranger breaks into your home, grabs you, and holds a knife at your throat. There are basically two ways to respond, out of either compassion or fear. Coming from a place of spiritual strength does not mean that we do not take action to physically defend ourselves. Clearly we would take action to stop the assailant and to prevent this person from committing a crime that would manifest as more unconscious guilt. Yet regardless of the actions the person shares our humanity. We have to be very careful not to project our guilt onto other people, regardless of their appearance, in our attempts to facilitate true justice.

Psychologist Kenneth Wapnick in his book *Forgiveness and Jesus* (1983) has this to say about justice.

Our response to injustice is one of love and concern, not fear or desire for revenge. We "protect" ourselves, not to punish or because we are frightened, but because we wish to help all who are present in the situation. We have heard our "assailants" call and seek to answer; our attitude of non-attack teaches they are loved even as they sought to hate. The judgment we make in this situation, therefore, is not based on condemnation but on a desire to help, seeing in the others' attack their need for love. Self-protection in this context becomes more than a defense against attack. It has become a loving response to a call for love that we share. It should be added that we need not feel this love totally. To be completely without fear would involve a level of sanctity few if any of us have attained. If our love was that perfect, we would not need Heaven's aid. Thus our simple desire to see the situation differently, despite our fear, is enough to allow the Holy Spirit to work through us.

Painful experiences can be our greatest learning opportunities. This is especially true when we are practicing true justice based in forgiveness. This form of justice does not focus on the pain that was endured but on the perception that there is nothing to forgive. We see the situation with spiritual eyes and see the situation in a different light. This can happen only when *our* guilt has been healed and thus we have no need to place unconscious guilt on someone else. When this is the case we don't place all those negatives we unconsciously think about ourselves on someone else. As a result we view the perpetrator in a different light. If we don't place our negative thoughts or guilt on the perpetrator then we are more likely to see this person as needing help. Forgiveness gets us to this place of understanding. Forgiveness helps us recognize our common humanity. Forgiveness enables our minds to be healed.

There is one additional point I would like to make concerning the issue of justice. Our perceptions can easily become distorted, especially when we assume we know what is best. It is easy to spot the injustices in this world. Once we have identified injustices we feel that we know how to deal with them. We think we know what is best in any given situation and are the ones to teach "lessons" to others. This is our arrogant ego speaking again. How can we know what is best for others especially when it is impossible to be totally aware of everything that has happened to that person—past, present, or future? In order to judge a situation correctly, we would have to make sure our perceptions are not distorted so that our judgments would be fair to everyone. No human being can possibly be in a position to do this. To think that we can is truly arrogant, and it is easy to cloak our arrogance in the name of justice. We need only to think about how much blood has been spilled in the name of God to realize that this is so.

Related to this is the issue of suffering. Suffering is based in perception and believing you are stuck in the victim role. We strongly believe that suffering is the effect of what has been done to us: that our pain is the result of causes beyond our control. People do suffer unjustly experiencing psychological and physical pain yet beyond this level of pain is another level of which we are very much unaware. This deeper pain comes from how we have interpreted our reality. It comes from our strong identification with that part of ourselves that is hooked into a very limited way of thinking and not from a place of psychological and spiritual maturity. Although people and circumstances can create situations that lead to suffering, our thoughts and beliefs are also creating our pain that we alone are totally responsible for. Only you can affect yourself.

Suffering is the *effect* of our belief in the ego or false self, which is its *cause*. Thus, whenever we choose to identify the cause of our suffering as external to us—be it another's attack, the cruel vagaries of fate, or the injustices done to us in the past—we are falling into the ego's trap of denying the true cause of our problems, the ego itself. Healing, whether individual or social, that does not have as its ultimate aim the reawakening of the spiritual self will eventually fail. Therefore, when we react to suffering we should not focus on another's weakness. Rather, we should unite with the strength, the spiritual essence that is in all of us. If we don't, then we are uniting with someone's form of darkness rather than the light of the spirit that always shines. In practicing true empathy, we are identifying with another's compassion and strength, the light of the soul, rather than with one's cruelty and weakness, the darkness of the soul (Wapnick, 1983).

How do we practice true justice? We heal our guilt, which is not only an attack on ourselves, but also what keeps us from hearing the voice of a higher consciousness. As long as guilt continues to plague our minds, it also makes it impossible to see the light of that self in others. Attacking someone, no matter how justified it seems, is nothing more than projecting our guilt. We conceal the voice of wisdom by our cloud of guilt. Only when we see someone else's attack as a call for help coming from a place of *their weakness*, will we be able to forgive and see the situation through the eyes of true justice.

14

With Love We Can Heal the Future

John Plummer's Story

"We cannot change history, but together we can go forward and do good for the world to promote peace."

—Kim Phuc

IT WAS VIETNAM 1972. A young army captain coordinated a napalm bomb-drop over a village in South Vietnam. A firestorm of napalm is captured on film, and an image is frozen in history. This image of a nine-year-old girl running naked and in terror from her Vietnamese village burning from napalm fire became the catalyst for what is to follow. John Plummer was the young army captain responsible for coordinating the napalm attack. The nine-year-old girl was Kim Phuc. This is John's story of his healing and his search for forgiveness. It is one of the stories behind the picture that touched the world.

John Plummer's Story

John was raised very close to Fort Bragg. The military was a viable alternative to going to college, particularly for those children whose parents could not afford to send them to college. John joined the National Guard while still in high school and four days after graduation went off into the army. When he arrived in Vietnam in April 1969, John was twenty-one years old and the father of three.

> MILITARY ACTIVITY WAS no stranger to me. Where I come from in rural North Carolina is a very patriotic area. We're people of the soil, linked to the very basic values of our country. I liked it in the army. The discipline didn't bother me because my father, an ex-first sergeant from World War II, brought me up with that same kind of disciplining. It was a time in our country when the army presented tremendous opportunities.

To give you an example of one of these opportunities, John told me how he was standing in formation one day when the first sergeant announced that people were needed to attend officer candidate school. John volunteered and became commissioned as second lieutenant when he was nineteen years old. You did not need a college education, only a clean record and a desire to make a career out of the army.

John exuded warmth as we talked about his experiences. He spoke with a kindness that comes only from someone who has gone through great pain and made peace with it in his heart. As he told me his story, I could not even imagine the torment he must have gone through. John continued.

> IT WAS A very uneventful day in June of 1972. I was the Assistant G-3 Air for the Third Regional Assistance Command, part of the Military Assistance Advisory, Vietnam. Part of my job was coordinating preplanned and immediate air strikes for III Corps. On this particular afternoon, I received a call from an American advisor with a South Vietnamese unit that was pinned down and

unable to make progress against an enemy force in the village of Trang Bang, northwest of Cu Chi along Highway 1. I knew there was a battle going on out there, but it surprised me that the American advisor was requesting air support. He requested an immediate air strike against the enemy unit that he said were in bunkers and trenches on the outskirts of the village. We had a list of air support on standby. I turned to that list and knew exactly what I wanted as far as the munitions. I wanted napalm and high explosives because they were both very effective against dug-in troops. I went down the hall to the air force desk and told the U.S. Air Force coordinator to scramble the standby aircraft. I checked with the advisor to inquire about the location of the civilians in the area before I determined the target coordinates. I saw that the coordinates were on the very edge of the village. We had target clearance requirements. We were not allowed to bomb within a certain distance of friendly troops or villages. I asked at that time if there were any "friendlies" in the area. The advisor said no, that all the villagers had gone. So I took the actions to get the aircraft in the air, but I told the air force officer not to release the planes until I double-checked to make sure that there were no "friendlies" there. I then called the district HQ to confirm and was again told that the area was clear of civilians. The target area was inhabited only by main force VC military units. I released the planes to make their attack and went forward with the air strikes. We got word that the mission was successful and that all the targets were destroyed. Everything went as normal so I did not give the day any more thought.

The next day as I walked into the mess hall, I picked up a copy of the *Stars and Stripes* newspaper for military forces in Vietnam. I was shocked to see the now-famous photograph on the front page. The graphic nature of the photograph took my breath away. Seeing the little girl naked and running in fear, the little boy with his face contorted in screams, and the napalm smoke in the background ripped me apart. As I read the caption, I discovered to my horror that the little girl was from Trang Bang. My knees nearly gave way as I realized she had been hit with the napalm I had coordinated the day before. Her name was Kim Phuc, and her photograph was indelibly burned into my heart and soul. It haunted me for many years. My heart was wracked with remorse at the realization that it was I who was responsible for her injuries, and it was I who had sent the bombs into her village. That is when my life began to fall apart.

When I saw the photograph at that time I was so confused by what had happened and what I had been a part of that it took awhile for me to sort out any kind of solution. I began to have nightmares from seeing that photograph almost immediately. That is when I started to drink more. I would go to bed at night and wake up with a nightmare. The nightmare was always the same. It was simply that black-and-white photograph except that in the nightmare I could hear the screams. The screams would wake me up. But if I drank enough to pass out, then I would not have the nightmares. That is why I drank. I knew exactly what I was doing. I was able to function at work and luckily I wasn't thinking about this twenty-four hours a day, but I became much more careful about observing target clearances. I felt very responsible for what happened. That in itself became an issue. People told me that I shouldn't feel responsible. I did everything I could to clear the strike. Well, they are probably right. Yet I still felt responsible. I have come to understand that it's not the incident that precipitates feelings that are important, it's the feelings themselves. That has been very helpful to me in counseling other people. I didn't feel guilt because I knew I was doing my job. What I did feel was tremendous remorse. That child was hurt as a result of something I was involved in. In war you expect to kill people, and you expect people to be killed. That is the horrible nature of war, but you are never prepared for civilian casualties, especially children casualties. Having three children of my own, I related so closely to that little girl.

I finished the remaining five months of my tour and came back to the States. I never knew that that photograph had appeared anywhere other than in the *Stars and Stripes* newspaper.

Therefore, it was a shock to me when in the spring of 1973 *Life* magazine ran an article about Vietnam and had that photograph in it. It startled me that the photograph became so famous, that the incident itself became so famous, and that people around the world were familiar with that photograph. I guess at that time I went underground as far as that incident was concerned. I shared with very few people my involvement in that.

This was something that I was not proud of. So I turned it all in toward myself. The problem with that is that I couldn't share my feelings, and I didn't want people sharing feelings with me either. I felt that if anybody shared their feelings with me I would be responsible for them, and I knew that I wasn't very good with responsibility.

In 1974, a year and a half after I came back from Vietnam, the army was cutting back on soldiers. Since I did not have a college education, I was kicked out. I was a flight instructor at that time in Alabama but because of the cutback I was going to lose the career that I loved very much. On top of everything else, I felt that I did not measure up as a soldier and felt like a failure. It was a very bad scene and a really difficult time. Even though I was able to procure a job as a civilian flight instructor at Fort Rucker, I lost the status and success that I had achieved. I became a captain when I was twenty-two years old, and all of that was suddenly taken away. I had one failed marriage and remarried, but that marriage was destined for failure from the very beginning because of my reactions to Vietnam. I believe my behavior during this time was directly related to the napalm incident. I began to be unfaithful to my wife. We lived near Fort Rucker, and I led two very different lives.

I got caught up in a vicious cycle of drinking. The more nightmares I had the more I drank. When I got off at six-thirty I would start drinking at the officers club, and I would keep on drinking until midnight. There were nights that I would be so drunk that I could not drive home and would end up staying at a friend's house. In order to cover that up, I would lie to my wife, making up some sort of story. She was not sympathetic at all to my talking about Vietnam. She was not the least bit interested in hearing about what had happened to me. I didn't even talk to her about the picture. Since she was not interested in the war stories, I just clammed up. I don't remember sharing anything with her until it was too late, basically when our marriage was over.

When I was at home, I was a model citizen. I took my wife and son to church and did all the things that a person was supposed to do. But when I went to Fort Rucker where I worked, I went to all the parties and hung out with my drinking buddies. I would even bring girls into the officers club even though everyone knew that I was married. I didn't care. I shut people, including my parents and my own children, out of my life. I went a year and a half one time without seeing my own children from my first marriage. I was so centered on myself that I could not let anyone else into my life. I guess it was during that time period that I realized that the only way I could get rid of my remorse was to ask for forgiveness from the little girl. But I didn't know anything about her. I didn't know her name. I didn't know if she was still alive. And if she were alive, she would be in Vietnam, and I couldn't go back over there. During that time, Americans could not go there. I was in a quandary. I carried this heavy burden yet there was no way I could get rid of it. This caused me to sink deeper and deeper into my misery.

I told very few people about what happened at Trang Bang even though there was seldom a day during the next twenty-four years that I didn't think of that little girl and what I had done to her. I felt as if I was falling deeper and deeper into a black hole as my life continued to fall apart. I battled alcohol abuse and I turned all my emotions inward, sharing with no one. I had two failed marriages. I hurt a lot of people by focusing only on what I wanted at the moment and not respecting or considering other people's needs.

Then to my surprise, there was a turn of events. I was very fortunate to find someone who made her way into my heart. This became a catalyst for my healing. Joanne also became my third wife! Over a period of eight years, I began to very slowly evolve into a more caring, receptive person. It was during this period that I left my job as a defense contrator and became a Methodist minister.

Then one evening in June of 1996 while Joanne was in California, I was alone reading with the sound of the TV keeping me company. I happened to glance up from my book, and there appeared the photograph that had haunted me for nearly twenty-five years. I quickly jumped up from the couch to turn up the volume. The TV program was called "Where Are They Now?" I was so startled! As I continued to listen to the program, I learned several things: First that Kim was alive. Second, her name, and third that she lived in Toronto, Canada. It was all I could do that night to keep myself from jumping into the car and taking off for Toronto. I imagined myself knocking on her front door! Of course, I didn't know where she lived or anything else, but I was really excited about my discovery!

When Joanne came back from California, I told her, "She is alive, that little girl is alive and she lives in Toronto!" Joanne was very excited too.

A few weeks after seeing the television show, John attended a Vietnam veteran's reunion for helicopter pilots and crewmen. He browsed through the table of books and there again was *that* picture, this time with a poem alongside it. John became lost in tears. The poet was nearby and without asking for an explanation, shared a moment of prayer. Then John asked,

WHY DO YOU have that picture?
Sensing there was a reason for the question he replied, "Why do you ask?"
I shared with him that I was the staff officer who coordinated the air strike in which Kim was burned.
"I have so desperately wanted to meet her. I need to ask her to forgive me!"
The man told me that they had not actually met, but they talked on the phone.

"I wrote a poem about the girl in the photograph, and this is how we connected."

I went back to Virginia to find messages on my answering machine from this man. I could not get myself to call him back. He began to send messages to me through a mutual friend. Finally, in November, he sent a message telling me that Kim was going to be at the Vietnam Veterans Memorial on Veterans Day. My heart began to race. I knew in my heart that now I was supposed to meet her. I felt like I was standing at the threshold and needed help taking the step across. What if she rejected my request and didn't forgive me? No matter what the consequences were to be I had the responsibility for asking for her forgiveness. I knew that fate had a hand in this because we were having a small reunion of helicopter pilots in Washington that same weekend. We were also planning to be at the wall on Veterans Day.

From the time of the bombing in Trang Bang in June of 1972, even though our lives had followed wildly divergent paths, something was bringing us back to the same place at the same time. I was stunned by the news. I didn't know this at the time but Kim had made a trip to California and met this man who told her about me. I do not know how she found out that I was going to be at the wall, perhaps from this man in a later phone conversation, but at any rate when she got to the wall she knew that I was there.

That night before Veterans Day there were a bunch of the guys sitting around in my living room. In a very hesitant voice, I said, "There is something that I need to tell you. It's about an incident in Trang Bang, in 1972, in which I was involved."

There was dead silence among the group and then I began.

"To tell this story is extremely difficult. I probably never told more than ten people about the incident.

"Tomorrow I will have the opportunity to meet Kim Phuc. Will you stay with me at the wall to help me get her away from the press for a few minutes?"

I want to say that I am sorry she got hurt. I want her to know that this was not just an incident that I shrugged off. I suffered in my own way for twenty-five years because of what has happened, and I want her to know that I cared for her even though I knew nothing about her.

The group agreed. Eighteen went to the wall the next day. We did not know under what circumstances we would see her. We did not know if she was going to be alone or if there was going to be a press entourage. We did not know anything so I kept walking to the wall looking for an Asian face.

Finally at one o'clock a crowd began to gather, and the formal program began. Suddenly there was a disturbance in the crowd along the west wall. I looked over and noticed that Kim was right in the middle of the group. I was excited. I was scared. I was nervous. I just wanted to run over to her right then and there, but I knew that was impossible. Security people were surrounding her. Kim was escorted to the stand where the other VIPs were. It felt as though everything was spinning around me. Then suddenly I heard Kim being introduced. It was during her introduction that I learned two of Kim's brothers were killed that day in the bombing. That revelation took me right over the edge, and I broke down crying. Not only did I cause so much pain and suffering to Kim, I also killed two other children that day. I found out later that these two children were cousins, not brothers, but that does not lessen the tragedy. I was reeling with emotion. Then Kim spoke.

Dear friends. I am happy to be with you today. As you know, I am the little girl who was running to escape from the napalm fire. I do not want to talk about that day because I cannot change history. I only want you to remember the tragedy of war in order to work to stop fighting and killing around the world. I have suffered great physical and emotional pain. Sometimes I thought I could not live, but God saved me and gave me faith and hope. Even if I could talk face-to-face with the pilot who dropped the bombs, I would tell him we cannot change history, but we should try to do good things for the present and for the future to promote peace.

Although I was not the pilot who actually dropped the bombs, I knew she was referring to me as well. I do not remember if she actually used the word forgiveness but that was the implication. At that moment, I felt peace and knew it was going to work out; everything was going to be all right. Then I got very emotional. In fact I almost fell to my knees had it not been for my friends surrounding me and holding me up. They were like a herd of elephants surrounding a wounded one. There was one guy behind me holding me up, one friend had me on one side, and the other had me on the other side. Another friend backed up to my front so I could have my privacy. At that moment I felt like a psychological wreck. Then I became concerned with how I was actually going to meet Kim with all the security around her. So I wrote her a note that simply said "Kim, I am that man. I would like to speak with you a moment."

After I wrote that note, I gave it to a park police officer to deliver to her. I found out later that when she got the note she just put it in her pocket and didn't read it. In the meantime, another friend was standing near a woman who was the executive secretary for the Vietnam Veterans Memorial fund, who had sponsored Kim's trip. He mentioned to her, not knowing who she was, that his friend was the one who called in that air strike.

She asked, "Is he here?"

"Yes!"

"Please get him. Kim wants to meet him."

Then he came and grabbed me and took me over to the woman, Libby Hatch. By this time, Kim was leaving the wall. Libby and I got inside the security and walked behind Kim up the sidewalk to a place that was relatively quiet. Libby conveyed to Kim's escort that I was the man Kim was looking for.

He leaned over and asked Kim, "Do you still wanted to meet Reverend Plummer?"

In a quiet voice she said, "Yes."

Her escort told her to keep walking and that Reverend Plummer was walking right behind her. She took about two or three more steps and then stopped to turn around and look at me. I fell apart.

I looked into her eyes, and all I could say was "I'm sorry. I'm so sorry. I didn't mean to do it."

She looked at me, and all that I could see was love. Her look was so clear. I began to sob.

I kept repeating, "I'm sorry, I'm just so sorry that you got hurt. I did not mean to do this."

She held out her arms and patted me on my back. "It's OK. I forgive. I forgive."

Then she held me in her arms as I cried, and she kept saying, "It's OK. I forgive, I forgive."

This was the most emotional moment of my life. The twenty-four-and-a-half years of remorse and pain just fell away. By those two words, Kim lifted it right off my shoulders. It was everything I hoped it would be. Suddenly, I felt like I could fly. I remember those feelings so distinctly. She forgave me, and I was free.

I kept trying to explain to her what happened, but she didn't want to hear it. In fact, to this day she has never let me explain what happened. She has moved past it. In Kim's view, we have the opportunity to start over. This is what Kim has done.

We had about two minutes together and then she left. In that brief moment, I was forgiven, and it was complete. In the meantime, Kim had gone back to her hotel and sent one of her friends to ask me to join her. My wife and I and a couple riding with us went to her hotel, and we met her in the lobby.

We spent two wonderful hours together. I remember trying to tell her the story and every time I started, she would interrupt me. It wasn't like she was rude, but she kept saying,

"We can do good, we can share our story, we can do things together."

"I want to come to your church and give my testimony."

Kim replied, "I want to come to your church and give my own testimony."

We found ourselves making rudimentary plans for some kind of ministry. The time passed quickly. Kim talked with my wife for a few moments and with the other couple. She was very polite. My friends went outside to give us time together, but it was very cold and the lobby was very small. They didn't want to be in the way. They came in and stood in the hallway. Kim then went and got them and brought them in to where we were, which was so kind and considerate to everyone. That was where my friend took the photograph that was published in *Guidepost* magazine and others that showed Kim and me together that day. That snapshot has become almost as famous as the original pictures. What is more incredible is the whole process of how we both learned to forgive. Hopefully, the second photo will have an even greater impact because of what it represents. That is my emphasis and Kim's emphasis. The *Guidepost* picture does not represent the events that happened in Trang Bang; it is the end of this story, and yet unfortunately it is the press that has wanted to concentrate on the events of that day in June 1972. Our intention is to talk about the reconciliation and forgiveness aspect of it and how it has set us both free.

John's Personal Healing

Why was it so important for John to ask for forgiveness? It began with the issue of self-responsibility. John felt like a perpetrator because he was one of the people responsible for what happened to Kim. Many perpetrators feel justified in what they have done either because of certain beliefs they hold or because their minds are twisted, and they usually don't care about their victims. They are usually so psychologically wounded and filled with guilt, albeit unconscious guilt, that they are unable to respond appropriately. Although John suffers with the same emotional reactions as most perpetrators do, he knew he did the responsible thing in terms of checking for "friendlies" around the village. So he didn't feel guilt as such but did feel a sense of responsibility and remorse.

In spite of this, John was dealing with his own woundedness, which was the result of what we now call post-traumatic stress disorder. He had experienced a great deal of trauma while serving in Vietnam. Unfortunately we did not know how to take care of our vets when they came home, and many of them had become drug addicts, alcoholics, or worse, suicide victims. The point is that their psyches and souls were wounded and most of them didn't seek or receive treatment for it. John took to drinking and using women. Two marriages were destroyed because John was not capable of building strong, intimate relationships. He was in too much emotional pain and remained silent about that. So often he was hoping that someone would ask him if he were a Vietnam vet and then say to him "Good job!" Given the antiwar climate in the United States at the time, most vets were not given a warm welcome when they returned home and had to struggle with the demons within themselves. In a way, John was lucky. He had inner strength and the love of a partner who listened. He had enough strength within himself to want to function as a helicopter pilot, which he loved doing. He was lucky to have fallen in love with someone who did want to hear about Vietnam and was extremely supportive. He also carried the burden of the world-famous picture and was haunted by it. After John married for the third time, he made the decision to really commit to his marriage and that led John and his current spouse, Joanne, to attend a marriage encounter weekend. This is when a profound healing took place.

During the weekend, the attendees were asked to write a love letter to their significant other, discussing feelings they had that they knew would surprise their spouse. When John thought about writing his letter, he was surprised at his lack of feelings. He recognized that his absence of feelings was a sign that he was cut off from his spiritual source and was preventing him from going any further in his life. John began to cry, realizing that what he wanted most he had cut off from himself.

John said, "I could not write another word. As I began to weep, I felt something come over me as though there was someone else was in the room. Call it what you want, for me I felt it was the Holy Spirit. Then I knew that being cut off from my spiritual essence was no longer true."

Joanne came into the room and John handed her the one sentence he had written. She was startled, looked up at him, and said, "You need not worry, it is not true any more."

At that moment John recognized that he was being catapulted to his healing journey. Throughout the following year John focused a great deal on his inner healing. John later commented,"I went on that weekend with an attitude, but in my heart of hearts, I prayed for an inner healing. This was a surrender for me, a letting go, and the powers that be knew I was ready to listen. I believe that this is the way it works. When we are ready to listen, our divinity within us knows that and knows we are going to act on what is revealed. At that moment, grace was revealed. The truth is what happened here was the culmination of a very long process that began in 1972.

I asked John that although he said he did not feel responsible for what had happened that day in 1972, he did want to ask for forgiveness, which implies that in fact he did feel responsible.

John responded, "We all need to develop humility. All too often people associate humility with wimpiness. What humility really has to do with is realizing that there is something greater than oneself. Humility led me to realize that I am not the important one. The one who has been hurt is the important one and the relationship is more important than the incident. That is why humility is so important."

I was very touched by these words and wanted to know more about how people can come to a place of asking for forgiveness, and so I asked John about how he was able to do it.

John replied, "It is about forgiving yourself first. If people are able to heal their grief, pain, guilt, and anger and work on becoming whole human beings, then you know that if they ask for forgiveness from others it is genuine. The problem is that you can't skip any steps in your own healing process and too often people are left to rot in jail without getting the help they really need."

As John spoke, the thought crossed my mind that we can become victims and perpetrators twice over. We become victims twice over by first having the horrific experience and then by being trapped in the experience again and again by our inability to heal ourselves. If we cannot forgive, nor absorb the pain, we can't make the decision to move on. When we fail to forgive someone, we are keeping ourselves captive to the event. Our lack of forgiveness hurts not only the perpetrator but ourselves as well.

We become the perpetrator again by first committing the act and then not getting the psychological help we need to heal the inner dynamics that acted as the motivating force to commit the act in the first place.

Forgiving ourselves is a very painful struggle. We forgive ourselves in the same way we forgive others, and it leads us down the same path, reconnecting with the essence of who we are. There is no faking this because when an inner transformation does take place, it will manifest in actions you take in the outer world. For some, it becomes the desire to ask for forgiveness. For others, asking for forgiveness is a stepping stone for taking positive social action.

Healing of Post-Traumatic Stress Disorder (PTSD) and Forgiveness

John shared the following about PTSD and forgiveness.

WHEN I CAME back from Vietnam I had no idea about PTSD, yet I had many of the symptoms: the nightmares, the drinking to cover up my pain, and the feelings of hopelessness. I was fortunate to have a supportive family and friends who helped me in a sense to reconstruct myself. Part of that reconstruction was to get in touch with my pain and my suffering and the guilt I was feeling for what I had done with my life, not only during my years in Vietnam, but before and after as well. I was completely out of touch with the feelings I had toward myself until one day at a spiritual retreat I was doing an exercise in which I was to write down all of those things that kept me from accepting my spiritual nature. I wrote down what seemed like pages of incidents where I hurt people, including the women I had been married to, but I did not write down Trang Bang.

I was trying to block Trang Bang from my mind because first of all, it was too painful, and second, I felt I never could be forgiven for it. I felt that only the little girl in the picture could forgive me and for many years I did not think she was alive. I didn't realize how important the forgiveness process would be in helping me heal from the symptoms of PTSD until the day Kim and I met. Timing here was very critical. I was ready. I was learning to forgive myself and in doing so I was also helping myself feel worthy of being forgiven. Until then, asking for forgiveness would have been impossible.

We don't know what a greater plan may be about, or even if there is a grand plan that all of us are living out, but I have to wonder. Why on that fateful day in June of 1972 was there a little girl who happened to be at a certain place at a certain time and suffered for so many years to become a wonderful spiritual teacher. She was joined by a man who in a sense was responsible for her suffering but who then becomes a changed man and a wise teacher himself. Are these incidents just coincidences, or is there a higher meaning? It certainly makes me wonder why we all are here to begin with and what our lives are really about.

15

What *You* Can Do for Yourself

"To refuse to forgive is to refuse to repair a broken relationship. To forgive is to save that relationship. In the 'divine comedy' that plays out its course down to the end of historical tragedies of humanity, forgiveness is the way of divine victory."

—BRIAN FROST, WRITER

NOW THAT YOU have learned about the specific skills needed to forgive and have read about how others have gone through the forgiveness process, it is time for you to deepen what you have learned to help in your healing process. Here you will be given some more resources that you can use to help you along the way.

Your forgiveness journey is never over. Just when you think you have worked through all your strong emotions, there is a surprise. More emotion seems to come out of nowhere. That's part of the process. The tools given below are meant to be used over and over again. Feel free to adapt them to your purpose if that helps. Many of you will soon discover that your ability to forgive will become easier and your life far more rewarding.

Rating Your Progress

Some of you may have started to work through a situation and feel that you have completed a process while some of you may feel that you have just begun. Still others may be somewhere in between. That's OK. You may want to think about your situation once again and write about it to see if your thinking has changed in any way after reading some of the stories in this book. You may also want to revisit some of the steps if that is appropriate for you. Once you feel you have completed the program, rate yourself again.

Following this paragraph is the rating scale to use when you feel you have completed the program. With this rating scale, you will be able to evaluate how far you have come with the forgiveness process and where more work needs to be done. This is the time to evaluate the steps that have been more difficult for you, if you still need to work through an issue, or if you need to revisit it. Complete this rating scale and compare your answers with your responses before you started the program and at the end of each step. As you compare your ratings now with the ones you did earlier, see if any patterns emerge. Keep in mind that change can be slow and therefore any improvement is important. Once you have finished the ratings, go back to the rating scale and rate the scales themselves in terms of their importance to your personal forgiveness process. Use the same seven-point system with number 1 being the most important and 7 being very unimportant. See if a pattern emerges when you compare both sets of rating scales.

Step One: Getting Started

How clear was your understanding of forgiveness at the end of this program?

VERY CLEAR   **NOT CLEAR AT ALL**

| 1 | 2 | 3 | 4 | 5 | 6 | 7 |

How often did you think about getting even with the perpetrator at the completion of this program?

I DON'T THINK ABOUT IT   **I AM OBSESSED WITH IT.**

| 1 | 2 | 3 | 4 | 5 | 6 | 7 |

How willing are you to forgive at the end of this program?

TOTALLY WILLING   **NOT WILLING AT ALL**

| 1 | 2 | 3 | 4 | 5 | 6 | 7 |

Step Two: Telling Your Story

How much emotional pain are you experiencing at the end of this program?

NONE   **FEELINGS ARE OVERWHELMING**

| 1 | 2 | 3 | 4 | 5 | 6 | 7 |

How difficult is it to share your emotional experiences at the end of this program?

NOT DIFFICULT AT ALL   **VERY DIFFICULT**

| 1 | 2 | 3 | 4 | 5 | 6 | 7 |

Step Three: Working with Anger

How angry are you at the person who hurt you after completing this program?

NOT ANGRY   **INFURIATED**

| 1 | 2 | 3 | 4 | 5 | 6 | 7 |

How well did you understand the deeper meaning of your anger at the time you ended this program?

TOTAL UNDERSTANDING   **NO UNDERSTANDING**

| 1 | 2 | 3 | 4 | 5 | 6 | 7 |

Did you see ways in which you were subtly nurturing your pain after completing this program?

VERY AWARE						TOTALLY UNAWARE
1	2	3	4	5	6	7

Were you willing to make changes to your own behavior according to what your anger taught you after completing this program?

VERY WILLING						NOT WILLING AT ALL
1	2	3	4	5	6	7

Step Four: Working with Guilt

How aware were you of your own feelings of guilt after completing this program?

VERY AWARE						NO AWARENESS
1	2	3	4	5	6	7

Were you willing to step back and accept that you were not seeing the total situation that needed to be forgiven at the end of this program?

TOTALLY WILLING						NOT WILLING
1	2	3	4	5	6	7

Could you acknowledge your guilt and take responsibility for your actions after completing this program?

TOOK RESPONSIBILITY						TOTALLY DENIED GUILT
1	2	3	4	5	6	7

Step Five: Reframing the Situation

Were you willing to shift your focus from yourself to the other person who needs forgiveness after completing this program?

VERY WILLING						NOT WILLING AT ALL
1	2	3	4	5	6	7

How difficult was it for you to walk in the offender's shoes after completing this program?

EASY						VERY DIFFICULT
1	2	3	4	5	6	7

How willing were you to see the situation differently after completing this program?

VERY WILLING						NOT WILLING AT ALL
1	2	3	4	5	6	7

Step Six: Absorbing Pain

How difficult was it for you to accept your pain at the end of this program?

EASY						IMPOSSIBLE
1	2	3	4	5	6	7

How complete was your process for mourning your losses after completing this program?

COMPLETE						NOT BEGUN
1	2	3	4	5	6	7

Have you been able to make your pain meaningful after completing this program?

VERY MEANINGFUL						NO MEANING AT ALL
1	2	3	4	5	6	7

Do you have a deep commitment to forgive after completing this program?

VERY DEEP COMMITMENT						NO COMMITMENT
1	2	3	4	5	6	7

Step Seven: Gaining Inner Peace

How well have you forgiven the offender after completing this program?

COMPLETELY   NOT AT ALL

1	2	3	4	5	6	7

Were you able to view the situation by seeing that this person was worthy of love after completing this program?

TOTAL SPIRITUAL SIGHT   NO INSIGHT

1	2	3	4	5	6	7

Has practicing forgiveness changed your life from the way it was before you started the program?

VERY MUCH   NOT AT ALL

1	2	3	4	5	6	7

You may find as you work through the rating scales that more work needs to be done or you may discover that there are more people or incidents requiring your attention. As time passes you also may experience new hurts that seem to appear out of nowhere related to an incident you thought you had finished working on. All of this is a natural part of the healing process. The more you do this work the easier it becomes, although there can be many struggles. Sometimes life events are so painful that it can take a very long time to heal from pain's cumulative effects.

Visualization Exercises

Visualization exercises can help you learn how to relax, reduce anxiety, improve self-esteem, and help with healing as well as give you insight into your thoughts and behavior. For all of these reasons, visualization can be a wonderful tool for healing emotions and setting the stage for forgiveness. In the upcoming sections of this chapter, you will be given visualization exercises for each step in the forgiveness program. Some will be relaxation techniques, which will help you get into a state of deep muscle relaxation, and others will be visualization exercises, which will help you specifically deal with the issues pertaining to that particular step.

To make best use of these visualization exercises, you may want to read them into a tape recorder. Over time you will discover that the more often you practice these visualization exercises, the greater effect they will have. As you listen to the tape you may find that your mind drifts in and out. That's OK. You can gently guide yourself back to the voice on the tape once you have recognized that your mind has wandered. You may also want to review the suggestions in Chapter 2 to help you with your visualizations.

Step One: Getting Started— Willingness Meditation

Go to a comfortable place where you will not be disturbed and where you feel safe. Sit in a comfortable chair or lie on a sofa; close your eyes, and take a few deep relaxing breathes. Breathe in for a count of four (pause), hold your breath for a count of four (pause), and then slowly breathe out for a count of four (pause). Do this three more times (long pause). Feel your mind and body begin to slow down. Now scan your body for any places of tension. Begin by focusing your awareness on your feet. Wiggle your toes a bit and then rotate your feet in one direction for a few moments and then in the opposite direction (long pause). Feel the relaxing energy begin to circulate around your feet. Then focus your awareness on your calves. Pull the muscles in as tight as you can, tighter, tighter, and tighter and relax. Pause. Feel the relaxing energy begin to move from your toes through your calves. Now focus your awareness on your thighs. Pull the muscles in your thighs as tight as you can, tighter, tighter, and tighter, and relax. Pause. Feel the warm relaxing energy slowly move up your legs. And now focus your awareness on your buttocks. Pull in the muscles as tight as you can, tighter, tighter, and tighter, and relax. Just let all the tension melt into the chair that you are sitting in or the couch you are lying on.

Now focus your awareness on your stomach. Pull in those muscles as tight as you can, tighter, tighter, and tighter, and relax. Feel the warm relaxing energy move farther up your body as you become more and more relaxed. Now focus your attention on your shoulders. Raise your shoulders up and back in one direction for a few rotations. Pause. Now move in the opposite direction and feel the tension being released from your shoulder muscles. Pause. Now lift up your arms and make a fist with your hands and pull the muscles in as tight as you can, tighter, tighter, and tighter, and relax. Feel this relaxing energy spreading throughout your body as you become more and more relaxed. Now focus your awareness on your face. We tend to hold a lot of tension around our jaw and around our eyes. Scrunch the muscles around your mouth and eyes and hold the muscles as tight as you can, tighter, tighter, tighter, and relax. Enjoy the sensation of relaxation throughout your entire body. If there is still a place where you are holding on to some tension, mentally go to that place and imagine the muscles loosening. Pause. Now at the count of three I would like you to be twice as relaxed as you are now; one, two, three. Pause.

Begin to reflect for a moment on what the word *forgiveness* might mean. Pause. What might it be like to bring forgiveness into one's life, into one's mind? Pause. Now I would like you to think about a situation in your life where you needed to forgive someone. Pause. Who is this person and how are you feeling about this person at the present moment? Pause. Did you have a past history with this person? Is this someone you will see again or was this a total stranger? What would your life look like if you continued it as it is now, unable to forgive the person for what has happened? Pause. What emotions do you experience and how are they affecting your body? Pause. Ask yourself: Is this something I wanted for myself? Can I lead my life in a better way? Get a clear picture of what your life looks like today and what it would look like if you could forgive this person and move on? Pause. How would you feel if thoughts of that person and the incident(s) were not taking up space in your mind, and you could be doing things that would make your life more rewarding? Pause. Visualize a scene where you are free of the thoughts you don't want and where you are doing things that bring you joy. Continue taking some deep relaxing breaths as you create your scene. Pause. When you feel that you have completed your scene and have a clear picture of how your life could be once you were able to forgive, remember what has happened, knowing that you can go back to this place at any time that you choose. Then slowly become aware of the sounds in the room, the chair or couch you are sitting on or the couch that you are lying on, and when it is comfortable for you, stretch a bit and then slowly open your eyes.

Step Two: Uncovering Feelings— Forgiveness Meditation

Take a few deep, relaxing breaths. Breathe way down into or out from your abdomen. As you breathe in, imagine breathing in a peaceful yet uplifting energy. As you breathe out, feel yourself letting go of tension. Again, breathe in a powerful and uplifting energy. And as you breathe out, feel yourself letting go of tension and daily concerns. Affirm to yourself, "I give myself permission to let go of my concerns for now. I give myself permission to enjoy greater energy and peacefulness now. . . ." Feel peacefulness growing within you. And as you breathe out, feel this peacefulness now radiating outward from your body. Feel yourself filled and surrounded by peaceful radiance. Take a few moments to enjoy this feeling now (long pause).

Now imagine that it is a beautiful cool summer morning. You are walking in a valley enjoying the invigorating fresh air. The sky is intensely blue, and there are flowers and grass all around you. The morning breeze gently caresses your cheeks and as you walk you feel the contact of your feet with the ground. Pay attention to what you are wearing and the scenery around you. As you look around, you notice a mountain towering close to you. Looking at its summit gives you a sense of great excitement.

While looking at the summit, you decide to climb the mountain. You follow the path you're on, which leads you through a pine forest. As you enter the forest, you can smell the fragrant aroma of the pine needles and sense the cool, dark atmosphere.

Feel the soft bed of pine needles under your feet as you walk toward the steep path of the mountain. Walking uphill, you can feel the muscular effort demanded of your legs and the energy that pleasantly fills your entire body.

The path ends and all you can see is rock. As you keep climbing, the ascent becomes more difficult. You sometimes have to use your hands to climb over the rocks. As you climb higher, the air gets fresher and more rarefied. The scenery is pristine, and you experience total silence.

As you approach the very top of the mountain, you see someone off in the distance. It is a person, wise and loving, ready to listen to what you have to say and tell you what you want to know. He or she first appears as a small, luminous point in the distance. You have noticed each other and begin to walk slowly toward each other. As you come closer, you feel the presence of this person giving you joy, strength, warmth, and love.

Now you are facing each other. Look into the wise person's eyes. Sit with this person and tell the person your story and where you have been hurt. Do not be afraid. You are totally safe here. This wise person supports and loves you and listens attentively. As you share your story you notice that whatever you need is instantly present. Take as much time as you need to say what has happened and how you feel. Pause. Feel the warmth and compassion of this person next to you. After you have shared your story, wait for a moment to hear what this wise one wants to say to you. Ask any questions you would like. Continue your conversation for as long as you feel comfortable. Pause.

When you are ready to say good-bye, thank this person for coming, knowing that you can meet again at any time you choose. After saying good-bye, begin your journey down the mountain. The climb down is much easier now, because it may feel that you have left a piece of your burden behind. As you get to the base of the mountain, you see the path leading out of the forest. Stop for a moment and reflect on how you feel now and what it was like to meet the wise one on the mountaintop. Pause. When you are ready you can begin to close your experience and become aware of the chair or couch that you may be on. Take a few deep breaths and become aware of the sounds of the room that you are in. Gently begin to stretch, and when it feels comfortable for you, slowly open your eyes.

Step Three: Working with Anger— Healing Your Heart from Anger Meditation

Begin by taking a few deep relaxing breaths. Pay attention to your breathing and be aware of sensations as you breathe in and out. Give your breathing your full attention. Breathe all the way down into your abdomen and let your belly gently rise. As you breathe in, imagine this peaceful energy filling your entire being. As you breathe out, feel yourself letting go of all the tension stored in your body. Again, breathe in a powerful and uplifting energy. Breathe out all of your tension. For the next two minutes, just focus your awareness on your breathing. If any thoughts enter into your mind just notice what they are, daydreams, planning, or memories; and label the thoughts and then let them go and focus your awareness back on your breathing (long pause). With each deep breath allow yourself to become more and more relaxed. Allow yourself to melt into the couch or chair that you are sitting on with every breath that you take in. Breathe in and feel the wholeness within your own being. Breathe out any illusions of inadequacy or inferiority. . . . And once again breathe in the wholeness of your entire being. . . . And as you breathe out, let go of any illusions that you are anything other than a powerful, lovable, and uniquely wonderful person.

Begin by slowly bringing into your mind the image of someone you are feeling anger toward. Gently allow a picture, a feeling, and a sense of the person to gather there. Remind yourself that what you see through the lens of anger is not the truth of who this person is. Allow your heart to open gently just for this moment.

Notice whatever fear or anger may arise; acknowledge it and gently let it go. See through the behavior of this person to his or her true essence. If you could say anything to this person, what would you say? Say it to them now. Pause.

Now give yourself permission to experience that person's spiritual essence. What is it like for you to feel his or her inner light? Pause.

Feel your heart open, if only for a moment, and allow for the possibility of forgiveness.

Let those prison walls of resentment around your heart come down so that your heart may be free, so that your life may be lighter. Feel what it is like to release the burden of anger. Pause. Allow that person to just be in the stillness and warmth of your heart. Let him or her be forgiven. Release the person from your anger and let him or her be on his or her way. Give yourself whatever time is necessary to allow that person to leave. What does it feel like now that he or she is gone?

Now gently think of someone who may have anger toward you, someone whose heart is closed to you. Invite that person, just for this moment, into your heart. Say whatever you would like to say to this person. Pause. Hear what the person may have to say to you. Pause. Ask the person to let you back into his or her heart and to forgive you for whatever you may have done that has caused pain. Speak from your heart as you ask for forgiveness. Allow yourself to be touched by the person's offer of forgiveness. Allow yourself to be forgiven. Allow yourself back into that person's heart. Feel what it is like to be forgiven. Pause. Take in all those feelings as deeply as you can.

Now gently say good-bye to that person and thank him or her as you feel what it is like for two people to join together in forgiveness. Slowly become aware of the room you are in, the couch or chair you are lying or sitting on, and the sounds of the room. Slowly begin to stretch and when it feels comfortable for you, open your eyes and go on with the rest of your day.

Step Four: Working with Guilt— Healing Guilt Meditation

Find a comfortable position either sitting in a comfortable chair or lying down on a couch and gently close your eyes. Take a few deep relaxing breaths. Breathe in deeply through your nose and blow out through your mouth. Watch your breathing as you inhale and exhale. Slowly inhale. Slowly exhale. Keep focusing your awareness as you inhale and exhale and with each slow, deep breath you become more and more relaxed. Let your breathing gently rock you into a deeper and deeper state of relaxation. Allow your breathing to become slower and deeper. As you concentrate on your breathing, imagine a ball of pure energy starting from your abdomen and as you inhale, rises up the front of your body to the top of your head and as you exhale, goes down your spine, down your legs, and into the ground. Circulate this ball of energy as you breathe in and breathe out and as it moves up and feel the energy melt away all your tension as you move into deeper states of relaxation. As this ball continues to move around your body feel every cell of your body becoming more and more relaxed. Feel all the tension and tightness drain down your spine, down your legs, and into the ground. Continue circulating this ball for the next few moments as you become more and more relaxed. Pause.

Now in your mind's eye, create a place to go where you feel safe and secure. It may be an imaginary place or your favorite room or somewhere in nature that you enjoy going to. It doesn't matter what you create as long as you feel safe and secure. Sense the beauty of this place and look at every detail. Notice what is unusual to you about this place. Take in the colors and smells that surround you. Feel the comfort of what you are standing, sitting, or lying on. Feel how good it is to be in this place.

As you look around allow yourself to drift back in time when you felt ashamed about something or when you felt judged, emotionally abandoned, or unworthy or unloved. Now let the adult in you who is kind and compassionate meet your inner child who is in need of comfort and love. Let the adult in you be fully present, offering unconditional love and acceptance to the inner child.

Ask your inner child what it wants to say to you that it never before could say. How has this inner child felt shamed? Unworthy? Not deserving of love? Pause. Hold your inner child and comfort it. Offer your inner child love and safety as he or she tells you about his or her experience. Open your heart to this inner child. When the child's story is over, remind the child of the "truth" of who the child is. Remind this child that he or she is a beautiful spiritual human being totally worthy of love and respect. Let this inner child feel this love that you are giving at its deepest levels. Let this inner child feel this unconditional love within every cell of his or her being. Pause. Remind this inner child that he or she has already been forgiven. Let this inner child feel this forgiveness permeate his or her entire being.

Now imagine yourself as you are today carrying this healed inner child within you. Feel what it is like to let go of your guilt and shame. Feel what it is like to empower yourself to take positive healing actions that enable you to let go of your guilt. Pause. Look at the motivation behind the acts that now you might feel guilty for. Recognize the fear. Open your heart to yourself and listen compassionately to your fears and recognize them as cries for help. Pause. Answer those cries with your love and acceptance. Affirm your fundamental innocence, for the truth of who you are is always worthy of love. Feel that love you are so worthy of. Pause.

Now gradually return to your breathing and let your breath bring you back to the room you are in. Become aware of the sounds of the room, the couch you may be lying on or the chair you are sitting in. Move around a bit and begin to stretch. When you are ready, slowly open your eyes and go on with the rest of your day.

Step Five: Reframing the Situation— Spiritual Vision Meditation

Find a comfortable position either lying on a couch or sitting on a chair and gently close your eyes. Focus your awareness on your breathing. As you breathe in, breathe in relaxation, and as you breathe out, breathe out all the tension stored in your body. Keep focusing your awareness on your breathing—breathing in relaxation and breathing out tension. If any thoughts come to mind, notice what they are and focus your awareness back to your breathing.

Now I would like you to visualize seeing a black number five on a white curtain or a white number five on a black curtain. . . . If you have trouble visualizing, imagine yourself finger painting the number five, or hear it in your mind's ear. If possible, do all three. See it, finger paint it, and hear it. . . . Now, the number four . . . see it, finger paint it, and hear it, or do all three. Pause. Then do the same with the numbers three, two, and one. When you see the number one, imagine it's a gate. At the other side of this gate is a person you want to forgive. What would your life be like if you could forgive this person? Pause. How much freer will your life be if you could forgive? For a moment, imagine what this person's life has been like before you were hurt. Try to walk in the shoes of this person. Feel what it is to live this person's life. Pause. When you are ready, go through the gate. You see the other person waiting for you. You feel very safe and secure and are totally in control of the situation. Say to this person whatever you want to say. Ask him or her to tell you about his or her pain. Pause.

As this person finishes talking, you see a set of steps leading to a door. Now walk up the stairs and open the door. You will find a room with stairs leading up into a sacred space. You notice a figure surrounded in blue-white light coming down the stairs. As the figure comes closer, you experience it as a warm and friendly being. Whatever form it takes is OK as long as it feels warm and friendly to you. This being is your inner guide. Ask its name. Tell it you want to speak to your higher self. Let it take you by the hand and begin climbing the stairs. Your guide takes you to the door of a large temple. As you walk in, you see sacred objects. You are attracted to a beautiful and precious being. You realize this is your higher self. Take a moment to embrace your higher self. Ask your higher self to help you see the person you just spoke to at the gate with spiritual vision. How can you see the situation that caused you so much pain differently? Pause. How can you open your heart to this person who has hurt you and see the situation from a place of wisdom? Pause. Once you have your answer, thank your higher self and walk back to the door. Your inner guide is waiting for you.

Let your guide take you down the stairs to the gate. Pause. You stop for a moment and see the person once again. If there is anything you want to do or say take the time now. Then walk through the gate and take three deep breaths. Feel the life coming back into your feet and toes as you see the number five. Then feel the seat you are sitting in or couch you are lying on and your clothes on your body as you see the number four. Then feel the energy in your hands. Let it come up through your arms into your neck and shoulders . . . now see the number three. Feel your whole brain wide awake. Breathe in deeply. Tell yourself you will remember this experienc and you will stay with the images even if you don't fully understand them. Now see the number two and feel yourself fully awake as you see the number one.

Step Six: Absorbing Pain— Healing Pain Meditation

Find a comfortable position, either sitting or lying, and gently close your eyes. Loosen any tight clothing and move around a bit until you are at ease. Once you feel nice and settled begin to focus your awareness on your breathing. Become aware of your abdomen gently rising as you breathe in and gently falling when breathing out. Imagine that resting in your abdomen is a ball of light. As you breathe in slowly and deeply, watch the ball move to the top of your spine. As you breathe out, watch the ball fall back down to your abdomen. Feel your belly gently expand as you breathe in and contract as you breathe out. Watch the ball rise up and sink down with each complete breath. As you breathe in, breathe in relaxation, and as you breathe out, breathe out all tension as your body becomes more and more relaxed. Feel your breath bring you into deeper states of relaxation. Allow your breath to empty your mind even if for only a moment. If any thoughts come to mind, let them float away as your mind becomes quiet and still. Feel the stillness. Let your thoughts drift away with each outgoing breath as your body becomes more and more relaxed.

Now imagine a place where you feel safe, at peace, and secure. Choose a place that you may be familiar with, or an imaginary setting, or somewhere you have always wanted to be. It doesn't really matter. It could be a majestic pine forest where you are sitting next to a stream or the ocean's shore where you can hear the waves rhythmically beating white sand. It doesn't matter where you go as long as you feel safe and secure and your place feels nurturing and comforting to you. Look all around and notice where you are. Take in all the images around you: the colors, the sounds, the smells. Enjoy the surroundings as you take in everything you can that is around you. Notice what time of day it is and what time of year. Do you feel the warmth of the sun or are there clouds adding interest to the sky? Notice what clothes you are wearing. Are they worn or ordinary, comfortable, or something very special to you? What is it that you are walking on, cool velvety grass, a crackling bed of pine needles, or warm beach sand messaging your feet? Feel your feet as they make contact with the ground and if you are sitting or lying feel the beautiful earth beneath you. Listen carefully to the sounds that surround you. Hear the steady sound of the waves of an ocean as they hit the shore, or scampering animals running through the forest floor, or birds singing in the distance, or the sound of waterfalls or a rushing stream. It doesn't matter what it is—just listen for it—for it could also be the faint sound of the wind rustling through the leaves of the trees or beautiful tall grass. Just allow yourself to take in the sights and sounds of your sacred space cradling you and bringing you peace.

Now imagine that a gentle breeze is blowing ever so slightly as you feel it gently caress your face. It may feel crisp and cool or balmy and damp. Feel the peacefulness of your sacred place permeate every cell of your being as you take in everything you can of your surroundings. With every in breath take in all the peacefulness that surrounds you; with each out breath release any tension that may still remain in your body. Focus your awareness on your breathing as you become more and more relaxed. In this wonderfully peaceful state you begin to sense an energy around you and with this energy is a feeling that something wonderful is about to happen. This energy makes you feel very joyful as though something you want is about to happen.

Gradually you become aware that you are not alone any more and that there is a very loving presence somewhere nearby. This presence is someone or something which will protect you and give you guidance. You feel that this presence knows you, totally understands you, and accepts you for who you are. You feel a very strong link with this guide and are opened to what this guide has to say. As you feel its presence you feel your heart begin to open. Notice what this feels like. Allow the warmth of this presence to melt away any heaviness that may be around your heart. Share your pain and as you do, allow this being to become the container for your sorrow. Ask your sorrow what it needs to heal and ask your guide to support you in what you need. Allow the gentleness of this being to embrace the sorrow that may also be tucked away in your heart. When the time is right, allow yourself to feel the grief and pain that has been hidden within your heart. Give yourself permission to feel the pain and grief of betrayals or violations or woundedness caused by someone else. Embrace your pain. Give it the room it needs so it can heal. Allow grief's tears to cleanse your heart. Breathe life back into your broken heart by feeling everything that is in there. Know that you are strong enough to see what is there and feel your vulnerabilities. And when the time is right you will know how and when to let go of the pain and sorrow as your heart opens once again. Feel the warmth and love that are emanating from your guide, and energize your heart. Know with your entire being that your heart is healing. What was shattered by grief is coming back into wholeness. There is nothing within you that can't be healed within your own heart. Feel your pain and sorrow melt away. Allow the hurt and pain that has been buried so deeply feel the warmth of this gentle loving presence. Breathe in the warmth of this gentle healing energy. Take in more of this energy with each breath and as you breathe out, breathe out your pain and sorrow. All those tears cleanse your grief as you let the love of this guide fill your entire being. Take all the time you need for your grief to dissipate with every breath you take. Pause. Just be gentle with yourself as you give yourself permission to open your heart in a safe and protected environment.

As you breathe and feel the warmth and love, become aware of your scared place. Become aware of the colors surrounding you that may have become brighter and the sounds more vivid. You realize that it is time to go although you know that you can come back any time you choose. Thank your guides for being there and for creating your healing space. Say good-bye for now. Slowly bring yourself back to the room you are in. Become aware of your breathing, the sounds in the room, and what you are sitting or lying on. Begin to move your arms and legs and stretch a bit and when it is comfortable for you, move around a bit more, open your eyes, and slowly sit up.

Step Seven: Gaining Inner Peace— At-Oneness Meditation

Begin by taking a few deep relaxing breaths. Pay attention to your breathing and be aware of sensations as you breathe in and as you breathe out. Give your breathing your full attention. Breathe all the way down into your abdomen and let your belly gently rise. As you breathe in, imagine this peaceful energy fill your entire being. As you breathe out, feel yourself letting go of all the tension stored in your body. Again, breathe in a powerful and uplifting energy. As you breathe out, release tension and daily concerns. Give yourself permission to let go of everything for now. Say to yourself, "I give myself permission to enjoy greater energy and peacefulness now." Feel peacefulness radiate outward from your body filling the room you are in. Feel what it is like to be bathed in this light. Take a few moments to enjoy this feeling now (long pause).

As you continue to breathe in feel the wholeness within your own being. Breathe out any negativity you may be holding. Once again breathe in the radiant energy. And as you breathe out, let go of any negativity from every cell of your body. As you breathe in, remember that you are a loving and beautiful human being. For the next few minutes, continue to breathe in peace and harmony and to breathe out all the negativity within you (long pause).

Now I would like you to imagine that you encounter someone you have wanted to forgive. Take a moment to notice your thoughts. Instead of seeing the person through eyes of anger and judgment, see him or her with the inner recognition of his or her light, the spiritual essence that exists within all of us. Pause. See this person with the eyes of forgiveness. Allow yourself to see this person with your heart, not with your mind. Pause. Allow yourself to see the fundamental goodness that exists within everyone.

If you are struggling with feelings of anger or hatred, step back from this person and remind yourself that whatever was done to you was coming from a place of that person's woundedness. See the person's anger for what it is, an expression of fear. Recognize that what he or she needs the most is not your anger in return, but love and respect. If you see a person acting out, consider that his or her behavior is an expression of woundedness and offer, if only in your mind, compassion and understanding. Pause. If you are experiencing any resistance, ask your higher self, "Why am I holding on to my resistance? What inside of me needs to be healed? What is my pain saying to me?" Open yourself up and listen to whatever your higher self needs to say to you. Pause. And as you listen to the message of your higher self, hold yourself in gentle loving light. Feel the divinity within you. See yourself with spiritual sight and give yourself permission to see beyond the outer appearances of others, to their divine light. Open yourself to grace.

As you see the light in others, feel the light within you becoming stronger and more beautiful. Pause. Remind yourself that each person you see has a divine nature regardless of his or her outward appearance. . . . Remember the person's true essence. . . .

Practice seeing with spiritual sight. Pause. Remember that no matter what situation you find yourself in, you can take appropriate action and also come from a place of spiritual wisdom. You can take action while keeping your heart open. See each day with fresh eyes, not from past conditioning. Feel the beauty of your divine nature. Feel the love coming from your spiritual essence. Pause.

Feel what it is like to see the world through the eyes of this love. Pause. Remember that each moment provides an opportunity to choose once again. And so we can choose peace and forgiveness at any moment. Remember that you can always respond with this divine love in your heart. You can always choose to see with spiritual vision and feel the peace it brings.

When you are ready, slowly become aware of the couch you are lying on or the chair that you are sitting on. Become aware of the sounds in the room, and when it is comfortable for you, gently begin to stretch and slowly open your eyes.

References

Introduction
Strom, S. "Elie Wiesel Levels Scorn at Madoff." *New York Times*, February 27, 2009.

Chapter 1
A Course in Miracles. Tiburon, CA: Foundation for Course in Miracles, 1975.
Enright, R. D., L. A. Gassin, and C. R. Wu. "Forgiveness: A Developmental View." *Journal of Moral Education* 21 (1992): 99–114.
Frost, B. *The Politics of Peace.* London: Darton, Longman and Todd, 1991.
Hope, D. "The Healing Paradox of Forgiveness." *Psychotherapy* 24 (1987): 240–44.
Mawson, C. O. S., and K. A. Whiting. *Roget's Pocket Thesaurus.* New York: Pocket Books, 1923.
Muller-Fahrenholz, G. "On Shame and Hurt in the Life of Nations: A German Perspective." *An Irish Quarterly Review* 78 (1989): 127–35.

Chapter 2
Braden, G. *Walking Between the Worlds: The Science of Compassion.* Bellevue, WA: Radio Bookstore Press, 1997.

Chapter 3
Botcharova, O. "Implementation of Track Two Diplomacy: Developing a Model of Forgiveness." In *Forgiveness and Reconciliation: Religions, Public Policy and Conflict Transformation*, edited by R. G. Helmick and R. L. Petersen. Philadelphia: Templeton Foundation Press, 2001.

Dutta, S. "Why Revenge Isn't the Right Answer." *Newsweek*, May 3, 2004, 15.
Herman, J. *Trauma and Recovery.* New York: Basic Books, 1992.

Chapter 4
Shantideva. *A Guide to the Bodhisattva's Way of Life.* Dharamsala, India:
  Library of Tibetan Works and Archives, 1979.

Chapter 5
A Course in Miracles. Tiburon, CA: Foundation for Course in Miracles, 1975.

Chapter 6
A Course in Miracles. Tiburon, CA: Foundation for Course in Miracles, 1975.

Chapter 7
A Course in Miracles. Tiburon, CA: Foundation for Course in Miracles, 1975.

Chapter 10
Henderson, M. *All Her Paths Are Peace: Women Pioneers in Peacemaking.*
  West Hartford, CT: Kumarian Press, 1994.
Piguet, J. *For the Love of Tomorrow.* Richmond, VA: Grosvenor, 1985.

Chapter 11
Bole, W., Christiansen, S. J., and R. T. Hennemeyer. *Forgiveness in International Politics.* Washington, DC: United States Conference of Catholic
  Bishops, 2004.
Eckert, B. Speech given to Japanese delegates of the *Peace Boat*, August 8,
  2003, New York.
Morrow, L. "The Case of Rage and Retribution." *Time*, September 12,
  2001.
Titus, J. Address given at Kalamazoo College, May 2003, Kalamazoo,
  Michigan.

Chapter 13
Wapnick, K. *Forgiveness and Jesus.* Farmingdale, CA: Foundation for a
  Course in Miracles, 1983.

Chapter 15
Frost, B. *The Politics of Peace.* London: Darton, Longman and Todd, 1991.

Resources

Books for Forgiveness

Augsburger D. *Freedom of Forgiveness.* Chicago: Moody Press, 1988.

Casarjian, R. *Forgiveness: A Bold Choice for a Peaceful Heart.* New York: Bantam Books, 1992.

Dalai Lama XIV and V. Chan. *The Wisdom of Forgiveness: Intimate Conversations and Journeys.* New York: Riverhead Books, 2004.

Enright, R., J. North, and D. Tutu, editors. *Exploring Forgiveness.* Madison, WI: University of Wisconsin Press, 1998.

Flanigan, B. *Forgiving the Unforgivable: Overcoming the Bitter Legacy of Intimate Wounds.* New York: MacMillan, 1992.

Gobodo-Madikizela, P. *A Human Being Died That Night: A South African Story of Forgiveness.* New York: Houghton Mifflin, 2003.

Griffiths, B., and C. Griffith. *The Road to Forgiveness.* Nashville: Nelson Books, 2001.

Jeffress, R. *When Forgiveness Doesn't Make Sense.* Colorado Springs, CO: Water Brook Press, 2001.

Khamisa, A. *Azim's Bardo: A Father's Journey from Murder to Forgiveness.* Los Altos, CA: Rising Star Press, 1998.

Kornfield, J. *The Art of Forgiveness, Loving Kindness and Peace.* New York: Bantam, 2002.

Kushner, H. *How Good Do We Have to Be: A New Understanding of Guilt and Forgiveness.* Toronto: Little Brown, 1997.

Larsen, E., et al. *From Anger to Forgiveness.* New York: Ballantine, 1992.

Lomax, E. *The Railway Man: A POW's Searing Account of War, Brutality and Forgiveness.* New York: W. W. Norton, 1995.

McCullough, M., C. Thoresen, and K. Pargament. *Forgiveness: Theory, Research and Practice.* New York: Guilford Press.

Morris, D. *Forgiving the Dead Man Walking.* Grand Rapids, MI: Zondervan, 2000.

Muller-Fahrenholz, G. *The Art of Forgiveness: Theological Reflections on Healing and Reconciliation.* Geneva, Switzerland: World Council of Churches, 1997.

Nouwen, H. *The Return of the Prodigal Son.* New York: Doubleday, 1992.

Patton, J. *Is Human Forgiveness Possible? A Pastoral Care Perspective.* Nashville: Abingdon Press, 1985.

Renard, G. *The Disappearance of the Universe: Straight Talk About Illusions, Past Lives, Religion, Sex and Politics and the Miracle of Forgiveness.* Carlsbad, CA: Hay House, 2004.

Richards, N. *Heal and Forgive: Forgiveness in the Face of Abuse.* Nevada City, CA: Blue Dolphin, 2005.

Safer, N. *Forgiving and Not Forgiving: A New Approach to Resolving Intimate Betrayal.* New York: Avon, 1999.

Smedes, L. *Forgive and Forget: Healing the Hurts We Don't Deserve.* New York: Harper Collins, 1984.

Tutu, D. *No Future Without Forgiveness.* New York: Doubleday, 1999.

Wapnick, K. *Forgiveness and Jesus: The Meeting Place of "A Course in Miracles" and Christianity.* Roscoe, NY: Foundation for a Course in Miracles, 1983.

Wiesenthal, S. *The Sunflower.* New York: Schocken, 1997.

Books for Relaxation and Stress Management

Benson, H. *Beyond the Relaxation Response.* New York: Time, 1984.

Benson, H. *The Relaxation Response and Beyond the Relaxation Response.* New York: Harper Collins, 1975.

Charlesworth, E. *Stress Management: A Comprehensive Guide to Wellness.* New York: Ballantine, 1984.

Harvey, J. *Total Relaxation: Healing Practices for Body, Mind and Spirit.* New York: Kodanasha America, 1998.

Kabat-Zinn, J. *Full Catastrophe Living.* New York: Delta, 1998.

Lazarus, J. *Stress Relief and Relaxation Techniques.* Lincolnwood, IL: Keats, 2000.

Audiotapes for Forgiveness

Hay, L. *Anger Releasing.*

Hay, L. *Forgiveness/Loving the Inner Child.*

Kornfield, J. *The Beginner's Guide to Forgiveness: How to Free Your Heart and Awaken Compassion.*

Naparstek, B. *Health Journeys: A Meditation to Help with Anger and Forgiveness.*

Audiotapes for Relaxation and Stress Management

Bodhipaksa, D. *Guided Meditations for Developing Calmness, Awareness and Love.*

Bodhipaksa, D. *Guided Meditations for Stress Management.*

Gawain, S. *Creative Visualization Meditations.*

Kornfield, J. *Meditation for Beginners.*

McManus, C. *Progressive Relaxation and Autogenic Training.*

McManus, C. *Relaxation Body Scan and Guided Imagery for Well-Being.*

Pitkoff, B. *The Gift of Relaxation: Stress Relief * Sleep * Wellness.*

Salzberg, S. *Insight Meditation: A Step by Step Course on How to Meditate.*

Simmons, R. *Creating Calm in Your Life: A Guided Meditation and Stress Reduction.*

Websites

Bruderhof Forgiveness Guide gives great insight into forgiveness, including a guide to other forgiveness websites. forgivenessguide.org.

Campaign for Forgiveness Research lists research in forgiveness funded by the John Templeton Foundation. forgiving.org.

Catherine Blout Foundation facilitates the demonstration and teaching of the healing power of forgiveness. catherinebloutfnd.org.

Cooperative Communication Skills provides a number of resources, including free e-books as well as down-loadable essays and papers. coopcomm.org/index.htm.

A Course in Miracles offers a wide variety of information about *A Course in Miracles*, as well as interactive activities you can participate in. acim.org.

Forgiveness Foundation integrates psychological and spiritual approaches to forgiveness. forgivenessfoundation.org.

Forgiveness Project explores personal forgiveness stories from around the world. forgivenessproject.com.

Forgiveness Reading Room is a library of articles that is part of the Forgiveness Web. forgivenessweb.com/pages/readingrm.htm.

Forgiveness Web includes a comprehensive listing of websites concerned with different aspects of forgiveness. forgivenessweb.com.

Foundation for a Course in Miracles provides in-depth information on *A Course in Miracles* and what it teaches. facim.org.

Miracle Distribution Center makes the teachings of *A Course in Miracles* more accessible, aiding students in their practice of its transformational principles. miraclecenter.org.

Murder Victims' Families for Reconciliation is an organization of family members of murder victims who oppose the death penalty. mvfr.org.

Worldwide Forgiveness Alliance celebrates the healing power of forgiveness worldwide and broadens awareness of forgiveness. forgivenessday.org.

Index

Feedback Questions

———— ❧ ❧ ————

HEARING ABOUT YOUR experience in finding forgiveness is important to me. Knowing the problems you faced, successes you achieved, what worked, and what didn't work will provide invaluable information that can be passed to others. I have, therefore, developed questions to solicit your feedback. Please e-mail your responses to dreileenborris@cox.net or go to my website at dreileen borris.com for contact information. I encourage you to include in your message (or post on my website) whatever information you would like to add that is not covered by the following questions. Make sure to include a way I can contact you in return.

- What situation did you focus on in this forgiveness process?
- How did you first feel before you started the forgiveness process?
- What was it like working through the different steps of the forgiveness program?
- Where did you get stuck and why? How did you work through it?
- What changes did you notice in yourself as you worked through the forgiveness process?
- What have you learned about yourself and your situation as a result of the forgiveness program?

- How did you feel at the completion of the process and has this affected any of your relationships?
- How has your future changed as a result of your ability to forgive?
- Has anything happened to you as a result of using this program?
- Was there a story in this book you identified with?
- What did you find most helpful in this program? Why?
- What didn't work for you?
- Is there anything you would like to add or change in this program?

About the Author

SINCE THE 1980s, Dr. Eileen Borris-Dunchunstang has been on the frontlines of forgiveness from the personal to the political arenas. As a clinical psychologist, she teaches her clients about forgiveness and how to implement it in their own lives. As a political psychologist, she helps rebuild war-torn countries around the world through forgiveness healing, training workshops, and conflict resolution.

Dr. Borris-Dunchunstang not only goes to worn-torn countries, she leads the charge by training high-profile diplomats, peacekeepers, and humanitarian organizations. She is the director of training and program development for the Institute for Multi-Track Diplomacy (IMTD), designing and implementing programs in international peace building, forgiveness, and reconciliation.

She is a popular speaker on the nuances of conflict and forgiveness. By invitation, she has spoken at the United Nations about forgiveness and reconciliation. She has consulted with the United States Agency for International Development (USAID), the United Nations Development Fund for Women (UNIFEM), and the United Nations Development Programme (UNDP) in Liberia, training the Ministry of Foreign Affairs and Foreign Service Institute in multi-track diplomacy. She has shared the podium with such prominent people as Mary Robinson, former president of Ireland, and His Holiness the Dalai Lama. She is currently spearheading a project at the United Nations concerning forgiveness and the healing of nations.

Dr. Borris-Dunchunstang has made more than thirty radio and television appearances and has appeared in *Real Simple* and *O* magazines. She conducts workshops and training programs around the world to help countries heal from the pain of genocide and war. In addition to public speaking, she is also available to work with organizations and the nonprofit sector to resolve disagreements and enhance work cultures. For further information, please go to dreileenborris.com.